SHAPING PSYCHOLOGY

SOURCES IN SEMIOTICS, VOLUME X

John Deely and Brooke Williams, Series Editors

SHAPING PSYCHOLOGY

HOW WE GOT WHERE WE'RE GOING

by

Timothy Gannon

revised and edited in collaboration with

John Deely

UNIVERSITY
PRESS OF
AMERICA

Lanham • New York • London

University Press of America®, Inc.
4720 Boston Way
Lanham, Maryland 20706

3 Henrietta Street
London WC2E 8LU England

This book is published as a volume in the
SOURCES IN SEMIOTICS series under the General
Editorship of John Deely and Brooke Williams

Library of Congress Cataloging-in-Publication Data

Gannon, Timothy, 1904-
Shaping psychology : how we got where we're going / by Timothy
Gannon ; revised and edited in collaboration with John Deely.
    p.   cm. — (Sources in semiotics ; v. 10)
Includes bibliographical references and index.
    1. Psychology—History.
    I. Deely, John N.   II. Title.   III. Series.
BF81.G36   1991   150'.9—dc20   91-17860 CIP

ISBN 0–8191–7757–1 (cloth : alk. paper)

 The paper used in this publication meets the minimum requirements of
American National Standard for Information Sciences—Permanence
of Paper for Printed Library Materials, ANSI Z39.48–1984.

Brevitatem sectantes otiosum videbitur morosa praefatione diffundi, vel Spiritus Sancti sententia id praedamnante: «Stultum est ante historiam diffluere, in ipsa vero historia succingi».

— *from a "Preface" by John Poinsot* —

It is useless to put off with a wordy preface those who appreciate brevity—in the words of the Spirit: «There would be no sense in expanding the preface to the history and curtailing the history itself.»

Timothy Gannon in the summer of 1978. Photograph taken by Dr. John Joyce.

AUTHOR'S FOREWORD

Every attempt to unfold the development of psychology necessarily involves some evaluative judgments. These judgments will show up in the relative emphasis given to individuals and their work in the field.

This book is the culmination of teaching undergraduate and graduate psychology courses over fifty-six years, including courses in the history of psychology over nearly thirty-five years. It reflects the views of one who has seen a number of new and promising movements come and go, and who, in 1934, created his own introductory course as the basis for founding a department of experimental psychology.

In my evaluation of theories and movements, I have been guided by a single principle: psychology, at every point, must be true to the whole person.

LIST OF PLATES AND ILLUSTRATIONS:

CONTENTS

THE SHAPING OF PSYCHOLOGY

AS A SCIENCE

This is a book about origins: in the background, the book deals with the origins of psychological ideas in philosophical tradition; in the foreground, however, the book treats of the origins of scientific psychology, and of each of the main movements which have arisen within that psychology to shape and define its development, including, finally, psychology's involvement with semiotics, which the author sees as a new background against which to envision psychology's second century of growth. Thus, the idea for this book is at once retrospective and prospective. Let me explain.

RETROSPECTIVE DIMENSION OF THE WORK

The retrospective dimension can be well explicated through a remark made by Cole (1977: 1), in presenting in English the personal account of Soviet psychology given by Alexander Romanovich Luria [1902-1977]: "the history of psychology is still short enough to make it possible for the career of one individual to span all, or almost all, of its brief history as a science".

It was exactly this idea that had first led me to suggest, in the spring of 1988, that Professor Gannon consider transcribing and editing with me for publication the series of lectures in history and systems of psychology, as seen from an American point of view, that he had given at Loras College during the 1978 fall term, lectures which had been taped on some eighteen cassettes entombed in the Instructional Resource Center of Loras College.

I knew from close personal contacts that Timothy Gannon (born in 1904 and dedicated to experimental psychology since about 1934; see the Biographical Appendix at the back of this book) contained in his person a rare resource for providing an antidote for what Cole describes as "the general amnesia that afflicts the ahistorical discipline of psychology", which makes it "difficult to recover the dilemmas" that were the shaping influences upon the development of psychology as a science. The idea of capturing in more public and permanent form these shaping influences, the objective substance of Professor Gannon's experience as a professor, lay behind my suggestion for this book.

PROSPECTIVE DIMENSION OF THE WORK

A secondary idea, more speculative, also arose in our discussions: the idea of suggesting how the perspective of semiotic might influence the perspective of psychology as a science, of specifying in this particular how "semiotics as a moment of consciousness expands outward over the whole realm of knowledge and belief to elicit from within each of the disciplines objectively constituted an actual awareness, more or less reluctant, of the semioses and semiotic processes virtually present within them by their very nature as finite knowledge" (Deely 1990: 107).

This is what I would call the book's prospective dimension, as well explained through Boring's observation (1929: vii) that, "strange as it may seem, the present changes the past". For, as he amplified, "as the focus and range of psychology shift in the present, new parts of the past enter into its history". Thus, for example, the reader will find this one of the first works of mainstream psychology to mention the contribution to our understanding of the relational nature of psychic events made by John Poinsot, a heretofore neglected figure in the history of psychology; or to insist on the importance of Locke's introduction into our lexicon of the term "semiotic" for understanding the way knowledge derives from and grows within the experience it structures.

Dr. Gary Shank of the Department of Psychology at St. Meinrad College, one of the psychologists most active in the Semiotic Society of America, served as our main consultant on this point. Besides providing several extremely useful memoranda and other items of research, he also spent three days of consultation with us at Loras College, including giving a public lecture under the title: "Psychology: Cognitive Skirmish or Semiotic Revolution?".

Thus the project of this book, reflected in its title, is not merely to take a backward glance over the shaping of psychology, but, at the same time, to contribute to the shaping by suggesting where psychology, given where it has come from, might go from where it already is. How might the traditionally established discipline of psychology, in particular, be transformed by considering the sensory process as essentially a sign function, rather than the original atom of knowledge?

This is the question to which our author addresses himself in the final chapter of his book, having first "established his credentials" for so conjecturing in the previous eleven chapters. The idea, as he puts it, of a perspective for psychology equidistant "from psychophysical parallelism à la Wundt" and "from reductivistic materialism à la Sechenov" is, for one who knows the history of the discipline, not merely revolutionary indeed, but much needed for the maturation and further integration of this developing discipline now in its second century.

From my own point of view, it is in the area of personality theory—one of the more recent and promising areas of psychology's development, but one which is far from scientifically mature and theoretically unified—that part of the greatest promise for psychology lies. The contrast between organism as a primarily physical structure and personality as a whole, which is primarily a socio-psychological reality and the psychological phenomenon *par excellence*, is yet another of the contrasts which the flexibility of the action of signs makes more intelligible and amenable to scientific interpretation. For just as an organism develops and depends upon physical interchanges with the environment, so a personality develops through social interchanges which are distinct from the physical interchanges that carry them precisely inasmuch as social interchanges involve the further dimension of sign activity, or *semiosis*.

Personality, in its multi-relational nature, is as much a complex of sign phenomena as organism is a complex of physiological phenomena, and just as irreducible. At the same time, just as the living processes of physiology are irreducible to the bare physical processes and elements they involve and rest upon, so the semiotic processes of personality formation and integration are irreducible to the bare organismic physiological processes and organs the personality involves and rests on. Understanding the integration of these two dimensions or levels of process in the person, of cells and tissues with hopes and fears—"the unity of human behavior", as he put it in his 1954 text—has always been, in Gannon's view, the aim of psychological investigation.

CIRCUMSTANCES OF THE WORK

Writing a book always involves peculiar sets of circumstances which make the task more or less difficult. In our case, the difficulty was much reduced by the assistance in the library work needed to pin down the author's reflection which we received from the Spring 1990 Loras All-College Honors class which served as a small team of researchers. I daresay the group learned more about libraries in that one semester than in their previous four years!

Three individuals, however, one from the class and two from the library staff, were of such outstanding assistance in the work as to deserve special mention and thanks here: Mary Hense and Robert Schoofs of the Loras library staff, and Paul Barton of the class. Ms. Hense handled the whole volume of interlibrary loans, even securing books so rare (such as Sechenov 1873) we can still hardly believe she got them. Mr. Schoofs took over whenever our student researchers met the—for them—dead-end of having to go to German and French sources to pin down our references.

Paul Barton, under my direction, became the over-all coordinator of class bibliographical results. He it was who truly learned the use of library resources—and also how little our neophyte research team successfully accomplished in the semester of work. For, luckily for me, he continued his services as our research assistant well into the summer, when, as he put it, "about 90% of the needed work actually got done." The final list of references well reflects his yeoman service to the completion of this book.

Yeoman service in proofreading the final manuscript was provided especially by a team of Gannon's colleagues in the Loras psychology department—Eugene Smith for Chapters 1 and 2, Paul Chara for Chapter 3, John Naumann for Chapter 4 (and the inclusion of footnote 8, p. 62) and Chapter 5, Bob Dunn for Chapter 6, Steve Milliser for Chapter 7, Mary Johnson for Chapters 8 and 9 (where Dr. Johnson substantially contributed to clarification of the treatment of clinical and counseling psychology), Tom Pusateri for Chapter 10, Rose Deluhery for Chapter 11, and again Tom Pusateri for Chapter 12 (and help with the subdivisions therein).

STYLISTIC DEVICES AND REFERENCE CONVENTIONS

Two technical points concerning style need to be noted for the reader's convenience.

First, life dates of individuals are placed throughout the work in square brackets, whereas dates in parentheses always refer to particular writings detailed in the final list of References. The life dates are included at the first mention of a person's name in the unfolding of our history, and perhaps a second time if the name reoccurs in a more primary context later in the work. Even this device, however, does not always succeed in placing the relevant dates at each reader's disposal whenever desired. So, to avoid the tedious and sometimes lengthy task of paging back (or forward) to a first mention of someone's name, we have also included at the back of the book an Alphabetized Chronology where all the dates are gathered in one place.

Second, the professional psychologist reading this book is likely to be puzzled by the choice of reference style for citations: Why did we not use the Style Sheet of the American Psychological Association, choosing instead the newer Semiotic Society of America Style Sheet from outside the psychology discipline proper?

The answer to this question is that the Style Sheet of the Semiotic Society of America is the only style sheet that is organized according to the principle of the historical layering of sources, and, as such, is the reference style best suited to the clarification of origins which, as stated above, this book is all about. Historical layering requires that primary reference dates always be taken from within the lifetime of the author cited, with the relations to translations or later editions of the source work set forth in the complete reference list. The main merit of this style of reference is that it establishes an invariant reference base of sources across all the linguistic, chronological, and editorial lines of access volumes used. This is an outcome so useful to the scholarly community as to recommend the adoption of historical layering as the organizing principle for all style sheets, the APA included.

Bringing rationality into the matters of reference conventions across the disciplines is a thankless but worthy task; in this connection, one other uniquely rational feature of the SSA style which creates consternation in the face of the logical inconsistency to which most other style conventions have habituated us is in the use of quotation marks relative to punctuation marks: punctuation marks are placed outside quotation marks except in those cases where the punctuation itself is part of the quoted material. This procedure follows as a logical consequence of the purpose for which quotation marks are to be used, as stated, for example, in *Webster's* dictionary: "to indicate the beginning and the end of a quotation in which the exact phraseology of another or of a text is directly cited" (see Deely, Prewitt, and Haworth 1990).

Beyond the historical layering principle and the logically consistent use of quotation marks, the differences in detail between the SSA style and the APA style (or, for that matter, the MLA style) are of little significance. These details are set forth in the Semiotic Society of America Style Manual, published in *The American Journal of Semiotics* (1986) 4.3/4, 193-215. We would hope that consideration of the merit of historical layering, rather than a-priori rejection of a style from "out of discipline" based on a convention demonstrably inferior, would weigh in the minds of professors recommending books to their students.

We have tried by these various stylistic devices adopted in this book to provide our readers with a handy guide for following the ongoing process of the shaping of the scientific discipline of psychology.

John Deely
Loras College
18 January 1991

SHAPING PSYCHOLOGY

Chapter 1

PSYCHOLOGY IN ANCIENT GREECE

This work represents a somewhat different approach to the history of psychology, in that its chapters attempt to trace the ongoing relationship between psychology and philosophy through the vicissitudes of the new psychology as it struggled to find its place among the established scientific disciplines. The work takes into account the changing relationships with philosophy as psychology develops new interests and new directions. Thus, the emphasis throughout is on the continuing relationships between scientific psychology and philosophy as its parent discipline, relationships that continued in the nature of the case even over that decisive period when psychology, as part of its effort to achieve independent

1

status and recognition as a modern science in its own right, felt it necessary and expedient to play down or even deny the continuance of any such relationship.

In contrast, the usual presentation of the history of psychology emphasizes the break with philosophy that came with the opening of the first laboratory and the efforts of the new science to make clear the distinction between the new psychology and the traditional treatment of psychology as a part of philosophy, based on rational analysis rather than on laboratory findings. Having pointed out the initial opposition between the new psychology and the older rational psychology, most histories of psychology proceed as if the relationship between psychology and philosophy ended there. This early, casual dismissal of the bearing of philosophy on psychology, however, obscures an important fact, namely, that academic psychology in America during the first fifty years of its development was under the complete domination of the philosophical doctrine of Associationism, the doctrine that the mind is made up of simple elements in the form of ideas that come from sensory experience and are related by associations. Because of its centrality as an original formative influence on psychology as a science, accordingly, the reader will find it useful to take note from the outset of what associationism as a psychological doctrine basically is.

Chaplin, in his handy and generally excellent *Dictionary of Psychology* (1985: 37-38), says that "the doctrine of associationism began with Aristotle's essay on memory and became a dominant theme in British philosophy during the seventeenth and eighteenth centuries", and this has become an accepted way of putting the matter. Nonetheless, this accepted convention stands in serious need of revision, because it blurs the distinction between the *factual observation* that association plays a prominent role in relating our ideas to one another in relation to experience, an observation on which all agree, and *the modern philosophical and psychological doctrine* that the higher thought processes can be reduced to relations of association among simple sensory data, which is quite another matter.

This hypothesis that ideas can be considered *in toto* as the residuum of sensory experience connected by associations, as we shall see over the course of this book, is a doctrine quite foreign to Aristotle's philosophy of soul or mind. "The crystallization of associationism as a formal school of philosophy" in the sense of the doctrine, as distinguished from Aristotle's matter-of-fact observations, "took place", as Chaplin rightly points out (ibid.), "under the leadership of David Hartley [1705-1757]. However, the foundations had been laid by Thomas Hobbes [1588-1670], John Locke [1632-1704], George Berkeley [1685-1753], and David Hume [1711-1776]. It reached its highest development in the works of James Mill [1773-1836]. All of these philosophers emphasized contiguity and similarity as the basic laws of association (a position taken by Aristotle as a small part of his theory of cognition), although they presented varying interpretations of the laws and stated different corollary principles.[1] In present-day psychology there is no school of associationism as

---

[1] By the turn of the 20th century, it was customary for introductory psychology texts to include a diagram of the brain. In these diagrams, the areas of sensory input and motor direction were carefully noted. The rest of the cortex was labeled "association areas". Thinking was reduced to forming associative bonds. Thus when Thorndike, an early student of William James, appeared on the scene as a professor and theorist in his own right in the early 1900s, academic psychology was prepared for his "connectionism" and his S-R Bond theory which then became the basis for elaborate learning theories developed throughout the first half of the 20th century.

such, but its influence remains in theories of verbal and animal learning."

The doctrine of Associationism, thus, as it dominated the formative years of psychology as a new science, was not an Aristotelian influence properly speaking but rather an essential offshoot of empiricist philosophy in its oppositional development with rationalist philosophy in the classical modern period from René Descartes [1596-1650] to Immanuel Kant [1724-1804]. Outgrowing this domination forms much of the story of the maturation and shaping of psychology as a science in its own right. Nonetheless, this "philosophical hangover" of Associationism was the main reason why mainstream psychology was so unprepared for the return to cognition that the cognitive revival burst on the psychological scene with all the novelty and force of a revolution.

This, then, is the background of the present book. It would be important, I think, to realize that this developmental approach to the history of psychology is an attempt to tease out some of the items of specific psychological interest that have appeared very early in our thinking about ourselves, and then to trace somewhat the course of these items' development over time.

Suppose we begin with a very basic issue: What is a human being? How do human animals differ from nonhuman animals with which the human being has much in common? In other words, what about the soul, from which psychology gets its name? Scientific or experimental psychology has never been comfortable with the concept of the soul, and very early has pretty much transferred that discussion into terms of mind. But if we take mind, especially as intellect or intelligence, a good point to begin with is to inquire how we come to know things--the problem of knowledge or the problem of cognition. This is a good example of a very early and very important psychological problem that surfaced even among the ancients. Other examples can be found also, especially in the areas of behavior, such as volition and motivation.

The problem of cognition takes one right back to some of the earliest speculations about the ability of the human being to think. One might think that the matter of the formation of concepts was settled by psychology at least 50 years ago: that concepts and language are entirely explained by association, by simply attaching appropriate names to objects and their representations in the mind. But Russian psychology has challenged this view from the beginning, and more recently American psychologists have reopened the topic and have turned to an older view of concept formation.

In other words, although psychology is a relative newcomer among the scientific disciplines, the problems that it deals with are very old and it is important to realize that what is new about this discipline is not the subject matter, but rather the approach and the method of dealing with it. It is also important to realize that a certain tension has existed between experimental psychology and philosophy, as psychology tried to dissociate itself from the philosophical approach to the study of mind. In order to gain acceptance by the older and better established sciences, the founders of experimental psychology felt that it was necessary to declare their complete independence from philosophy, where by "philosophy" is meant the idealism of Kant and Hegel.

This has proved unfortunate for two reasons. First, the divorce has not worked. The evidence for this is the fact that after a hundred years of experimental psychology, there are signs of a return to some of the concepts that were elaborated in philosophical systems that go back beyond the beginnings of our era. Second, while eschewing all connection with philosophical traditions, the new psychology fell completely under the spell of Associationism, a concept of mind that was elaborated by the School of British Empiricism at the outset of the modern era (see note 1). Added to this was the doctrine of psychophysical parallelism that was adopted provisionally at the Third International Congress of psychology (1896) as the best basis on which to proceed with empirical investigations. Both of these doctrines represent philosophical positions without scientific data to support them. Taken together, Associationism and Parallelism have delayed the recognition of the psychosomatic unity of human behavior for half a century.

A final reason for adopting an approach to the history of psychology that pays some sustained attention to older philosophical approaches to human behavior is that psychology, while starting out with a declaration of independence from philosophy, has in recent years shown an interest in drawing closer to philosophy. For some time there has been a rising tide of criticism of Associationism as a satisfying explanation of human intellectual life. This opens up the whole question of how we arrive at our knowledge and how reliable our knowledge is. Cognitive psychology has come into its own in recent years, and surely this topic was not neglected by thinkers of the Ancient and medieval ages, as we shall see. So, let us begin with Socrates.

SOCRATES [c.470-399BC] AND PLATO [c.428/7-348/7BC]

In taking up Socrates, it is important to realize that we cannot distinguish between him and Plato with any degree of assurance. It's very, very difficult to tease apart how much of Plato's dialogues were actually spoken by Socrates, even though he is the protagonist in a number of the dialogues, but not all. In the later Dialogues, Plato tended to go into rather prolonged discussions and leave Socrates out. But to the extent that the dialogues represent Socrates at all, they enable us to say that Socrates brought the matter of psychological and ethical problems to the fore in his day. Prior to him, philosophy was mostly concerned with the cosmos, the world, and the material universe. By shifting attention to the cognitive and conative issues, in a sense, Socrates introduces psychology—for instance, in the dialogue *Laches*, where he tries to relate courage to different parts of the soul; or in the *Meno*, where he tries to show how memory can draw profound ideas from an earlier existence. Socrates' insistence on clear ideas was for the purpose of dealing with problems of values and ethical concerns. All of these have bearing on psychology, at least in the sense that they are dealing with problems of thought and behavior regulated by choice, rather than about the physical universe, the origin of the world, and the four elements.

With Plato we find an elaborate development of psychological thought, and we can still go back to him for the very first expression of a position that probably has never been absent entirely from psychological thought, namely the position of psychological dualism. What defines psychological dualism is the view that there is separation and independence of mind and body. So, with Plato you begin with the mind-body problem. Strangely enough, at the beginning of the modern era a person who has been very influential in all modern thought, including psychology, namely René Descartes [1596-1650], holds to the same dualism of mind and body. For him there is no possibility of any substantial interaction between them. The soul has some capacity to govern the body, but the body is of a lower substance and a lower order of things, and therefore has nothing to contribute to true knowledge of reality. It was by a similar line of reasoning that Plato was led to his particular theory of cognition, namely, reminiscence.

Reminiscence included the concept that the soul or spirit has a prior existence and that, through some misfortune, it has become enchained to or imbedded in a body. This is the situation of present existence. Plato maintained that the soul or mind, in its prior untrammeled existence, was in direct contact with the world of pure forms, often spoken of as the world of ideas. And, of course, if you have a mind or a basic principle of intelligence and cognition in direct contact with the pure ideas or essences of things, the result is perfect knowledge. This is a perfect match: pure intelligence apprehending true reality with nothing intervening to obscure the cognition. There is direct apprehension, with no reason for any sensory data interfering or intervening at all. In other words there is direct contact between an intelligible object and a knowing mind. Plato maintained that the souls existed in this world of ideas, and that the ideas are the prototypes of the actual existing things in the world of change. Then something catastrophic happened and the soul fell from this perfect state and became immersed in the heavier stuff of the body. It lost the immediate contact with those clear ideas, and could only recapture them by reminiscence. The function of the bodily senses is simply to facilitate this reminiscence, to start the train of reminiscence by which one can recall vaguely and imperfectly ideas that were clear in a former existence.

There is no comprehensive synthesis of Plato's views in any final or definitive work. His views on any topic must be gleaned from a number of Dialogues, and it was not until the third century that Plotinus [205-270AD] worked out a synthesis and a complete formulation and interpretation of Plato known as Neo-Platonism. But the basic ideas, and especially these basic contrasts between mind and matter, soul and body, are clearly set forth in several of the Dialogues, where the contrasting terms are described in ways that are totally incompatible with each other. We may say then that whenever discussion moves toward the mind-body relationship, in a sense it is harking back to the third century BC.

The significance of the Platonic and Neo-Platonic position for the development of psychology lies in the manner in which it discounts and downgrades the senses in the formation of concepts. Among the Christian thinkers of the West, St. Augustine [354-430AD] shared this view, but in a less extreme manner. As we shall see presently, it is precisely on the value of sensory knowledge that Aristotle [c.384-323BC] and after him the greater number of medieval and renaissance thinkers differed from Plato.

Along with these two most basic dogmas defining the psychological standpoint of Plato—extreme psychological dualism and the doctrine of reminiscence as an explanation of the origin of our knowledge—a third point worth mentioning would be his concept of the soul as tripartite, that is, consisting of three parts. At the top is the *nous*, the intellectual or rational soul. Below and farthest removed from this is the vegetative soul, while between these two is the irascible soul. The rational soul resides in the head, the irascible one in the thorax, the area of the chest, heart, lungs. Finally there is the lowest soul, which you might call the vegetative or plant soul. It resides in the intestines, or lower abdomen, and has to do with the maintenance of the basic metabolism of the body.

Plato carries this tripartite division over into the Republic or the "body politic". The ideal state must have wise rulers (philosophers), courageous citizens to maintain security within and without (soldiers and policemen) and temperate and dedicated workmen to support it.

As a final point on the elements of psychology that one finds in Plato, one might mention the position of Socrates which Plato seems to have shared. It is the idea that ignorance is the only evil. If human beings only know what is right they will not fail to do it. Not many clinicians would say that this view of human nature coincides with their experience in the office, but it does appear to have some resemblance to Carl Rogers' optimistic "insight therapy". Translated into everyday experiences this would seem to imply that if a person really understands the nature of his disorder, he will certainly move to correct it. This appears to be far from the rule in practice.

ARISTOTLE [c.384-323BC]

As we move from Plato to his pupil, Aristotle, it is well to recall that the whole purpose in going to the ancient and medieval philosophers is to trace to their origins the topics of psychological interest, not to review philosophy as a whole. At the same time, it is interesting to note that many of these topics have surfaced again and again in contemporary psychology.

At the outset, it is important to realize the extreme contrast between Plato and Aristotle. It would be difficult to imagine a greater contrast between teacher and disciple than the one that came to exist between Plato and Aristotle. Plato was an Athenian by birth; Aristotle was a Macedonian, born at Stagira, in what is now Turkey. Plato was a poet until he met Socrates; Aristotle was the son of the court physician of

Philip, the father of Alexander the Great. From early youth Aristotle was interested in observing nature and studied marine forms that he collected along the seashore. He is regarded as the earliest biologist. In today's terms, Plato was an idealist, while Aristotle was an empiricist. Aristotle believed in writing and kept a good record of his observations. Plato, at least after making the acquaintance of Socrates, was convinced that dialectic, the open dialogue, was the only way to philosophize, and its results could not be committed to writing.

When Aristotle came to Athens as a young man, Plato was already the head of a school located in the grove of Academe. Plato was apparently quite well born and had all the advantages of the more affluent Athenian youth in the early period of artistic and intellectual achievement in Athens. Before he met Socrates he had been a rhapsodist, but was won over by the great simplicity of Socrates. When Aristotle came to Athens, Plato was already the head of the Academy, an institution of considerable renown, of which Aristotle became a part. However, it seems that he continued his own style of scholarship even under the tutelage of Plato, where he remained for a period of about twenty years. The relationship between them is rather strange. There is a saying that Plato referred to the house where Aristotle lived as "the home of the reader". This was not a flattering term, because Plato was convinced that philosophical development takes place only in actual dialogue, presumably Socratic dialogue. So spending one's time studying, reading and writing was not Plato's idea of the best way to do philosophy. However, Aristotle was of that very studious caste of mind, and would probably consider a lot of discussion pretty much a waste of time.

Aristotle wrote a tremendous number of books, but many of them have been lost. Among the important survivors are his works on poetry, rhetoric, ethic, part of his metaphysics, the *De Anima* (or "Treatise on the Soul"), and a number of short treatises on physiological and psychological topics which are of particular interest in psychology today, as we will see in subsequent chapters. Finally, there are his logical works, the *Analytica Priora*, which first sketched the problematic of formal logic, and the *Analytica Posteriora*, which treated of scientific proof or demonstration.

The works of particular interest to psychology are the master work, "On the Soul", and the shorter works including "On the Sense and Sensible" (in other words, sensation), "On Memory and Reminiscence", "On Sleep and Sleeplessness", "On Dreams", and even "On the Interpretation of Dreams".[2]

---

[2] To these primary references I add a recent secondary source of exceeding value, *Aristotle's Psychology* by Daniel N. Robinson (1989). This work came to my notice through the attention it received in the bulletin of Division 24 of the American Psychological Association, *Theoretical and Philosophical Psychology*, 10.1 (Spring 1990). Robinson's excellent work contains invaluable insights, especially in its quotations from neglected areas of Aristotle's writings. The special value of Robinson's work lies in the fact that he has teased out numerous examples of Aristotle's psychology from non-psychological sources, such as the *Rhetoric*, *Politics*, *Topics*, and *Ethics*, both Nicomachean and Eudaemonian.

Taken together, these citations from the spectrum of Aristotle's writings beyond those that are *prima facie* psychological, add up to a comparative (animal) psychology by Aristotle himself. His mentions in particular of human emotions in diverse works shows the integral mind-body responses to life situations. Robinson uses citations from various non-psychological works as concrete laboratory demonstrations of the basic psychosomatic unity of living things operating in human choices and ethological behavior of subhuman animals.

In recalling the parallels Aristotle noticed between human behavior and the ethologically directed behavior of sub-human animals—parallels we would

These are topics that still appear in some form in any basic psychology text. This is not to say that they will be treated in the same way that Aristotle dealt with them. But here we are interested in the formulation of the problems which psychology will later claim for its province, and the insights which may have a bearing on the ways in which that claim might need some readjustment. Our interest however, will be focused more on the treatise, "On the Soul", and some of his logical works that deal with the problems of contemporary psychology. As noted earlier, psychology has never been on easy terms with the idea of a soul and until recently would usually enclose it in quotation marks when the occasion to use the word might arise. But we must remember that modern psychology has never had a workable concept of the soul, having first reduced it to mind and later dispensed with it altogether until very recent times.

So here is one of the very great minds of all time, and one that is very clear on the fact that our knowledge has to be grounded in observation. In other words, we have here in the writings of Aristotle the first reply to the extreme rationalism and idealism of Plato. And that reply is Empiricism, which is the very opposite of Plato's contention that true knowledge is dependent on some former existence, in which we were able to make contact with the true realities, the essences of

---

now subsume under the unitary rubric of zoösemiosis—Robinson shows that the differences between human behavior and the behavior of animals of kindred biological species are not as great as the literature of experimental psychology has often presented them to be. The distance between animal behavior under ethological controls and human behavior under the direction of the will is not as great as psychophysical parallelism made them out to be. In fact, examples of ethological behavior show the act of volition as always taking place amidst and under the influence of the demands of animal appetition.

things. According to Aristotle, on the contrary, we have to gain our knowledge by deriving it from the senses. This means that we have no knowledge that does not come ultimately from sensory data. In other words, there are no innate ideas. This is the direct opposite of Plato's position. Aristotle is saying that the only knowledge of reality that we possess comes ultimately from the senses. This does not mean that our knowledge of reality remains at the sensory level, but that it must begin there. He is firmly rooted in what you might call a scientific and empirical approach to things. All this is in line with Aristotle's emphasis on observation and his interest in biology and embryology. Yet even while Aristotle is a thoroughgoing empiricist, he is not a reductive empiricist, like Hobbes or Locke, who in the end reduce knowledge to a sensory content.

There is another important contrast between Aristotle and his teacher. Plato was very much dedicated to mathematics. After all, mathematics is very near to his ideas of the importance of changeless forms and infinity. On the other hand, there is no evidence that Aristotle ever spent much time with mathematics. How much of it he knew or did not know we can only speculate about, but in his physics he was not dealing with such problems as would later give rise to the principle of Archimedes [c.287-212]. He was not dealing, as far as it appears, with any of the attempts to introduce measurement into the problem of the motion of bodies in space, or anything like that. His physics continued and expanded cosmology of earlier times, but it was, at least, a sound physics in the sense that he was fully convinced of the reality of this world and of its intelligibility within experience. This is because he was fully convinced of the value of sensory knowledge, while at the same time aware of its limitations for defining the whole of scientific knowledge.

The difference between Plato and Aristotle is basic: it has to do with the whole concept of reality. With Plato, the world of sense is only a kind of pseudo-reality. The true reality exists in the world apart from this world. Knowledge then has to come from some kind of action of the mind within itself, rather than through an interaction with sensory data, with the changing world, because senses only register change. And that very radical difference carries through all of the subdivisions of philosophy, and certainly affects the areas of psychology in particular.

The Greek title of Aristotle's basic work, "On the Soul", is *Peri Psycheis*. So the term, psyche, provides the root of all the terms that name psychological disciplines and therapies. The term, psyche, in contemporary usage usually refers to the mind, but the Greeks have another word for mind or intellect. That word is *nous*. Psyche had a broader connotation for them and included the whole range of living functions. What has happened in the Western World is that the term "psyche" or "soul" simply became translated as "mind" or "conscious principle". It was Descartes who was largely responsible for narrowing the term to consciousness.

Note that with Aristotle psyche or soul is not simply the principle of consciousness or of conscious life; it is the principle of all life, even in the absence of consciousness, as in the realm of plants. Soul is simply the vital principle. To capture this broader biological notion of the Aristotelian soul, many later authors would speak instead of the "entelechy". Probably the best definition of entelechy is a vitalizing or animating principle. What Aristotle is saying is that the entelechy is what makes the difference between living and non-living things, between organisms and inert matter. And for Aristotle, every living organism has this entelechy or soul.

Note that in the discussion of entelechy Aristotle gives his final word eliminating the possibility of a Platonic or Cartesian separation of body and soul, in that the union of entelechy and prime matter is at the lowest possible level. There can be no division below this level, because, without this union of prime matter and substantial form, there is no being.

But although not all substantial forms are souls, neither are all souls of the same type or level. Souls are rational, sensitive, or vegetative. And so you encounter in Aristotle something of a reflection of Plato's tripartite division, but it must be understood that for Aristotle each organism has but one soul. Even when he speaks of the three souls as if they were distinct, in any organism there can be but one entelechy or activating principle. In human beings, whose soul reaches the level of rationality, the rational soul activates the vegetative, perceptual, and sensorimotor functions. In this manner Aristotle safeguards the unity of the living organism at all levels.

So, then, the divisions of the soul according to Aristotle's philosophical scheme are into the vegetative or plant soul, the sensitive or sensori-motor or animal soul (nonhuman animal), and the rational soul. The function of the rational soul is thought, best expressed by language. According to Aristotle, only human beings have a rational soul. Nonhuman animals have vegetative and sensorimotor souls, but lack the highest level of soul, and, as a consequence, are incapable of rational thought and its expression in true language.

In this view of the human organism, Aristotle anticipates the Russian School founded by Vygotsky [1896-1934]. His followers maintain that language is as typical of the human being as flying is of the bird or swimming is of the fish. On the contrary, most American behaviorists have worked from the hypothesis that human language is but an outgrowth of animal communication, and much time has been spent in attempting to teach chimpanzees to speak or to learn a sign language. These experiments have demonstrated the upper limits of the chimps' ability, but have not shown that their communication amounts to a true language that makes possible the exchange of ideas. The results amount to a falsification of the hypothesis that led to the experiments in the first place.

The vegetative soul governs the nutrition, growth and reproduction—in general the basic metabolic changes that support the life of the organism. The animal soul adds sensorimotor functions and locomotion to the basic vegetative activities—that is to say, the entelechy at the animal level sustains the basic metabolism, and also makes possible locomotion and the sensory functions that guide it. It is at this point that consciousness, as we know it, enters. With locomotion comes the need for sensitivity to pleasure and pain, putting the organism in touch with its environment, and giving rise to the approach or avoidance movements that enable it to stay alive. At the human level the entelechy assumes rational powers, manifested by thought and language and a much more sophisticated and flexible use of signs. But this higher soul also activates and governs the vegetative and sensorimotor functions that human beings share with lower orders of life.

In coming to terms with Aristotle's concept of the entelechy, it is very important to keep in mind that, although he speaks freely of the three kinds or levels of soul activity, he never considers that a living organism can have more than one soul. For him the soul or entelechy is the principle of unity as well as the principle of diverse activity. This is guaranteed by a reference to his metaphysics and his hylomorphic doctrine--the doctrine that individuals are composites of matter and form. In order to explain change, Aristotle had recourse to the two incomplete principles, potency and act. As applied specifically to the material world, he called these two principles primary matter and substantial form; and in living organisms, the substantial and determining form is the entelechy or soul. Where there is more than one form, there is more than one being, and if there are two entelechies, there are two organisms.

In addition to providing a sound and workable concept of the soul, Aristotle contributed the outline of a dynamic approach to the whole process of cognition. In the process of concept formation Aristotle finds place for the lower activities of sensory input, imagination, sensory memory and the operation of a central function that integrates the input of the various senses. In all of this the contribution of the senses is vital, providing the starting point for the whole process. A very old adage sums up Aristotle's view of the importance of the senses in sense knowledge and the process of thought: "there is nothing in the intellect that was not formerly in the senses". In other words, all knowledge has its origin in the sensory data. Professor Deely suggests (1987: iii-vi) that, in the light of what we have learned about the essential function of signs in all phases of knowledge, a supplementary adage needs to be taken into account: "There is nothing in thought or in sensation which was not first in a sign", the first sign consisting in the relations of sensory data.

Aristotle's theory of concept formation will receive more attention in conjunction with the exposition of the views of Thomas Aquinas, so we shall postpone a fuller exposition of Aristotle's views until that time. This actually follows the order of historical development in this area, since it was in the Latin period from the 12th through the 17th centuries that the epistemological ideas of Aristotle were taken up systematically and worked out in remarkable detail. For the present let it suffice to say that the X-ray provides a helpful parallel: just as the x-ray can penetrate through the surface appearance of things which the ordinary camera presents and reveal solid material underlying, so the intellect can penetrate through the changing surface qualities and grasp the underlying structure of things.

In addition to his exposition on the soul, Aristotle presents some interesting insights on the virtues in his ethical treatises. He presents virtue as occupying a midpoint between extremes of undesirable conduct. For example, the virtue of courage holds the middle ground between timidity and temerity, and prudence regulates behavior between recklessness and the unwillingness to take any risk.[3] Because of its appeal to reason, this view of the natural virtues had great appeal for the Stoics who came later.

After the Golden Age of Socrates, Plato and Aristotle, philosophy went into a sharp decline. A number of unfortunate events contributed to this failure to sustain the high level of speculation, and a period of skepticism began. In this atmosphere of uncertainty, interest turned to ethics and conduct, as the Stoics and Epicureans, with their emphasis on ethical and practical matters, took over. At the same time the center of intellectual life shifted to Alexandria, and mystical religions from the East began to filter in. Out of all this a tightly integrated interpretation of Plato's doctrine called Neo-Platonism emerged.

---

[3] And, as we noted above, Robinson (1989) has presented numerous examples of Aristotle's psychology appearing in many other of Aristotle's treatises.

NEOPLATONISM

Plotinus [205-270AD] and his disciple, Porphyry [c.232-300/306AD] developed a well integrated and highly intellectualized interpretation of Plato's idealism. Plato's true reality, the world of forms, was unified in the Nous, the supreme intelligence just lower than the One. Next in the hierarchy was the World-Soul, which was responsible for the order in the world of change.

Porphyry, to whom we owe the written record of Plotinus' teaching, is remembered, in his own right, chiefly for his introduction to the Categories of Aristotle, called the *Isagoge* (c.271), or *Quinque Verba* (the "five words"), which in the translation of Boethius served as a part of the logic that was a basic book in the medieval library.

The interest of psychology in Neo-Platonism is the manner in which it separates mind from matter as a further example of the psychological dualism of Plato. In addition to this, there is the important historical fact that St. Augustine was brought to Christianity by discussions with friends who were Neo-Platonists—important because of the great influence Augustine's thought had on succeeding generations of medieval Latin students. Indeed, it was the tradition of St. Augustine, stoutly upheld by the Franciscans at the University of Paris, that formed the greatest opposition to the Aristotelianism that St. Thomas introduced in the thirteenth century.

Chapter 2

PSYCHOLOGY IN THE LATIN AGE

The Roman Empire was in an advanced stage of collapse by the 5th century. With that collapse, contact with the Greek language was also lost. By the time of Boethius' execution in 524, the Latin-speaking peoples of Europe were on their own, and so began an indigenous intellectual development that would span eleven centuries and absorb many influences, before the national languages would emerge as the dominant vehicle for science and culture. That indigenous Latin development, "the Latin Age", begins with the work of Augustine [354-430], culminates in Aquinas [1225-1274], and ends roughly in the time of Descartes with the last writer of genius inspired by Aquinas, John Poinsot [1589-1644].

AUGUSTINE OF HIPPO

St. Augustine's significance lies in the fact that he is the most important connection between the rising Christian Schools of the Middle Ages and the decline of the classical schools of Greece and Rome. He is also the single most influential figure of the Latin times, transcending even the renaissance split of Christianity into Protestant and Catholic. The son of a pagan father and a saintly Christian mother, he studied rhetoric at Carthage and taught it for a few years at Milan, where he made contact with some Christian followers of Neo-Platonism. Under their influence he converted to Catholicism, prepared for the priesthood, was ordained, and later became the Bishop of Hippo. He became a powerful voice against the heresies of his time. His writings, filling many volumes, became the most important resource of the libraries of the monastic and cathedral schools when they began to appear late in the seventh century. In the vacuum created by the loss of contact with the Greek writings, it is not difficult to comprehend the extent of his influence on the intellectual and cultural life of the early Middle Ages.

Augustine was unacquainted with Aristotle, but what he knew of Plato appealed to him as a support for the Christian approach to God. In response to the skepticism and agnosticism that was prevalent, he placed great weight on the testimony of inner consciousness, rather than relying on evidence of a sensory nature. He, however, does not discount the value of the senses entirely, as Plato had done. On the other hand, he by no means placed the kind of weight on sensory experience that Aristotle did. Sensory input was a *sine qua non* for the start-up of intellectual knowledge, but once the intellect had taken over, Augustine considered the insight provided by consciousness adequate of itself, without need to recur back to the sensory experience of material things. Augustine's view of the process of cognition was dynamic, and somewhat parallel to Aristotle's, but he held that an inner power of illumination takes over and leads the person to a sure grasp of the truth of the situation. So much weight does he place on this inner source of light that he has been accused by some of depending on divine intervention in the process of cognition. This seems like an exaggeration, but he did believe that the grasp of truth occurred within a divine though natural illumination in the soul's center.

On the question of the union of the soul and body, Augustine avoided the extreme dualism of the Platonic tradition and discarded most of the baggage of his attraction to Manicheanism, the heresy of his time which held that the body and all functions of the body are inherently evil. But, aware of the strength and pervasiveness of the sexual drive in his own life, and led by a deep mystical yearning, he tended to overemphasize the difference between body and spirit. This was probably the result of his own experience rather than any attachment to Platonic dualism.

Augustine would be important for psychology if for no other reason than his book of *Confessions* (399AD), which is the first recorded example of self analysis. Some have designated him as the first psychologist on the basis of this book, which is indeed a classic. For one thing, one will find in this book a careful analysis of the existential will in operation. Here, his skill with words combines with a deep understanding of the self to give psychology a moving commentary on what it means to be human.

While we have touched only on the topics of psychological interest in the work of this powerful and versatile thinker, it is important to realize that his influence on the thought of the Middle Ages was on a par with his genius. Indeed, when we take up the effort of Thomas Aquinas to introduce Aristotelianism into the University of Paris in the thirteenth century, it will be in a prevailing climate of Augustinianism maintained especially by teachers of the Franciscan order.

During the years between the death of St. Augustine in 430 and the coming of the works of Aristotle to the schools of the West around 1150, there seems little evidence at present that anything of particular interest to psychology transpired. The schools from which we get the term "scholastic" began as little more than grammar schools in which medieval Latin became the language of scholarship, religion and diplomacy for all of Central Europe. In the beginning there was a great scarcity of books, since the great libraries of Greece and Rome had not survived the years and the surge of the Huns and Vandals from the north. This shortage of books was gradually remedied, partly by the occasional recovery of a book that had been lost, but mostly by the copying of existing manuscripts by assiduous monks and other persons who shared their concern for writing.

The only work of Aristotle that graced the early medieval libraries were his logical treatises. Along with them was the brief introduction to them by Porphyry, called the *Isagoge* (also *Quinque Verba*), which we mentioned above. These works had been translated by Boethius [480-524AD], the last scholar of early medieval times who possessed knowledge of the Greek language, and who also left extensive *Commentaries* on the translated works. For the early medieval period, up till the mid-12th century, Greek writings not translated by Boethius were unavailable to the Latin West. The logical treatises of Aristotle, called collectively the *Organon* or "Instrument" after the third century, provided, thus, along with Porphyry's short treatise, the logic texts of the schools, where they served as the philosophical component of an otherwise literary and ecclesiastical tradition. Boethius had concluded his translation with the question of the *Isagoge*: Where do universals exist? In the mind? In the name? Or in the object? It was on these questions of both logical and psychological interest that Scholastic Philosophy got its start, and the dialectical part of the *trivium* led to discussions of a metaphysical character. In this engagement in philosophical questions, Peter Abelard [1079-1142AD] played a significant role. His brilliant and original development of logic lost much of its impact through the historical accident of coming at the very moment when new translations of the whole of Aristotle's logical writings were introduced to the Latin West. Indeed, it is only in recent years that the thorough serious study of Abelard's logical theories has begun. Thus we may say that, as far as continuous historical development was concerned, the follow-up on his brilliant writing was derailed by the reintroduction of Aristotle to the Latin West through translations done in Arabic centers in Spain and Persia (today's Iran).

THOMAS AQUINAS

Thomas Aquinas came to the University of Paris just as the translations of Aristotle both from Arabic and from the original Greek to the Latin of the Schools were becoming available. For some time, the works of the celebrated Greek philosopher had been filtering into the monastic and cathedral schools of the Continent by way of Spain. These were Latin translations of Arabic versions that had suffered from the insertion of glosses and commentaries into the text in a manner that made it difficult to determine what was Aristotle's teaching on a point and what was the interpretation of the Islamic commentators. With more able translators, it was possible to sort out the authentic Aristotle. St. Thomas had the advantage of a translator in his own Dominican Order who prepared treatises directly from the Greek texts for him to study and comment on.

It is said that the blood of most of the royal families of Europe flowed through the veins of St. Thomas. His home, the town of Aquino in southern Italy, was near the base of Monte Cassino, where one of the most eminent Benedictine Abbey Schools was located. There, the boy Thomas received a solid grounding in the original seven "liberal arts," that is the *trivium* (grammar, rhetoric and dialectic) and the *quadrivium* (astronomy, geometry, mathematics and music). Thus prepared, he entered the new Dominican Order and was enrolled in their course of studies, first at Naples and later at Paris and Cologne. He had the advantage of a splendid teacher, Albert the Great [c.1193-1280], a fellow Dominican and a student thoroughly convinced of the great value of Aristotle's philosophy and also of the splendid mind of his student. Thomas Aquinas went with Albert to Cologne for three years and thereupon returned to the University of Paris to begin his teaching career.

His acquaintance with Aristotle through his studies under Albert had convinced him that Aristotle's philosophical system had great value as a framework for the intellectual support and development of Christian belief. In this project he had an advantage over his teacher in the new translations that were coming out, which vindicated Aristotle from some of the views on which accusations of unorthodoxy that were being circulated by some of the champions of the Augustinian tradition had been based. In particular, Thomas had the support of William of Moerbeke, a fellow Dominican in Paris, who was translating Aristotle from the Greek text. When William had finished the translation of any work of Aristotle,

Thomas would comment on it in his lectures at the convent of St. James, which was a part of the University of Paris.

Early in his career he achieved a great breakthrough in the opposition to Aristotle when, with the aid of William of Moerbeke he was able to prove that a work that had circulated widely in Paris under the title, *The Theology of Aristotle*, was spurious. He successfully traced it to Porphyry, the Neo-Platonist disciple of Plotinus. This cleared Aristotle of any charge of pantheism and did much to soften the prevailing opposition to Aristotelianism.

Thomas continued to lecture and comment on the separate works of Aristotle even as he began his masterwork, the *Summa Theologiae*, the greatest of the Scholastic syntheses of philosophy and theology. During his lifetime of teaching and study, he was trying to clarify the position of Aristotle, to make it acceptable to Christian thinkers, and to demonstrate that, although it came from a pagan source, it was not contaminated by doctrines incompatible with Christian faith. That, very briefly, is the background from which the Thomistic synthesis emerges. Although the main work is called *Summa Theologiae*, which is translated as a summary or synopsis of theology, it is also full of philosophy. The reason for the title is that because Thomas himself was a believer, and because he did not hesitate to call on the insights of faith to assist him in his answers to questions, he therefore titled his work theological, if you will, or summary of theology. Only a person who depended entirely on reason would be a philosopher. So you find in the *Summa* that St. Thomas normally refers to Aristotle as "the philosopher". To me this says that, as far as St. Thomas is concerned, here is the greatest philosopher who had appeared up to that time. Aristotle is the philosopher par excellence, because he has evolved whatever insight he has entirely by way of reason, whereas St. Thomas would consider himself, by contrast, to be a theologian, no matter on what subject he is speaking, because he was able to supplement reason with the insights of faith.

The psychological material of Thomas Aquinas as regards cognition is found especially in Questions 75-89 of the First Part of the *Summa* (c.1266-1273), in his commentary on the *De Anima* (c.1269-1273), and in his commentaries on the so-called *parva naturalia* (c.1266, 1266a), those briefer works of Aristotle like "Sensation and What is Sensed" and "Memory and Reminiscence"; his treatment of emotions is found in the First Part of the Second Part of the *Summa*, Questions 22-61.

The first and most important issue for psychology in the work of Aquinas is the nature of the soul and its relation with the body. Here, in other words, is where he faces the mind-body problem and the prevailing psychological dualism, part of the Neo-Platonic heritage of the early Latin philosophers. Both in the questions in the *Summa* and in his commentary on the *De Anima*, St. Thomas is in agreement with Aristotle. Like Aristotle he holds that the soul is the animating, vitalizing and unifying principle of the person.

He holds that the rational soul is not only the principle and source of consciousness and mental activity, but it also activates and governs the vegetative and sensorimotor functions as well. St. Thomas subscribes to the hylomorphic (matter-form) concept of Aristotle, so there can be no question of the division of the person into mind and body. The soul is the basic or substantial form and principle of all the operations of which the human organism is capable. Without the soul, the organism does not exist.

When we come to the question of how we acquire knowledge, St. Thomas explains the operation in terms of a process he calls abstraction. The intellect extracts the essential and unchanging features from particularized characteristics of individuals and proceeds to give the object a name. Although the operation takes place in a split second, several steps are involved. These involve the combined activity of the internal senses: sensory memory, imagination, the common senses, and the estimative power, the *vis cogitativa*. This is the function which provides an immediate and quasi-instinctive evaluation of experienced objects as beneficial or harmful.

Following Aristotle, St. Thomas describes these steps in the following terms. The sensory presentation elicits similar sensory experience from the past to form a sort of composite picture, the phantasm. At this point the active intellect illuminates the phantasm and impresses the essential features on the passive intellect. This activity suggests again the analogy mentioned earlier with the x-ray plate in contrast to the ordinary photograph. The photograph faithfully records the surface characteristics of the object, while the x-ray penetrates to more solid structures within. In a similar way the intellect grasps the essential nature and disregards the sensory qualities that are constantly changing.

It is clear that this is an active or dynamic operation throughout, the rational powers seizing on the raw data of experience and reworking them into the abstract concept that can be given a name. This dynamic view of mind is in complete contrast with the static view of mind which we will encounter in radical empiricism. The doctrine of Association, which we noted at the outset of our study as the dominant philosophical influence forming the backdrop of psychology in its initial attempts to become an experimental science, was the derivative of that radically static view, not at all of the Aristotelian views we are considering now.

One of the internal senses merits special comment (see Deely 1971: 55-83 for an extended textual analysis). According to Aristotle and Thomas Aquinas, the *vis cogitativa* had a parallel at the subhuman level. This was called the *vis aestimativa*. This highest of the internal senses involves also learning by experience in higher animals, but always centered around a core of unlearned and species determined awareness that served to warn the animal of predators and assist it in the search for food. This kind of unlearned apprehensive response was denied by the Behaviorists in the 1920s, only to be brought back under the name "species-specific behavior" in the 1950s.

When we focus on the school of British empiricism, which was the main proximate background of scientific psychology, we shall find that all this matter of the internal senses and the active and passive intellect has been discarded as useless and unnecessary to account for the acquisition of knowledge. In this project of streamlining, empiricism constantly appealed to "Ockham's razor", a principle to the effect that the simplest explanation is always to be preferred in accounting for phenomena. This principle is explicitly stated and adhered to by Thomas Aquinas in a number of forms. In his *Summa theologiae* (c.1266), he cites, as part of an objection (I, Q. 2, Art. 3, Objection 2), a common principle generally accepted by the Latins, and, in replying to the objection, he takes no exception to the principle: "what can be achieved through fewer principles does not happen through many" ("quod potest compleri per pauciora principia, non fit per plura"). Indeed, in his *Commentary* (c.1268) on the *Physics* of Aristotle, Book I, Chapter 6 (Lectio 11, n.95), he expounds the principle in question—to interpret the operations of nature in the most economical way possible—as the ground of the most general and basic of all the principles of natural science: "It would be superfluous for what can come about through fewer principles to be brought about through many."

Straightforward statements of the principle in question are not as easily or clearly found in William of Ockham, ironically, since it has been Ockham whose name came to be associated with the principle by those who admired his rejection of many scholastic distinctions. But in fact the principle now called "Ockham's Razor" was a common scholastic property a full century and more before Ockham came on the scene, and existed throughout the Latin age in a variety of forms (e.g., "entia non multiplicanda sunt sine necessitate"—"theoretical entities should not be multiplied beyond what a hypothesis requires"; "frustra fit per multa quod potest fieri per pauciora"—"it is useless to postulate many factors to explain what could be accounted for with fewer postulates").

This points to the problem of applying the principle, that is to say, the problem of establishing when the simpler explanation or theory *really accounts* for the phenomena to be explained. In its application to psychological data "Ockham's Razor" has too frequently amounted to an over-simplified explanation that fails to take all the data into account. It has served as a front for reductionism. In attempting to streamline and simplify the complex process of knowing, the British Empiricists exaggerated the role of sensation, assuming that sensations themselves are meaningful and supply basic bits of knowledge without qualification. What is particularly objectionable about this exaggerated reliance on the senses is that it gives to the intellect only a passive and receptive role in the knowing process. This is the point of greatest contrast between the position of Aristotle and Thomas and the followers of Locke and Hume.

STRENGTHS AND WEAKNESSES

This fairly well sums up the history of the problem of knowledge or concept formation from the beginnings of the philosophical period of Greece to the High Middle Ages. It presents the intellect as actively synthesizing, penetrating and validating knowledge in the effort to explain how we get in touch with reality. However, when this problem and the question of the reliability of human knowledge became the absorbing interest of the philosophers of the modern era when the break with Aristotelianism and Latin tradition began in the works of Descartes and Locke, the intervening and irreducible zone of internal sense was ignored. In treating of sensation as if its content were wholly determined passively, while the understanding came to be viewed as little more than the juxtaposition of those sensory contents through further association, the essentially dynamic and purposeful function of consciousness was lost. In fact, this comparatively simplistic modern view set the stage and provided the agenda for the beginnings of experimental psychology, which has often made progress in spite of or by making explicit the arbitrary restrictions imposed by reductivist assumptions inherited from modern philosophy.

St. Thomas discussed the various powers of the soul and their relationship with one another. These discussions later gave rise to a doctrine of the faculties of the mind which came to be thought of as static compartments of the brain. It is important to remember that with Aristotle and St. Thomas the various powers or faculties were all unified in function by the entelechy or soul.

"The passions of the soul" was an expression used in Aquinas's time both for concepts, ideas and images, and also for what we would today call the emotional life. With Aristotle, Aquinas divided these "passions" into the irascible (energizing) emotions and concupiscible (pleasurable) emotions. These were presented in conjunction with the virtues that are needed to control them, rather than in terms of their involvement of the autonomic nervous system as states of consciousness that need to be accepted and studied as important human experience. The result is a somewhat over-intellectualized approach to human emotion that did not prove sufficiently resistant to the revival in modern philosophy of the old opposition between mind and body. Aquinas' discussion of the "passiones animae" would have benefitted from greater emphasis on the physiological component of emotion that Robinson has teased out of various less familiar and non-psychological works of Aristotle (Robinson 1989: 87):

> Consistent with Aristotle's comparative psychology, his theory of emotion regards the human emotions as just the more sharply delineated forms of what is found among all the advanced species. Any number of animals display "gentleness or fierceness, mildness or cross temper, courage or timidity, fear or confidence, high spirit or low cunning, and, with regard to intelligence, something equivalent to sagacity" (*History of Animals* 588b1). In some instances, the differences are only quantitative; in other instances, the respective states and capacities are analogous.

In terms of Aristotle's comparative psychology, the emotions of subhuman animals are seen to merge with the human in a manner which Christian writers generally have failed to take into account. The philosophical contrast between soul and body was overemphasized and erected into an unhealthy dualism by ascetical writers even before Descartes' proposals gave rise to the doctrine of psychophysical parallelism.

A further appreciable benefit to be gained from Aristotle's comparative psychology is the understanding that the emotions provide the rock-bottom basis of the existential will.

All human choices involve a blend of sensory animal appe-
tites or seekings and distinctively human intellectual seekings, and the animal component is always basic. This sensory
component[4] often requires some volitional neutralization
when the choice of a remote goal is effectively made. Study
of affective life in its relation to purpose and will is something that has been sadly lacking in behavioristic tradition
within psychology. The affective states have been considered
as nonexistent or irrelevant to the study of motivation.

THE PERIOD FROM AQUINAS TO POINSOT

We conclude this survey of the psychological questions that
were dealt with by the thinkers of Greek and Latin times
with a word about the fate of the intellectual development
inspired by the work of Aquinas, whose *Summa Theologiae* in
particular, composed between 1266 and 1273, was a monu-
ment to the intellectual achievement of the schools of the
Middle Ages. This Aristotelo-Thomistic synthesis of ancient
and medieval thought could not have come about were it not
for the amazing sequence of events that opened up Aristotle
to the teachers and students at the University of Paris in the
12th and 13th centuries.

During the transition to the modern era, Scotism and
Nominalism emerged as rival schools competing in subtlety
alongside Thomism. This development greatly heightened
interest in logic, but also brought about a rise of skepticism
in some ways comparable to what occurred after Greece's
"golden age" of philosophy. The English Franciscan, William
of Ockham [c.1285-1349], a brilliant logician, brought the

---

[4] —what we will call, in light of our concluding chapter, a zoösemiotic
component of human behavior and experience—

movement known as Nominalism into the mainstream,[5] and contributed to the movement in several ways: the complete separation of faith and reason, his position with regard to universals, and use of the famous logical "razor" somewhat unwarrantably attributed to him, as we have mentioned. Another name for Ockham's razor is the principle of parsimony, which readily lends itself to a radical reductivism.

When you see discussions of reductivist tendencies in any contemporary discussion of psychology, you will be dealing with basically the same principle, namely, that the simplest explanation is always to be preferred. In other words, you do not postulate the existence of anything unless you can demonstrate it with data that can be measured. This easily becomes a principle of positivistic thinking: you do not consider anything to be real unless you can see, feel, hear or otherwise sense it. Insofar as psychology has subscribed to Positivism, it has denied to the human person the possibility of ascending beyond the level of sensory knowledge.

Even in the fourteenth century great changes were taking place that would usher in the modern era and make it entirely different from and often contemptuous of the medieval period just closing. Some of these changes were the Black Death, decimating the cities, the end of Feudalism and the beginning of the modern states, the discovery of the New World, the Renaissance, the religious revolution and the dawn of the scientific era.

---

[5] This revived the old question with which Boethius had concluded his translation of the *Isagoge* of Porphyry back in the sixth century. That question is: Does the universal concept reside in the object? in the mind? or in the word that names the object? Experimental psychology has attempted to straddle the issue by responding with a strange combination of Idealism and Positivism, as Cardinal Mercier has pointed out (see Chapter 7).

In philosophy, however, the return to an interest in logic brought with it also a turning inward and a concentration on psychological concerns that had been passed over previously. Originally developed at Paris under the stimulus of debates provoked by Ockham's discussion of concepts as "natural signs" (see Deely 1986: 5-34, 1990: 110-113), these concerns were imported into Thomistic circles by Dominic Soto on his return to Spain after some student years in Paris. His logic book called *Summulae*, published at Salamanca (1529, 1554), sparked a series of debates that spread throughout the Iberian university world and turned the analysis of concepts decisively in the direction of what we call today semiotics. But this development, culminating in the *Tractatus de Signis* of Poinsot (1632), unfortunately was to have no influence at all on the mainstream figures outside Iberia who would define modern philosophy, and has been left to our own times to rediscover. We will see more of this in our closing chapter.

CONCLUSION

This brief look at some genuinely psychological problems that have been dealt with in the past should inoculate us against the naive assumption that the problems themselves were discovered by scientific psychology. As we follow the movements of experimental psychology, note that some of these problems recur in different guises.

Note also an essential difference between the review of the Greeks and Latins and the attention to philosophers of the modern era: with the modern philosophers, we deal not with broad philosophical viewpoints that set the stage for further psychological development, but with philosophic doctrines that have been incorporated into the fabric of experimental psychology and have determined its development.

Chapter 3

THE BEARING OF MODERN PHILOSOPHY

ON PSYCHOLOGY

As we move from a consideration of the psychological problems that emerged in the discussions of ancient and medieval philosophers to the beginnings of the modern era, an important difference is to be noted. Whereas the discussions of psychological problems in the epochs of Greek and Latin philosophy have had very little influence on the course of development of experimental psychology, the philosophers that we are about to take up were responsible for setting the agenda and providing main ideas that dominated scientific psychology in its early attempts to achieve acceptance as an experimental discipline.

The transition that set the stage for modern thought should have occurred naturally within the Italian, and to some extent also, the Iberian schools where the natural philosophy or "physics" of Aristotle had been specifically developed around the narrower focus of the *De Anima* in establishing the foundations of a "philosophy of man" and the outlines of what would later be called "rational psychology". What happened instead was a radical departure from the medieval period, in which a dynamic view of rational psychology degenerated into a static and mechanical "faculty psychology" as a result of the emphasis on sensation as the unit of consciousness by the English, Scottish, and American schools of thought. The manner in which this contact with the Aristotelian tradition was distorted and diminished at the beginning of the modern era is so radical that it requires some comment on the changes that accompanied and fostered it.

In this transition from medieval to modern, nearly every aspect of European civilization underwent significant change in the years between 1300 and 1600. Not all of these changes were fully realized but they were all in motion. Take, for example, the change in the political scene. What was the big change in the face of Western Europe? Feudalism had disappeared and in its place the modern nationalistic state was taking shape. The loyalty and fealty that was the bonding element of feudalism was disappearing. Serfs were freed from their indenture to the land and were moving to the towns. Gunpowder has rendered the castle no longer an asset.

In the religious sphere the Protestant revolution and the break up of Christendom was in the making. Culturally, the Renaissance sponsored a revival of ancient, and therefore secular, learning. Gothic architecture came to be regarded as crude and primitive, and there was a spate of rather ribald books, all aimed at ridiculing the Church. In general, the Renaissance championed a worldly and secular view of life, rather than the otherworldly emphasis of medieval religion. A spirit of revolt against the past was in the air.

Geographically, the great voyages and the great discoveries came at the same time, and the whole so-called Copernican Revolution in astronomy did much to alter radically our species' view of itself and of our place in nature.

From the biblical view of humankind as the paragon of the universe, the human being is reduced by the advances in astronomy to an insignificant observer on one of the least impressive heavenly bodies. In this whole period, as in any period when a very serious reversal or very serious upheaval in the general climate occurs, a great amount of doubt and questioning, as well as overall widespread skepticism, results. Indeed, even the "Golden Age" of Greek philosophy was succeeded first by Stoicism with its emphasis on the civil and political, then by a growing skepticism. Similarly after the height of the middle ages: the subtleties of Duns Scotus gave way to the Nominalism of Ockham as a note of skepticism began to dominate in philosophy very early in the 14th century. This spirit of radical questioning was augmented by the cataclysmic changes which affected every walk of life.

The result of all this was a desperate effort to pin down human knowledge, to answer the doubts of the skeptic, and to discover a method or a formula of knowledge which would be absolute and reliable. And so we find illustrated again in the early modern period the attitudes of mind associated with the rationalist and the empiricist viewpoints. As the two positions assume a modern form, they are not totally different from the difference we noted between Plato and Aristotle. The rationalistic approach holds that one cannot rely on the senses at all—true knowledge has to be derived from the mind itself, from the careful analysis of what consciousness presents. In contrast, an empiricist approach holds that the senses alone are the origin and guarantor for what we know.

The empiricist viewpoint, that all our knowledge has ultimately come through the senses, had already been championed by Aristotle and Thomas Aquinas. The word "empirical" is probably best translated as coming from experience, or as based on or derived from sensation. But here in the origins of modern empiricism this theme from Aristotle and St. Thomas is taken up, first, in ignorance of their earlier interpretation of the theme, and, second, with an important difference. Empiricism always places great emphasis on observation, but this is radical empiricism that can be traced to the Englishman, Francis Bacon [1561-1626]. What does this mean? It is the doctrine that the only reliable knowledge is sensory in its content. This goes beyond the empiricism of Aristotle and St. Thomas by holding the position not only that all our knowledge depends ultimately on sensory data, but also that the only sure knowledge reduces to this sensory content. Later on, this position came to be known as Positivism. The doctrine is also referred to as Sensationalism or Sensism, because of its exaggeration of the role of sensation in the cognitive process. Later on, we will see, the development of semiotics will require a re-evaluation of this matter of the sensory origins of knowledge. It will appear that reliable knowledge involves the interpretation of signs, and the first level of this operation is with sensory signs. But this was not what the radical empiricism of the British School was asserting. Their position, rather, was that the only knowledge that can be relied on is at the sensory level and is throughout sensory in character.

By contrast, the rationalist position in its modern form kept faith with the need for some kind of innatism that we saw in Plato's views. Some idea that our basic concepts are inborn continues to characterize the modern version. Our ideas are not derived from experience. These two totally opposed positions taken together provide a summary of the attempts to discover how we come by our knowledge and therefore what knowledge is reliable and what knowledge is not. But at the same time they provide an illustration of how an abstract principle such as that of empiricism can yet be given radically opposed interpretations in the concrete.

John Locke [1632-1704] studied at Oxford, and after some minor appointments there he took up medicine but without much thought of ever practicing. As a young man he entered the service of the Earl of Shaftesbury and became involved in political questions of the troublesome period of the Restoration. He devoted considerable time to political issues at the time when the divine right of kings was being seriously questioned. In the debates growing out of the renunciations of the doctrine of the divine right of kings and the recognition of the rights of the governed, he saw the need for clear and distinct ideas as the basis of any discussion.

This led to his work on the origin of our ideas, which was published under the title *An Essay Concerning Human Understanding* (1690). It set the direction of British Empiricism and was picked up for comment and criticism by a succession of English thinkers who make up the school: George Berkeley [1685-1753], David Hume [1711-1776]. David Hartley [1705-1757], James Mill [1773-1836] and his son, John Stuart Mill [1806-1873]. The interest of this school is due in part to the fact that it provides a complete contrast to René

Descartes' *Discourse on Method*, which had appeared some years earlier. Locke's *Essay* resumed the emphasis on sensation that Francis Bacon and Thomas Hobbes [1588-1679] had earlier introduced.

What follows is perforce a slight simplification of what happened, but the outlines of the simplification are grounded in fact. When John Locke developed his position, very early in the modern era, he based it on a very literal interpretation of the familiar adage of Aristotle: *nil in intellectu nisi prius fuerat in sensu*—"there is nothing in the understanding that was not first in sense". This very literal translation is to the effect that there is nothing in the mind but sensory content. This denial of any knowledge above the sensory level is clearly foreign to Aristotle's concept of the human understanding and to his idea of the way the intellect works. When we recall Aristotle's total rejection of Plato's doctrine of ideas as coming from another world and being present from birth, it seems clear that this slogan is simply saying that there are no innate ideas. He is far from maintaining that the whole content of the mind is at the sensory level.

Another concept that had wide currency in the school of British Empiricism was the image of the mind of the infant as a *tabula rasa* or "blank slate", ready and waiting for the senses to project their data upon it. This leaves us with a very static, passive picture of the mind. It does not leave any room for activity on the part of the understanding to analyze and interpret sensory data as it comes in.

Locke's interpretation seems to reflect an over-simplified or very literal acceptance of this doctrine, and there is some evidence that the textbooks of Aristotle in use in Oxford in the time when Locke was there had already been streamlined too much, omitting ideas that seemed too complex. So, when we see the term "empiricism" applied to the work of Bacon,

Hobbes, Locke and Hume, we should perhaps use rather the designation "radical empiricism". This view is empirical to be sure—it holds for a dependence of knowledge on experience, but it construes this dependence to the point of making it a slavery. The freedom of the intellect whereby it inquires on sensible grounds into what transcends the sensory disappears on this view. The empiricism of the British School simply discarded the internal senses as useless baggage and with them the active and passive intellect. All of these powers of the mind fell victims to Ockham's razor. With them went a dynamic concept of the human mind at work trying to interpret the signs that the senses are continually sending in to the sensorium. In its place Association was given the task of accounting for human cognition.

Thus, by the late seventeenth and the early eighteenth century, the scientific movement was getting under way. With the breakthroughs in physics, chemistry and mathematics, the emphasis on scientific experimentation became very strong. The repeated successes in physics and chemistry gave gradual shape to the scientific method, a shape that became the paradigm for exploration in the life sciences as well, thus setting the stage for the emergence of experimental psychology more than a century later. Because of continued success in the fields of astronomy, physics and chemistry, empirical data were accumulating rapidly. Scientific experimentation seemed destined to unlock the mysteries of the universe. It was in this developing climate that Locke came up with his radical empiricism, which simply said that the only thing we have to rely on is sensory data. And the "ideas" of Locke and the "sense impressions" of Hume, are pretty much that—the raw data of experience.

As earlier indicated, the radical empiricism of John Locke is found chiefly in his *Essay concerning Human Understanding*.

In this work he emphasized the origin of all ideas from sensation and argued strongly against the possibility of innate ideas. From this point on, sensation becomes the central concept in his philosophy, and sensation thus becomes the backdrop for the beginnings of experimental psychology a century later.

Much of Locke's *Essay* is given over to the analysis of ideas into simple and complex, emphasizing that all ideas must come from sensory experience and hence cannot be innate. In the fourth edition of the *Essay* (1700), he added a chapter on association, but he does not develop this concept beyond pointing out how wrong associations or connections between ideas are a potent source of error in the opinions of men, which was his reason for writing the *Essay* in the first place. Later on members of the British School, especially David Hartley and John Stuart Mill, would exploit the function of association and develop the so-called "laws of association of ideas" that set the stage for the beginnings of experimental psychology and established its initial agenda.

Opposition to Locke's radical empiricism developed among his Scotch neighbors. Thomas Reid [1710-1796] and Dugald Stewart [1753-1828] were intent on preserving something of the concept of active powers or faculties of the mind, along the lines of traditional philosophy of mind. Unfortunately, they conceived these powers in terms of special areas or compartments of the mind, probably influenced by the extravagant claims of phrenology, which were being promoted by Franz Joseph Gall [1758-1828] (see Miles 1835). Reid's powers of the mind became the basis for the "faculty psychology" that was pretty much in command in the United States at the beginning of this century. Faculty training or "mental discipline" became the target for E. L. Thorndike (1906) and others in their attack on what they termed "armchair psychology". This was part of their attack on traditional education, as they tried to make education entirely experimental.

In appraising John Locke's contribution to the scientific approach to the study of psychology, one should place more emphasis on his radically empirical approach to knowledge than on his pioneering reference to the association of ideas, even though his followers (such as Hume, Hartley and Mill) would make of the doctrine of associationism—the theory, as we have seen, "which takes association to be the fundamental principle of mental life, in terms of which even the higher thought processes are to be explained" (Drever 1968: 11)—the central explanation of cognitive activity. By his lack of precision in the use of the terms "sensation" and "idea", he gave to sensation the first byte of meaning in the cognitive process. In a very true sense he laid the groundwork for Positivism, which became the trademark of the scientific movement.

Ironically, John Locke's name is being brought up today in quite a different connection. Toward the end of the *Essay*, he introduces a new term, "semiotic", which opens up a wholly different view of the value of sensations, not as building blocks of our knowledge, but as signs to be interpreted. This involves a dynamic, rather than a static, view of the mind, which takes us back to the Aristotelo-Thomistic theory of cognition and the dynamic interaction of the internal senses with the active and passive intellect. Although Locke's interest in semiotics seems to have come as an afterthought to his version of empiricism, it is interesting to speculate—and we will have to do just this in concluding the present work—on the different route modern thought might have taken if John Locke had gone on to a full-scale development of his semiotic insight, or had been familiar with John

Poinsot's [1589-1644] illuminating replacement of Aristotle's small logical treatise, *On Interpretation*, with a full scale *Treatise* on the role of signs in knowledge (Poinsot 1632). This treatise, in Professor John Deely's excellent bilingual edition, emphasizes the universal role of signs in all cognitive operations, beginning with the sensory changes produced in consciousness by the sensory impulse and extending to the level of the highest achievements of understanding. Poinsot's work, although published in the very year of Locke's birth and less than sixty years before Locke's *Essay*, remained unknown to the world of English philosophizing; for by Locke's time communication in the scholarly world between Northern Europe and Spain had almost entirely stagnated.

THE RATIONALIST POSITION—RENÉ DESCARTES [1596-1650]

Diametrically opposed to the radical empiricism of Locke and the British School was the doctrine of innate ideas introduced into the modern era by René Descartes. While modern psychology has drawn much more heavily from Locke and his followers, it also shows the influence of Descartes, as Cardinal Mercier has pointed out in his *Origins of Contemporary Psychology* (1897), discussed in Chapter 7. In fact one of its most basic concepts, that of the reflex arc, can be traced to Descartes. So psychology can be said to have drawn from both modern philosophical traditions, and, in its first phase, the contents were dictated largely by the philosophical precedents set in the modern era. Thus, as we get nearer to the beginnings of laboratory work in psychology, the influence of philosophical issues becomes more proximate and tangible. This focus of interest was due in part to the fact that the philosophical center had shifted in this same period from ontology, the study of being, to consciousness, which is also a main concern of psychology. Hence, the analysis of sensory consciousness became the primary problem of the researches in the first laboratory of the new psychology.

Both the empiricism of Locke and the rationalism of Descartes were attempts to discover the basis of true and reliable knowledge in response to the prevailing skepticism. Both had been brought up on the rather shallow Scholasticism that had survived the thirteenth century outside of Iberia and Italy. Both sought the basis of reliable knowledge in the idea, but at this point their philosophical reflections took opposite directions. Whereas Locke depended entirely on the senses for the true ideas that constitute reliable knowledge, Descartes, like Plato, placed no reliance at all on the senses. How did this radical difference come about?

Locke clearly shows the influence of Bacon and Hobbes, with their emphasis on the concrete and the practical. Descartes' answer to the skepticism of the day was influenced by a mathematical approach. A gifted mathematician, at an early age he had achieved a breakthrough in combining algebra with analytic geometry. Looking around him he saw philosophy in complete disarray, with followers of Augustine, Thomas, Scotus and the Ancients vying with one another, each relying on the authority of a favorite philosopher. He asked himself, Why could not philosophy be like mathematics? In that discipline, when a theorem was proposed, the theorem was put to test, and either successfully proved or discarded. The appeal was directly to reason in mathematics, while in philosophy the recourse was to authority.

Descartes decided to begin his work by cutting away all uncertain knowledge or opinion of any sort by his system of methodic doubt. This included all sensory knowledge, because the senses are unreliable, as the bent appearance of a spoon in a glass of water clearly shows. From here it was an easy step to sweep away all the philosophical doctrines and opinions of the past. This procedure is presented in considerable detail in his *Discourse on Method* (1637), and especially in his *Meditations on First Philosophy* (1641). His remedy for the skepticism of the day is to push doubt to its absolute limits, to see what might emerge beyond. He soon finds that he cannot doubt that he thinks, that he is conscious; and, if he thinks, he must exist. His famous words are: *Cogito ergo sum*—I think: therefore I am. It is important to note that in this formula the "I" stands for only a thinking subject or mind. It does not include assurance that I exist in or as a body. This fact must be proved by a series of deductions that proceed like a geometry text. In this series of proofs, the all-perfect existence of God is the fulcrum, which Descartes proceeds to establish by his unusual version of the ontological argument, originally formulated by Anselm [1033-1109]. In the original argument, the contradiction in considering a-being-than-which-a-greater-cannot-be-thought as possibly not existing was alleged as proof that such a being must exist. In Descartes' variation, the fact that I can conceive of such a being is alleged as proof that such a being must exist as cause of my idea, since the cause of anything must be at least equal to the effect.

This summary sketch of Descartes' line of reasoning clearly shows his innatism and his repudiation of sense knowledge. In this he shows affinity to Plato, while his version of the ontological argument develops strains of thought that can also be found in Augustine.

What is more important for the development of psychology, however, is the manner in which he injected the mind-body problem into the modern background of psychology. Probably even before the time of Descartes it had become customary to think of the soul in terms of mind or principle of consciousness, rather than in terms of principle of unity in living things. Descartes reinforced this view and created an impassible gulf between soul and body, thus postponing the recognition of psychosomatic interaction for the first hundred years of scientific psychology.

This is psychological dualism as radical as Plato had proposed, and it is now introduced into the background of psychology by one of the most influential thinkers of the modern era. It involves the most complete divorce between the functions of mind and body.

For Descartes, the mind has only one attribute: consciousness or thought. Thought for him includes both knowing and willing and all other conscious operations. The body also had but one attribute, the attribute of all matter viz., extension. In fact, for him, the body was a machine, a very delicate and complex machine, but mechanical in all its operations. Apparently the model of the human body that Descartes had in mind was one of those ingenious water clocks or robots powered by the flow of water and found in the gardens of the aristocracy of his day. Clearly there is no possibility of any communication between two substances so completely opposed to each other in all aspects. Yet, somehow, the mind exercises control over the body. To bridge this gap he called on the "animal spirits", a term and concept that had considerable currency in his day. Even giving to animal spirits the contradictory attributes of spiritual or immaterial and material substance in the form of some very light fluid did not solve the problem of the interaction between mind and body. In a letter to the Queen of Sweden late in his life, Descartes used the analogy of a captain and his ship, but admitted that this simile really fell short of answering her questions.

At this point it is important to compare this image of human nature with that presented by Aristotle three hundred years before the beginning of our era and reaffirmed by Thomas Aquinas in the thirteenth century. In the mind of these thinkers, the human being is a rational animal. The soul of that animal is the substantial form of the body. Neither soul nor body is complete in itself and only in the combination of the two does a human being exist.

The contrast between the two positions is clear. For Descartes, the soul is the principle of consciousness alone; for Aristotle the soul is the single principle of life, the source of its unity and the activating principle of all parts of the body and of all that the body does. In this view there is no mind-body problem, because a single principle, the soul, activates all organic functions from metabolism to muscular exercise and all mental functions from sensory awareness to the grasp of complex meanings.

This unbridgeable gap between mind and body is the burdensome legacy of Descartes to modern psychology. Under the imposing title of psychophysical parallelism (a terminology in the Cartesian line coined by Leibniz within a few years of Descartes' death), it became one of the unproved assumptions of academic psychology, and it has postponed the serious study of the emotions for decades, creating an air of mysticism about psychosomatic disorders that has made the work of psychotherapist to appear like that of some magician.

Conclusion

As we leave this presentation of the remote and proximate philosophical heritage of psychology, it is useful to return to some observations made at the beginning of our discussion.

Our concern in going back to the ancient and medieval thinkers was to take note of the early appearance of certain problems that have proved to be perennial in psychology and to observe the manner in which they were handled by philosophers. Between what we have referred to as the proximate philosophical influence on psychology and the remote influence, this difference is to be noted: while it is almost impossible to trace any direct influence of the ancient and medieval thinkers on the development of the new science of psychology, the direct and formative influence of modern philosophy is clearly evident.

As we shall see when we come to the beginnings of experimental psychology, Descartes' emphasis on the conscious states and his radical separation of mind and body combined with the empiricism of Locke to open the way for the analysis of the conscious states that constituted the agenda of the first laboratory in Leipzig in the last quarter of the nineteenth century. Probably the chief example of this influence of modern philosophy on the new science of psychology may be seen also in the manner in which Associationism has dominated theory and research on learning in America for more than fifty years, while psychophysical parallelism received official approval in the Third International Congress of Experimental Psychology (1896) as the best philosophical base for the new science of mind that was emerging (Misiak and Sexton 1966: 15).

This heavy influence of modern philosophy with its mentalistic approach to the new psychology is not surprising when we recall that the philosophy of the modern era has moved away from the consideration of being and the world to a preoccupation with mind and thought. But we must at the same time take note of the fact that a scientific psychology, by its own development, strongly suggests that some of the older views of human behavior and psychology that modern philosophy filtered out are in need of being brought back into consideration, albeit in a framework and climate entirely different from that of Greek or Latin times.

Chapter 4

THE RISE OF

EXPERIMENTAL PSYCHOLOGY

Three movements contributed to the rise of scientific psychology. These were the development of the doctrine of Associationism within modern philosophy, the development of a systematic interest in physiology, and the development of statistical analysis within mathematics.

It was through the position known as Associationism that British Empiricism exercised a determining influence on the emerging scientific study of the mind. There is nothing new about the principle of association. Aristotle called attention to the fact that an idea in the mind easily becomes linked up with other ideas that are similar, or proximate, to it in time or place. Repetition tends to fix the linkage in consciousness and make it permanent, so that the reappearance of one term of the association automatically brings the other to mind.

What Associationism adds to this is the claim that the explanation of all higher thought processes can be reduced to such formation of associative bonds. It was mentioned earlier that John Locke had introduced the term, association, but did not reduce all cognitive activity to association. He was particularly concerned with the manner in which associations casually formed may lead to erroneous opinions that become very hard to dislodge.

It was David Hume who gave to Associationism its definitive form and formulated its so-called laws of similarity, contiguity and cause and effect (1748, 1750). Hume was extremely critical of Locke, and introduced a note of skepticism into all scientific endeavor by maintaining that the laws of the physical sciences are in reality only the result of associations formed by the mind. This was the disturbing position that Immanuel Kant [1724-1804] said awoke him from his dogmatic slumber. This was also the position formally reducing all thought activity to the formation of associations.

Coming from a medical background, David Hartley [1705-1757] reinforced the concept of associationism as the universal law of mental operation. He was greatly influenced by Isaac Newton's [1642-1727] explanation of the vibratory movement of light and sound. He translated the concept of minute vibrations to the central core of the nerve fiber, and thus moved nearer to the contemporary view of nerve action. In doing so he contributed to the demise of the animal spirits—a concept, it will be remembered, on whose magic properties Descartes had relied heavily—and substituted the concept of minute vibrations traveling through the nervous system. Throughout his life, Hartley tried to find the connection between these minute vibrations and the sensory changes which they consistently produce in consciousness.

Thus, in addition to setting the program for the new psychology by pointing to the laws of association as the key to the understanding of human mental life, Hartley pointed the way to an experimental grounding for psychophysical parallelism. This is the doctrine that mind and body run in parallel courses, the mind reflecting what is happening in the body, but neither controlling the other. It is in this manner that Associationism came to have such a predominant influence on the development of experimental psychology, an influence that lasted for more than half a century.

The next important contribution to the new psychology was physiology. It goes without saying that psychology as an experimental discipline could not have gotten started without some basic information on the brain and nervous system, displacing the mystical notion of "animal spirits". Long before the nineteenth century it had been generally recognized that the brain was the seat of consciousness, but the realization that different parts of the brain had different functions was not generally recognized until well along in the 19th century. The first significant datum concerning the brain was the recognition that the center for speech is located in the lower frontal lobe of the left hemisphere. This discovery was made by Paul Broca [1824-1880] in 1860. This fact of localization of function in the brain was followed by the report of Gustav Theodor Fritsch [1838-1927] and Eduard Hitzig [1838-1907] on the location of the center for general body control (Fritsch and Hitzig 1870). But the controversy over the extent of localization carried over well into the 20th century.

The most important breakthrough in the knowledge of the way nerves function had been reported earlier in the last century. This was the demonstration of the one-way law of nerve transmission by François Magendie in France, whose results did not appear in print (1818, 1822) early enough to close the window of cynical opportunity used by Charles Bell in a shamelessly chauvinistic way to claim the discovery for himself, on the basis of an 1811 work which sustains the claim only with a hindsight made possible by familiarity with Magendie's work.[6] Another development that contribut-

---

[6] Olmsted describes Bell's claim to priority in the work rightly established by Magendie in the following remarks (Olmsted 1945: 114): "Bell decided, now that Magendie's experiments and his clear-cut statement of the implications had drawn attention to the matter, that he would do well, even at this late stage, to publish his own views. He therefore brought out a book in 1824 entitled, "An exposition of the natural system of nerves of the human body, with a republication of the papers delivered to the Royal Society on the subject of nerves". These Royal Society papers were, however, so altered in their wording as to make their statements conform more nearly to the concept of the nervous system which followed from Magendie's 1822 paper than their original expressions would allow, and Bell made no mention of any changes, stating that these were "the papers which I presented to the Royal Society". Olmsted proceeds to detail the unacknowledged changes, showing them to be indeed changes such as "can only have been made in the light of knowledge gained subsequently to the writing of the original paper" (ibid. 115).

"At first," Olmsted notes (p. 118), "some British journals gave the credit to Magendie"; however, "by 1830 Bell's influence in London had become overwhelming. He was instrumental in bringing about the foundation of University College and was a leading spirit in the Middlesex Hospital. Anyone venturing to criticize Bell did so at his peril. Dr. Pattison, the first occupant of the chair of anatomy at University College said at the first distribution of prizes, 'Bell's mistaken idea that the fifth nerve bestowed motion and sensation on the parts on which it was ramified had been corrected by M. Magendie and Mr. Mayo.' He was cried down by the students, dismissed from his post on the charge of incompetence and half the professors in the university resigned in protest."

The ground for such a triumph of chauvinism was well prepared by Bell himself, who had published in the *Philosophical Transactions* of the Royal Society for 1823 (113: 299, cited in Olmsted 1945: 117) the following revealing remarks:

ed greatly to the beginnings of the new science of psychology was the work of the Berlin school of experimental physiology established by Johannes Müller [1801-1858]. He set forth the doctrine of the specific energy of nerves, in which he noted that the character of the experience in consciousness that results from stimulating a sense organ is determined by the cortical area to which it is transmitted, rather than by the kind of stimulus that is exciting the sense organ. All receptors respond to electrical stimulus but each receptor responds with the conscious experience that is specific to the sensory center in the cortex to which the nerve impulse is transmitted. Thus electrical stimulation of any receptor will result in the change in consciousness specific to the nerve tract and cortical center involved.

Because of the prestige of Müller's research in physiology, bright students from many countries came to learn his

---

When the popularity of these doctrines (those of Gall, Spurzheim and Magendie) is considered, it may easily be conceived how difficult it has been, during their importations to keep my Pupils to the example of their own great Countrymen. Surely it is time that the schools of this kingdom should be distinguished from those of France. Let physiologists of that country borrow from us, and follow up our opinions by experiments but let us continue to build that structure which has been commenced in the labours of the Munros and the Hunters.

Bell would have been well advised to consider yet another futurible in staking his claim: the observation in Hungarian folklore of the physicist who kept on his desk a sign advising his Hungarian colleagues that "It is not enough to be Hungarian". In matters of scientific advance, being of any nationality—not even, *pace* Bell, English—is not enough. This is an episode in the history of science which shames even the controversy between Leibniz and Newton (no mean feat, but hardly a feat to the credit of Bell—or the "English people" he thought himself so superiorly to represent).

method. Among them were Ivan Sechenov [1829-1905] from
Russia and Emil DuBois-Reymond [1818-1896] and Hermann
von Helmholtz [1821-1894] from Germany. Both of Müller's
German students later made significant discoveries in the
operation of nerves. DuBois-Reymond discovered the electrical discharge that accompanies the nerve impulse and von
Helmholtz measured the speed of the nerve impulse. In addition to these noteworthy accomplishments, Müller's work
provided the methodology that was adopted in the first psychological laboratory established by Wundt at Leipzig in
1879, and undoubtedly had something to do with Wundt's
choice of the expression "physiological psychology" in the
title of his 1873 work on the scientific approach to psychology. Many of the researches of the Berlin school involved
measurements of sensory functions and the nerve impulse.
These provided important data that could be incorporated
into psychology. They also provided a method of investigation that opened the way for psychophysics, the first name
given to the new psychology. At the same time they pointed
the way to methods that could become the model for the
further study of conscious functions.

The third discipline that contributed substantially to the
emergence of psychology as a scientific enterprise was
measurement. In fact it was the reliance on measurement and
quantification that supported the claim of the new psychology to be scientific, in contrast to the non-quantitative approach of philosophy. As psychology developed, statistics,
present in the first psychophysical measurements of Ernst
Weber [1795-1878] in elementary form, was destined to have
a constantly expanding role. Sechenov summarized the
importance of the statistical approach for the prospect of
subsuming human psychic events and action under laws as
follows (1873: 338):

The only thing that prevents us accepting the idea of the immutability of the laws governing our psychical life is the voluntariness of human acts. But modern statistics have thrown some light on this medley of psychical phenomena by proving that some undoubtedly voluntary human acts (marriages, suicides etc.) are subject to definite laws, if they are taken, not as individual cases, but in the aggregate, and for a considerable period of time.

With this background in mind, we are prepared for the birth of the new science of experimental psychology, first known as psychophysics. It began with a movement that has since become known as structuralism, a name that comes from the fact that it sought to understand the human being's conscious life by analyzing it into its basic structures or elements. With association as the accepted explanation of the manner in which simple ideas become integrated into larger meanings, the study of simple sensory experience seemed to be the logical basis for an understanding of more complex mental functions. The aim was to develop a chemistry of the mind, as John Stuart Mill once referred to it.

Even as we use the word, structuralism, to characterize the first school of psychology, we must warn the student that the same word, structuralism, has been used to designate the later school of Gestalt. It is very important not to confuse the two uses of the term, because Gestalt psychology came into existence in direct opposition to the structuralism of Wundt and the Leipzig school.

The first book that presented a method of measuring sensory experience was published in 1860 by Gustav Theodor Fechner [1801-1887]. It was called *The Elements of Psychophys-*

ics, and incorporated (pp. 112-198) work done earlier (1846)
by Ernst Weber on "just noticeable differences" (j.n.d.).[7] This
deals with sensory thresholds and involves the determination
of how much the stimulus must be increased or decreased in
order that a second stimulus can be correctly distinguished
from the first. In correctly discriminating weights on the skin,
Weber thought that, as weights were increased, he saw a
mathematical relationship between the increase or decrease
of the stimulus and the subject's ability to judge correctly the
direction of the change. Fechner proposed an algebraic
formula to express the relationship that Weber had observed.
This formula has been found to be only a rough approxima-
tion, but it had the effect of raising hopes that a psychology
could be developed that rested securely on scientific measurement. "Psychophysics" as the first distinctive name for
distinguishing the new psychology from the study of the
mind as a branch of philosophy was taken from the title of
this 1860 book of Fechner.

One should not fail to note the manner in which the first
name given to the new psychology reflects the doctrine of
psychophysical parallelism which originated with Hartley
and Alexander Bain [1818-1903], but which emphasizes the
fact that Descartes' fateful legacy of the mind-body dichotomy carried over into the very first movement in experimental
psychology. In fact, psychophysical parallelism was accepted
as the official position at the Third International Congress of
Experimental Psychology which took place in Munich in 1896
(Misiak and Sexton 1966: 15).

---

[7] Zusne (1984: 454) remarks that "Weber's other work was not as well
known at the time, and his discovery of the just noticeable difference in
sensation might also have passed unnoticed if Fechner, who was also at
Leipzig, had not made it into a cornerstone of psychophysics."

WILHELM WUNDT [1832-1920]

We are in a position now to date the beginnings of psychology as we know it. There is always some arbitrariness about placing a date on the beginning of something that has emerged gradually. The year 1874 is the date of the appearance of the first book that attempted to bring together the findings of various people who had been doing experimental work with the sense organs and the nervous system, combining that work with the data from psychophysics, and strongly advocating the launching of a new psychology of mind. This classic in the field, published by Wilhelm Wundt, went through four editions and bore the title, *Principles of Physiological Psychology*.

The author, Wilhelm Wundt, had done medical studies at Tübingen and Heidelberg, but it was his study under Müller at Berlin that shaped his decision to devote his efforts to establishing the new discipline of experimental psychology. After returning from Berlin, Wundt took a medical degree at Heidelberg where he worked with von Helmholtz and published the first volume of his *Principles*. In 1875, he accepted a position in philosophy at Leipzig where he established the first laboratory for experimental research in psychology in 1879. William James [1842-1910] had equipped a demonstrational laboratory at Harvard in 1875, but this gesture towards experimental psychology did not include the opportunity for advanced study and a doctoral degree, as Wundt's laboratory did. The novelty of the discipline and the dedicated work of Wundt attracted bright students from around the world. Among these were many Americans, a number of whom returned to this country to establish departments of psychology in universities and promote the acceptance of the new psychology.

In the quarter of a century that followed the publication of the classic *Principles*, the new discipline was launched. But the early shape of scientific psychology was so different from what psychology has become today that some exposition of Wundt's system must be added. Wilhelm Wundt left an indelible mark on, but also a very narrow framework for, the psychology he promoted with such tireless vigor.[8]

There is general agreement among psychologists that Wilhelm Wundt was the most important single figure in the founding of the new psychology. This is based on several facts. He wrote the first comprehensive work on the new discipline, his *Principles of Physiological Psychology*, the first volume of which appeared in 1873. He opened the first laboratory granting an advanced degree in the new discipline at Leipzig in 1879, where he had given experimental demonstrations in connection with his lectures from first assuming

---

[8] This point is of great importance for the final evaluation of Wundt's position in psychology and his discrepancy from his American disciple, Titchener, which we will have occasion to mention along the way. The new psychology was to be experimental in setting itself apart from philosophical theories of human nature, and Wundt played a leadership role in this regard. Unlike those who came after him, however, Wundt never considered that psychology in its totality could be rendered experimental. From experimental work he specifically excluded whatever of human thought transcended direct relation to immediate sensory stimuli, the so-called "higher thought processes". His own handling of the higher thought processes he reserved to his so-called *Völkerpsychologie* (i.1900-1920), which was much more in the broader German tradition of the *Geisteswissenschaften* (the "human sciences" as counterdistinguished from the "natural sciences") than the new psychology would turn out to be (see gloss in the References for Wundt i.1900-1920). It was as if Wundt thought the whole of what we now know as cultural anthropology could have been subsumed within psychology. In any event, Wundt's "larger definition" of psychology had no influence on the actual development of the discipline at large, which actual development is our sole concern in this work.

his chair there in 1875. In 1881 he established and edited *Philosophical Studies*, a journal devoted to the discussion of the new psychology. Thus Boring [1886-1968] describes Wundt as "the first man who without reservation is properly called a psychologist" (Boring 1950: 316):

> Before him there had been psychology enough, but no psychologists. . . . When we call him the 'founder' of experimental psychology, we mean both that he promoted the idea of psychology as an independent science and that he is the senior among 'psychologists'.

The use of the term "physiological" in the title of Wundt's 1873 text not only served to distinguish the experimental approach to psychology from its traditional philosophical discussion, but was meant to emphasize the physiological character of the scientific approach. Wundt has expressed his aim to analyze conscious states in terms of their physiological components in the *Principles* (1873: 228):

> It is clear that the forebrain, in which the most signifi-cant functions of the cerebral cortex are concentrated, transforms sensory stimuli into extraordinarily complex movements of many forms . . . . Everything which we call Will and Intelligence resolves itself, as soon as it is traced back to its elementary physiological phenomena, into nothing but such transformations.

From these and similar statements it is clear that for Wundt the science of psychology was to be the result of the perfect blending of the internal and the external contents of consciousness. It would be neither psychology nor physiolo-gy, but the combination of the two in a new discipline, physiological psychology. When the more complex states of consciousness had been reduced to elementary physiological data the new science, soon to become known simply as "psychology", would come into being. To analyze the internal states of consciousness he developed his rigorous introspective method. To acquire the introspective approach, the subject must be patiently trained to hold one object steadily in attention while taking note of the changes in sensory consciousness induced by the experimenter's systematically varying the conditions of the stimulation. The changes in the sensation must then be objectively recorded in a protocol. That is to say, these changes, verbally reported by the subject over the course of the experimenter's variation of stimuli, would be carefully written down in the experimenter's notebooks. Differences in individual reports could then be subjected to statistical analysis to determine quantitatively both the median or average of whatever sensory function was being measured.

The equipment of the Leipzig laboratory was simple. It consisted of a Hipp Chronoscope, capable of measuring time in thousandths of a second; a set of Helmholtz resonators for the analysis of sound stimuli; and a variety of devices for measuring sensory thresholds for the different senses. One of the experiments frequently used was the measurement of just noticeable differences (j.n.d.). Another was the very close measurement of reaction times, first known by the quaint name, "the personal equation". This sometimes included the time required when the choice of a simple motor response (the release of a key, for example) was involved. Skillful use of these devices permitted the accumulation of data concerning the temporal and spatial sensory threshold, reaction times, attention span and the like. Such studies made up a large part of the results reported in Wundt's psychological journal, *Philosophical Studies.*

In the fifth edition of his *Principles* (1902-1903), Wundt adds some further precision to his statement of the task of experimental psychology:

> Thus, the task we assign to our science is this: *first*, to investigate those life processes that, standing midway between external and internal experience, require the simultaneous application of both methods of observation, the external and the internal; and *second*, to throw light upon the totality of life processes from the points of view gained by investigations of this area and in this way perhaps to mediate a total comprehension of human existence.

On the program of Wundt's laboratory and its methods there is ample documentation, but concerning the influence of British empiricism and Associationism in Wundt's system, there has been considerable disagreement. An early evaluation of Wundt's position, based on Titchener's appraisal, was made by Edward G. Boring. In the first edition (1929) of his authoritative *History of Experimental Psychology*, Boring placed Wundt clearly in the Associationist position, and indicated that for Wundt the goal of psychology was the reduction of complex mental states to their irreducible sensory origins. According to this view, scientific psychology becomes a kind of mental chemistry; and the laws of association become the principles of cognitive awareness. Because of the regard for Wundt expressed by Titchener and the prestige of Edward Garrigues Boring as a historian of psychology, this view went unchallenged until 1947, when Arthur L. Blumenthal and his collaborators pointed out that the Titchener-Boring account amounted to a gross misrepresentation of Wundt. Since then a number of studies have pointed out that the standard version had avoided all reference to Wundt's rejection of Associationism and did not take into account Wundt's forthright assertion that he regarded his system as best characterized as Voluntarism. Another concept that looms very large in Wundt's conception of conscious activity is apperception, a term and concept he borrowed from Herbart [1776-1841]. Apperception is scarcely mentioned in Boring's version. This is an important omission because it is very probable that Wundt's claim that his system is a voluntaristic one comes from the fact that apperception for him was dynamic and active, sometimes amounting to selective attention. On the other hand, some of the opponents of the Titchener-Boring version would make of Wundt's Voluntarism a *Ganzheit* or holistic tendency. This is entirely unwarranted in view of Wundt's opposition to any metaphysical factor that might be considered volition.

Undoubtedly Wundt's particular and sometimes changing use of such words as "voluntarism", "apperception", and "association", compound the problem of teasing out his true system. In *Wilhelm Wundt in the Making of Psychology*, Rieber has provided a sustained rebuttal of the Titchener-Boring version of Wundt's systematic position. In fact, Rieber's remarks on the problem of definitively stating "Wundt's position" are very strong (Rieber 1980: 73):

The North American psychologist who wants to put Wilhelm Wundt's singular achievement into a broader historical perspective faces a peculiar difficulty. He will not find it easy to arrive at a fair and accurate characterization of Wundt's position on any of the fundamental issues of psychology, for to do that he would have to cut through a veritable thicket of misleading information whose roots run very deep. Although some paths have recently been hewn through the thicket (Blumenthal 1975; Mischel 1970), a great deal of clearing remains to be done.

It would perhaps help here to distinguish between *elementarism*, the view that the simplest psychological phenomena are sensations, and *associationism* as the doctrine which tries to explain how these elementary simple phenomena are brought into relation with one another and in the formation of higher cognitive states. It is clear that for Wundt, as for Locke and his colleagues of the British School, sensation is the simplest unit of experience, the "atom" of the molecular complex of consciousness.[9]

Perhaps the whole controversy about whether Wundt was a Sensationist or not comes from a failure to distinguish

---

[9] Feldman, for example (1932: 211), in his chapter-by-chapter summary of Wundt's *Principles*, notes that "Sensation is, unquestionably, the simplest psychological phenomenon; but it never occurs in isolation". We have become so accustomed to the phrase "simple sensation" that we have come to regard it as really the beginning of conscious experience—a received view which we shall have to reconsider in our final chapter. For conscious experience begins with a sensory impulse that alerts the subject to some change in the environment and sets up a relationship with some particular phase of the environment that demands interpretation. In other words, the simplest sensory experience is the sensory sign in consciousness, inducing considerable interpretation, and already on the way to meaning through the relations it sustains.

between "elementarism" and "associationism" as just distinguished. Elementarism and atomism come from simply considering sensations as the building blocks of one's knowledge. Associationism goes further, and asserts that all complex knowledge is built up from associations formed among sensory data, and the mind contributes nothing beyond permitting associations to form, as we have said. By contrast, Wundt showed great reliance on apperception. While it is not certain just what he meant by apperception, it is clear that there was a dynamic character about it. His preference for the term "voluntarism" to designate his system does not, in my opinion, entitle him to be called a "voluntarist" or "ganzheit" psychologist, but it does assuredly remove him from the school of simple associationism.

In response to the claims of Blumenthal (1975) that Titchener read an unwarranted atomistic interpretation into Wundt's discussion of Introspectionism, it should be kept in mind, as we will mention in concluding Chapter 5, that Max Wertheimer used this designation to point out the reason for the failure of Wundt's introspective analyses to account for the phenomenon of apparent movement.

In conclusion, we may say that Wundt held that sensation is the simplest state of consciousness, but Associationism does not bridge the gap between sensation and cognition, whether perceptual or intellectual. Associationism asserts that all complex knowledge is built up from associations formed from sensory data and the mind contributes nothing beyond the permitting of associations to form. Wundt's reliance on apperception is indeed dynamic and goes beyond the limits of Associationism. His elementarism, nonetheless, comes from this singling out of sensations as the elementary or "simplest" mental content.

One constant throughout Wundt's various attempts to reformulate the new science he was creating was the assurance that when the contents of consciousness can be expressed in terms of Fechner's psychophysical formula—the strength of the sensory experience is proportional to the logarithm of the stimulus—the new science of psychology has been born, and its claim to be scientific guaranteed by its quantitative expression.

Light is thrown on this issue of whether the accusation of Wundt's elementarism is atomistic stems from Titchener's mistranslation of passages of the *Grundzüge* by contemporary German Gestalt psychologists. Wertheimer used his demonstration of apparent movement to show the inadequacy of the atomistic approach to which Introsepctionism leads. Wertheimer's demonstration of the phi-phenomenon occurred in 1913, during the period of Titchener's translations of the earlier editions of Wundt's classic. It is unlikely that the contemporary Gestalt psychologists mounted their attack on introspection either on the basis of mistranslation or deliberate misrepresentation of Wundt's texts. Even granting Wundt's difficulty in sticking to a uniform vocabulary, this matter of interpreting the vernacular is too fundamental to be missed.

Fortunately, in this attempt to review the main lines of development of the new psychology during Wundt's lifetime, it is not necessary to pass a definitive judgment on the claims and counterclaims in this debate. The first generation of psychologists trained in Wundt's laboratory showed great enthusiasm for the master's promotion of the new science and his dedication to precision in the laboratory, but felt no obligation to be bound by his narrow limitation of the new field. In Germany there was an early infiltration of Brentano's emphasis on act and function rather than Wundt's emphasis on content. This influence moved the second generation of psychologists away from Wundt's narrow emphasis on content. In America the interest in the practical applications of psychology and the domination of the scientific field by mechanistic positivism crowded out Wundt's emphasis on the precise introspective analysis of the quality and intensity of sensory data.

The reason for this is that the power of Associationism and of Mechanistic determinism were so strong in America that the course of the new science of psychology had no choice but to follow the reductionist course of mechanistic positivism if it wished to be accepted as a science. In Germany, the emphasis on function suggested by Brentano, rather than Wundt's emphasis on content, was sufficiently strong to create an opposition to Associationism and the elementaristic analysis of psychology, and to move psychology in the direction of holism and eventually in personalistic directions. All this makes the consideration of Franz Brentano appropriate.

FRANZ BRENTANO [1838-1917]

With the first laboratory established at Leipzig under Wilhelm Wundt and a journal established to bring its researches to the public, one may say that experimental psychology was launched. As if to show that the time was ripe for the new discipline, we must take into account another person who demonstrated great interest and support for the new psychology, but along a line sharply contrasting with that of Wundt. In 1874, the same year that Wundt's classic textbook, the *Principles*, was completed, another classic in psychology was published. This was Franz Brentano's

Psychology from an Empirical Standpoint. This book makes clear that the psychology it presents is based on experience, and therefore is not to be confused with the rational psychology that had been taught as a part of philosophy up to this time. Although based on experience, as the title emphasizes, it was not experimental, and did not propose a laboratory approach, using controlled data. As a result, the book did not produce anything like the excitement aroused by Wundt's *Principles,* with its suggestion that it would be possible to study mental life by means of experiments that would yield data comparable to the advances of physics and chemistry. Hence, although Brentano's work was completely opposed to that of Wundt, it did nothing to dampen the enthusiasm for the project of applying laboratory methods to the phenomena of consciousness. The influence of Brentano in America came with the second generation of psychologists and the advent of Gestalt.

To understand the full import of Brentano's contribution, it is necessary to know something of his background. How did he arrive at a position completely rejecting associationism and insisting on an active and dynamic view of the mind? The answer is that he had a thorough-going knowledge of Aristotle that had been acquired in his study of St. Thomas with the Dominicans in preparation for the Catholic priesthood, and also as a young student under F. A. Trendelenburg [1802-1872], a renowned authority on Aristotle at the University of Berlin. We have noted earlier that Associationism and the exaggerated emphasis on sensation by the British Empiricists was probably due to a superficial understanding of Aristotle's logic at Oxford in the sixteenth and seventeenth centuries. Be that as it may, it is important to note that Brentano's was the only voice that affirmed the dynamic

Aristotelian view of concept formation when experimental psychology was struggling to be recognized as a scientific discipline.

A number of circumstances prevented that voice from being heard, and psychology was forced to develop under the constraints of the associationist view of thought and learning, even though Franz Brentano was highly regarded as a lecturer by persons whose approaches to psychology were as far apart as Edmund Husserl [1859-1938] and Sigmund Freud [1856-1939]. Brentano withdrew from academic life quite early. He became involved with the group known as Old German Catholics, who opposed the declaration of infallibility of the Pope made by the First Vatican Council (1869-1870). Unable to accept the doctrine of infallibility, he resigned his professorship and subsequently withdrew from the priesthood and married. Soon his sight began to fail, and he had to give up intellectual work. Husserl tried to arouse his interest in phenomenology, but Brentano remained aloof. As a result of all these circumstances, Brentano had little influence on the new psychology in its formative period, the period when it was attracting worldwide attention. Although he had originally projected a second volume of psychology, he was never able to bring it to completion.

Brentano's psychology, as set forth in his *Psychology from an Empirical Standpoint* (1874), has received the name "act psychology", because Brentano saw the task of psychology as the investigation of the three activities of conscious life: ideating, judging and loving or hating. His idea of psychology is entirely opposed to that of Wundt, whose structuralist position emphasized mental content, rather than function. For Brentano the most important act is that of "intending" the object presented by the senses. By this act of intending the object, the mind somehow brings the object within itself, not actually but intentionally. In other words, the act of knowing sets up a relationship between the object and a mind capable of knowing or understanding. The result is a meaning, something that establishes a fix in the flux of the sensory manifold, the constantly changing world of sense. Meanings or ideas do not result merely from the clustering together of frequently repeated experiences, but in an intellectual grasp and interpretation of the signals that come to us through the senses. Brentano does not revive the internal senses or the active and passive intellect of Aristotle and Thomas, but, by the use of the words, "intending" and "intentionality", he does present the mind as active and dynamic in the formation of ideas.

Brentano's contribution to the new psychology provides an interesting commentary on the history of ideas. Because of the great appeal of the laboratory and its promise of quantitative results, Brentano's seminal views received little attention in this country until fifty years after the 1874 publication of his *Psychology from an Empirical Standpoint*. Yet this work has shown remarkable vitality in connection with the cognitive revival, late in the twentieth century. In contrast, Wundt's introspection long since has been laid to rest. This makes one wonder what would have been the consequence for psychology if John Locke's contemporaries had chosen to pursue his tantalizing reference to semiotics at the end of his famous *Essay*, rather than to exploit his brief reference to the association of ideas.

Thus, despite its contemporaneity with Wundt's *Principles*, Brentano's *Psychology from an Empirical Standpoint* attracted none of the immediate and enthusiastic attention that Wundt and the Leipzig laboratory quickly commanded. It was only later that the outgrowth of Brentano's approach began to exercise its influence in terms of the Gestalt movement which had its origins in Brentano's emphasis on intentionality.

In assessing the progress of the new psychology in Germany, credit must be given to individuals whose contributions stand out because of their influence on subsequent developments of the field and to schools or movements that set the direction that psychology would later take.

Hermann Ebbinghaus [1850-1909] and Oswald Külpe [1862-1915] are examples of individuals who were not deterred by Wundt's restrictions, and refused to exclude the higher thought processes from the purview of the new psychology. Ebbinghaus' work on *Memory*, which appeared in 1885, based on an adaptation of Fechner's method, represents the earliest attempt to subject a higher thought process to experimental conditions. Although he had never studied under Wundt, he had been drawn to the possibility of the quantification of mental activity by Fechner's *Elements of Psychophysics*, which he had chanced upon in an English bookstore. He developed four methods of measuring the effects of memory. His method of investigating memory became the model for the memory and learning studies that preoccupied American psychology for a quarter of a century.

In addition to his pioneering work on memory and learning, Ebbinghaus was instrumental in establishing laboratories in several universities, including the university of Berlin, which later became the home of the Gestalt movement. After Leipzig, one of the first German universities to establish a laboratory for research in experimental psychology was Würzburg.

In 1894, Oswald Külpe assumed the chairmanship of the department at the University of Würzburg. Although he had been Wundt's laboratory assistant, Külpe had absorbed none of Wundt's desire to exclude the higher thought processes from experimentation. To the contrary, he refused to direct psychology to the analysis of sensory experience but led the way in devising methods to explore such experiences as insight, judgment, and choice.

In addition to the basic interest in ways of studying the higher conscious activities, the Würzburg laboratory was aware—as were all the German-speaking universities—of the early stirrings of the Gestalt movement. The contact with the beginnings of Gestalt thinking came through Christian von Ehrenfels [1859-1932] and Alexis Meinong [1853-1920], both of whom had been taught by Franz Brentano and had come to realize that in perception there is a quality of wholeness or form ("Gestaltsqualität") in addition to the sensory input involved. From this notion of a form-quality came the slogan "The whole is greater than the sum of the parts". With this introduction of "form quality" the contrast between act psychology, the psychology of function, and Wundt's content psychology began to be emphasized.

The Würzburg school gave free rein to the study of the higher processes. Karl Marbe [1869-1953] investigated the psychological activities involved in judgment; Narziss Ach [1871-1946] studied the existential aspects of volition; H. J. Watt [1879-1925] used introspection to study the steps involved in thought. Finally, Karl Bühler [1879-1963] opened up the question of imageless thought, the hypothesis that thought and the meanings involved are not dependent on a particular set of images—a contention that proved something of a decisive contribution of the Würzburg school. This contention aroused a conflict with Titchener in America and probably helped to discredit the introspective analysis of consciousness, in turn tending to make John Watson's denial of consciousness more acceptable in America.

Another German university engaged in experimentation in the new psychology was the University of Berlin. The Berlin laboratory was established by Hermann Ebbinghaus in 1886. Berlin is noted particularly for maintaining interest in the Gestalt concept. But it was Max Wertheimer [1880-1943] who gave special impetus to the Gestalt movement by his demonstration of the phi-phenomenon, the phenomenon of apparent movement, in a series of experiments conducted at Frankfurt in 1910-1912 (Wertheimer 1912). Wertheimer moved to Berlin in 1916, where he remained until 1929.

Wertheimer was joined in Berlin in 1921-1922 by Wolfgang Köhler [1887-1867], whose earlier work on *The Mentality of Apes* (1917) demonstrated the inadequacy of Associationism to account for the chimpanzee's problem-solving abilities. These two men were associated in their work with two other strong supporters of the Gestalt movement, Kurt Koffka [1886-1941] and Kurt Lewin [1890-1947]. Kurt Koffka, who had graduated from Berlin in 1909 and served along with Köhler as a subject in Wertheimer's crucial experiment of 1910, developed the laws of Gestalt and marshalled the other figures to demonstrate the Gestalt principle using the examples of ambivalent figures and unfinished designs. Kurt Lewin, who was also on the Berlin faculty from 1922-1932, extended the Gestalt principle into the social field and made it the basis of his group dynamics.

These four able exponents of Gestalt theory mounted a devastating critique of Associationism and Behaviorism and, in general, of any form of elementarism in psychology. As pressure from Hitler's Germany increased during the '20s and '30s, these four came to America (Koffka in 1924,

Wertheimer in 1933, Lewin and Köhler in 1935) and assumed academic positions in psychology departments—Lewin at the University of Iowa (later at MIT), Koffka at Smith College where he became Chair, Wertheimer at the "University in Exile" established at the New School for Social Research in New York, and Köhler at Swarthmore College. Thence they made the Gestalt influence felt on the American scene. We will have occasion to discuss their work further in Chapter 5.

William Stern [1871-1938] was a member of the second generation of psychologists who were not members of any group or movement, but whose contribution notably helped to shape the image of psychology. William Stern was the pioneer in insisting that personality should be the focus of the new psychology, rather than the conscious or the unconscious mind. Stern did both undergraduate and graduate studies at the University of Berlin, taking his doctoral degree in 1897. In his autobiography (Stern 1927: 340), he mentions his early devotion to philosophy that remained with him throughout his life, even though he found little of interest in the philosophy program at the university or among his peers. His interest in psychology was awakened by Carl Stumpf [1848-1936], then head of the department there. His life alternated between periods devoted to philosophy and time spent on psychological problems. In his first teaching experience at the University of Breslau, he became interested in intelligence tests being developed as a result of Binet's use of mental age as a unit of measurement. Stern is credited with coining the term "individual differences" to cover the whole range of mental testing. He also originated the term "intelligence quotient" (IQ) as a measure of brightness. He contributed the first formula for calculating the IQ (MA/CA x 100). He also devoted much time to the study of child development.

But more significant than his study of individual differences was his pioneering work in making personality the true center of psychological inquiry. He published the first paper on the person in psychology in 1917, and his subsequent writings show a consistent interest in making the person the central topic of experimental psychology.[10] Gordon Allport [1897-1967], who was more responsible than anyone else for bringing personality to the fore in American psychology, gives William Stern credit for his own choice of personality as his field of particular interest in psychology. Although Allport's "graduate years at Harvard were not particularly productive intellectually", he tells us (G. W. Allport 1967: 9-10), he was nevertheless "awarded by Harvard a Sheldon Traveling Fellowship, which gave me two years in Europe", years which proved "a second intellectual dawn":

> The German tradition in psychology was still strong in America. . . . I was not prepared, however, for the powerful impact of my German teachers who included the aged Stumpf and Dessoir, the younger Max Wertheimer, Wolfgang Köhler, and Eduard Spranger in Berlin, and in Hamburg, William Stern and Heinz Werner. . . .

---

[10] "Now, was this work determined through some definite tendency of the philosophy of the time? Can I claim to be a member of some school, a continuer in some definitely chartered way? This question I must answer in the negative. The professional philosophy of the day, at least so far as I had come in contact with it, could offer me no guidance in my search" (Stern 1927: 352). In terms of what has been said about Aristotle and his notion of soul as the unifying principle of life in the present study, then, Stern's further comment will be of particular interest to the reader (*ibid.*: 353): "The relation of my philosophy with that of Aristotle only came to my notice in the course of elaborating the system" of Personalism.

At that time Gestalt was a new concept. I had not heard of it before leaving Cambridge. . . . *Ganzheit* and *Gestalt*, *Struktur* and *Lebensform*, and *die unteilbare Person* were new music to my ears. Here was the kind of psychology I had been longing for but did not know existed.

Of course I realized that romanticism in psychology could poison its scientific soil. (I myself had been brought up in the Humean tradition.) At the same time it seemed to me that the high quality of experimental studies by the Gestalt school, the original empirical investigations at Stern's Institute, and the brilliance of the Lewinian approach (which I came to know at second hand) gave safe anchorage to the kinds of concepts that I found congenial.

This enthusiastic statement of his intellectual debt to this unusual group of psychologists which Allport found at work in Berlin, Breslau, and Hamburg is evidence that not many psychologists of the second generation in Germany paid much attention to Wundt's declaration that the higher thought processes were off-limits for experimental investigation by the new psychology. William Stern's pioneering work on personality between 1906 and 1935, as we have seen, extended the boundaries of psychology even further than the notion of "thought processes", and Gordon Allport, who introduced personality into American psychology as an important and acceptable area for scientific study at a time when academic psychology was under heavy behavioristic domination, freely proclaims his own indebtedness to Stern for having introduced personality as an area of experimental study.

It was America's good fortune that Hitler forced the leading Gestalt thinkers to migrate to the United States, where they made significant contributions to the growth of psychology in America. Their influence would not be felt until a later date.

This consideration of the beginnings and early phase of development in Germany sets the stage for the quite different development in America.

Chapter 5

THEORY OF PSYCHOLOGY IN AMERICA: FROM CONSCIOUSNESS TO BEHAVIOR

Something of the zest and enthusiasm for the scientific study of mind that Wundt was able to infuse into Structuralism in spite of its limitations can be gleaned from the interest the work created worldwide. Nowhere was it taken up with so much verve and optimism as in the United States. We have already noted that Wundt was able to attract bright and enterprising students from many countries outside Continental Europe. Among these were students who came from the United States, and, when they returned home, they found in a number of universities a favorable climate for establishing psychology departments equipped with laboratories. The list of these departments founded by Wundt's former students is impressive: Frank Angell [1857-1939]—Cornell and Stanford (opened the first laboratory at Cornell, inherited by Titchener); James McKeen Cattell [1860-1944]—Pennsylvania and Columbia (developed the use of statistics and individual testing); H. Gale [1862-1945]—Minnesota (established a laboratory); G. S. Hall [1844-1924]—Johns Hopkins and Clark (a promoter and herald of the new science, adopted an evolutionary approach, established the first American journal, and a founder of the American Psychological Association); C. H. Judd [1873-1946]—Chicago (held to the Leipzig line but early moved into education); E. A. Pace [1861-1938]—The Catholic University of America (helped maintain the voice of scholastic philosophy and therewith Aristotelianism within psychology); G. T. W. Patrick [1857-1949]—Iowa (came to teach morals and pedagogy, set up a laboratory); R. Pintner [1884-1942]—Columbia (early testing movement); W. D. Scott [1869-1955]—Northwestern (founder of industrial psychology); E. W. Scripture [1864-1945]—Yale; G. M. Stratton [1865-1957]—California; G. A. Tawney [1870-1947]—Beloit; E. B. Titchener [1867-1927]—Cornell (leader of the "loyal opposition" to abandonment of Wundt's limitation of the sphere of psychology); H. C. Warren [1867-1934]—Princeton; L. Witmer [1867-1956]—Pennsylvania (established first child's clinic in connection with an academic department); H. K. Wolfe [1858-1918]—Nebraska.[11]

Even more amazing is the fact that only one of these students of Wundt continued with the structuralist viewpoint

---

[11] The first American Ph.D. was G. Stanley Hall, who visited Wundt's laboratory in the year of its founding, but returned to the United States to receive his degree from Harvard under William James in 1878. Of the others on the list, we were able to determine that at least the following received Leipzig Ph.D.s under Wundt: Cattell in 1886, Angell, Pace and Scripture in 1891, Titchener and Witmer in 1892, Judd and Malcolm in 1896, Scott in 1900, Pinter in 1913.

and the dedication to introspection which had been the hall-mark of psychology at Leipzig. The exception was Edward Bradford Titchener who, through many years at Cornell University, continued to train students in the introspectionist tradition. As chairman of the department there, Titchener stood almost alone in trying to maintain Wundt's position. In upholding this tradition he provided an on-going critique of the Functionalist direction of American psychology. Since psychology in America took quite a different turn from Wundt's program, in spite of the fact that nearly all of the first flight of psychologists had gone to Leipzig for training, it is important to note the shape that psychology took on in this country from the beginning. These differences might be summarized by the following characteristics:

1. *Practical*—American psychology very early explored the possible ways in which psychology might be applied to life situations.
2. *Biological*—heavily influenced by an evolutionary view of mind and consciousness.
3. *Laboratory conscious*—a heavy emphasis on hardware and on the development of quantitative methods of investigation.
4. *Statistical Methods*—the collection of large masses of data subjected to statistical analysis to aid in their interpretation.
5. *Behavioral*—interest in response and behavior rather than on mental states considered apart from muscular and glandular reactions.

In a word, from the beginning, psychology in America was functional and pragmatic in outlook. Much of this attitude came from William James, whose influence on psychology in this country was dominant during the first period.

Born in New England to parents of means, William James, the brother of the novelist, Henry James, had the advantages of unusual educational opportunities supervised by his father. His earlier studies were divided between Europe and America, as his father became dissatisfied with the educational program in this country and sent his sons abroad, only to become anxious because of their lack of contacts with their peers on this side of the Atlantic. Going to Harvard, William James began his studies of physiology in preparation for a career in medicine. In 1865 he accompanied the famous naturalist, Louis Agassiz, on a trip to the Amazon in Brazil. Partly for reasons of health he interrupted his academic work and returned to Europe and visited several universities. He even toyed with the idea of joining Wundt and Helmholtz at Heidelberg. In this way, he became familiar with the beginnings of psychology in Germany and came to the conclusion that the time had come for psychology to enter the field of the sciences. This marks the beginning of his interest in psychology that was later to produce a textbook, *Principles of Psychology* (1890) that immediately became very popular and did much to arouse interest and to set the tone of the new science in America.

Returning to this country, William James spent several years battling depression and trying to regain his strength. In 1872 he was invited to teach physiology at Harvard, and in 1875 he offered his first course in psychology. This course included laboratory work, so he established the first laboratory for psychology in this country. This was actually a few years before Wundt established his laboratory in Leipzig, but James' innovation was more of a demonstration than a research laboratory. James' course did not lead to a degree in the new discipline, as Wundt's department provided. In 1892 James published a condensed volume, *Psychology: Briefer Course*, that was an immediate success. Its clear and engaging style recommended it to instructors throughout the country. The book established its author as a leading exponent of the new psychology and did much to gain interest for the science in America. As an example of his clean, terse style, I recall his statement of Johannes Müller's doctrine known as the "specific energies of nerves". What took Müller some ten propositions to state, James caught in a simple statement: "If, for instance, we could splice the outer extremity of our optic nerves to our ears, and that of our auditory nerves to our eyes, we should hear the lightning and see the thunder, see the symphony and hear the conductor's movements" (James 1892: 12).

For some years after the 1890 publication of the *Principles*, James continued to offer courses in psychology and to lecture to interested groups, but his heart was not in it. As the concluding paragraph of his text states, psychology was, at that time, not a science, but only the hope of a science, so he abandoned the field in favor of philosophy, where, with C. S. Peirce [1839-1914], he was very influential in establishing the school of philosophy known as Pragmatism. So complete was his disenchantment with psychology that, when he was about to be honored by Harvard University at the completion of fifty years of teaching, he expressed apprehension that the citation would include some reference to his work in the field of psychology.

Psychology for William James had none of the narrowness of Wundt's Introspectionism. Instead of viewing psychology as the analysis of conscious states, James simply regarded the discipline as the study of the mind in all its activities, including the awareness of bodily functions to which the study of mind leads. His difference from Wundt and the first wave of German psychologists began with a basic difference in the view of consciousness. James spoke of the stream of consciousness, rather than fixed states to be analyzed into their constituent elements, as Wundt proposed. James was prepared to include dreams, the unconscious, mental disorders, habit, and the emotions. His approach is essentially eclectic and holistic. There is more than a hint of Brentano in his stream of consciousness concept, and the act of intending is not incompatible with James' dynamic view of cognition. This opening to holism in James' work very probably comes from Brentano by way of Carl Stumpf, whom James met at the University of Berlin and found more interesting than Wundt, whom he regarded as too dry and pedantic.

James never had the patience to engage in collecting experimental data, and, when he retired from teaching psychology, he secured Hugo Münsterberg [1863-1916], a promising young doctorate from Wundt's school, to continue psychology at Harvard. If James seemed anxious to move out of psychology, American psychology moved away from James no less decisively. He was not sufficiently dedicated to the laboratory and experimentation to suit the psychologists who were busily establishing departments in universities across the land. He did, however, leave one imprint on the American scene. This was the famous Lange-James theory of emotion (stated as such in James 1890; independently in Lange 1885). Briefly stated, this theory maintains that instead of first feeling emotional excitement and then reacting physically, like seeing a bear and starting impulsively to run, the reverse is what happens. The sight of the bear triggers the flight reaction and the sensory experience from all the organs involved in running away is what we feel as the emotion of fear. Regardless of its lack of plausibility, to say nothing of its lack of experimental support, the Lange-James theory of emotion was laid to rest only within the last few decades. The hyphenated title comes from the fact that James shared credit for this theory with Carl Lange of Copenhagen, who came up with a similar idea at about the same time. Better understanding of brain function, in particular the role of the limbic lobe and of the reticular activating system, eventually made this theory completely disappear from psychological textbooks. Its prominence helped postpone the recognition of psychosomatic illnesses for half a century.

So one of the new psychologies little ironies in its history: despite his caustic statements in concluding his highly successful text of 1892, the *Psychology: Briefer Course*, disclaiming enthusiastic advocacy of the new psychology, nonetheless he, more than anyone else, is responsible for giving to American psychology its functional and practical turn.

Some years after William James had left the field, Edward Bradford Titchener, America's lone follower of the Leipzig tradition, coined the name Functionalism to designate the psychological viewpoints opposed to the position of Wundt. It was Titchener also who gave to Wundt's position on experimental psychology the name of Structuralism.

Since we have had occasion to mention Brentano in connection with James' functionalism, it may be well to recall the difference between Brentano's Act Psychology and the Functionalism (as it came to be called) mentioned in concluding the previous chapter, where we saw a whole range of attempts to bring higher thought processes within the purview of experimental psychology. Act Psychology merely shifts the goal of psychology from the contents of the mind to the acts of the mind: from sensory input and association to the activity of ideating, judging and feeling. This leaves psychology still preoccupied with consciousness only.

By contrast, Functional Psychology addresses the question: What purpose does consciousness serve in the life of the organism? What is its function in enabling the organism to adjust to its environment? What is its survival value? This line of questioning shifts the scene of inquiry from what goes on within the mind to the ways in which the mind helps to shape behavior, and psychology moves towards the study of behavior. This places psychology in the field of biological evolution. Later on, we will note efforts to demonstrate the evolutionary origins of human intelligence. Within a few years the term functional came to designate the mainstream of psychology in America, until Watson attempted to channel all psychology into Behaviorism. Titchener at Cornell, the loyal disciple of Wundt, remained almost the only exception to Functionalism.

William James thus provided the framework and direction for psychology in this country. He was followed by two distinguished experimentalists who shared none of James' later misgivings about the scientific aspirations of psychology. These were G. Stanley Hall and James McKeen Cattell.

G. STANLEY HALL [1844-1924]

G. Stanley Hall grew up on a small farm in Massachusetts and attended Williams College. He turned to the ministry and spent some time at Union Theological Seminary, but the theology taught there failed to satisfy him, so he went to Bonn and later Berlin. There he studied physiology as well as philosophy (1868-1871). Back in this country, he took a degree in theology and entered the ministry for a short time.

When Wundt's *Principles of Physiological Psychology* appeared in 1874, it immediately drew Hall's interest. He became further attracted to psychology at Harvard, where, in 1878 with a thesis on the muscular perception of space, he took his doctorate (Philosophy-Psychology) under William James. By this time Hall's interest in psychology had developed into full commitment to the field as a career, determining him to return to Germany (1878-1880). Going first to Berlin, he resumed his work in physiology, later transferring to Leipzig, where he became Wundt's first American student, but his experience there was disappointing, probably because his hopes for the new science ranged more widely than the narrowly introspective program of the Leipzig laboratory. He returned to Boston and was invited by Harvard University to do a Saturday series of talks to teachers. These lectures were well received and enhanced his reputation as a psychologist. In 1882 he accepted an appointment to the new Johns Hopkins University in Baltimore that was being modeled on the German university, with heavy emphasis on scientific research. After two years he was appointed professor of psychology and pedagogics. His laboratory was probably the first in this country after James' efforts at Harvard, and the first serious research laboratory in the United States.[12]

---

[12] The University of Iowa provides an interesting example of the manner in which psychology managed to get its foot in the door in most institutions. George T. Patrick was a student of E. W. Scripture at Yale when he received his appointment to teach philosophy, psychology, and didactic at the University of Iowa. This indicates how psychology got started in most universities. In the 1880s, most appointments to teach psychology came by way of philosophy, and the first efforts of the appointee were to establish an autonomous department of psychology, with a laboratory and a budget of its own. The tension between psychology and philosophy was clearly evident on most campuses. Under Wundt, psychology had declared its independence

The laboratory and department at Johns Hopkins achieved considerable renown, not so much because of Hall's researches as because of the productivity of some eminent students he had there, such as Cattell, Dewey [1859-1952], Jastrow [1863-1944] and Burnham [1855-1941]. Hall made up for his own lack of experimental research by opening up such fields as child development and adolescence to experimental study. In his later years he wrote the first psychological approach to senescence. Perhaps his greatest contribution was his vigorous promotion of psychology at every turn. He did this by establishing in 1887 the first journal in the United States, *The American Journal of Psychology,* and by introducing the *Pedagogical Seminary* (now known as *The Journal of Genetic Psychology*) in 1891. Even more significant for the future of psychology was Hall's initiative in forming the American Psychological Association (APA) in 1892. Some of these things were accomplished after he had been named president of the newly founded Clark University, an institution concentrating on work at the graduate level.

Hall went to Clark as its president when it opened in 1889. There, as might be expected, he formed a strong department of psychology, and continued as a regular member of the department during his tenure as president. The most dramatic event of his presidency of Clark University was the invitation of Sigmund Freud to the campus for a series of lectures in 1909. Freud came, accompanied by some of his most ardent followers, whom he had attached to himself as the guardians of orthodox psychoanalysis. This was not only Freud's first and only visit to America, but this series of

---

from philosophy, and philosophy returned the compliment by taking a very superior attitude towards the sciences in general and towards psychology in particular among the new experimental sciences.

lectures was his first effort to combine his writings on a variety of clinical subjects into a coherent statement of psychoanalytic doctrine. It is well to point out that Freud was a medical doctor, or psychiatrist if you will, and his audience was made up mostly of psychologists with a strong bias in favor of associationism. Responses were mixed, and Hall did not convert many of his peers to psychoanalysis, but Freud's visit did much to open up their thinking to the role of the unconscious and to a more dynamic view of mind.

From this review of his pioneering work it is clear that in G. Stanley Hall we have a person who, on this side of the Atlantic, contributed more than anyone else to the establishment of psychology, towards getting it accepted in academic circles and in creating interest among the general public. He would be comparable in some respects to Wundt in the impetus that he gave to the new discipline, while at the same time he relieved psychology of the artificial restrictions placed on it in the Leipzig laboratory. Because of his interest in genetics, child development, and a general evolutionary approach to consciousness, he was once referred to as the Darwin of the mind. He was particularly interested in the applications of psychology to pedagogy and education. His interests thus reflect most of the marks, noted earlier, that have characterized American psychology from the beginning. By the time of Hall's death, we can say that the new psychology had been securely launched in this country, but there are two other important names in the first wave of psychologists in America. The first of these was James McKeen Cattell.

JAMES MCKEEN CATTELL [1860-1944]

We have noted already that James McKeen Cattell was at Johns Hopkins when Hall opened his laboratory there, but this was but a sort of interim appointment on his way to a career in psychology. Born to a professor on a small college campus, he continued his studies beyond the bachelor's degree abroad. After a couple of years at Göttingen and Leipzig, Cattell took the Johns Hopkins appointment, and then returned to Leipzig to complete his degree in psychology under Wundt. Typical of his forthright manner, he did not offer his services as assistant to Wundt: instead one day he told Wundt that he should have an assistant, and that he, Cattell, would be it. Typical also was the fact that he did not seek direction for his research from Wundt, but pursued his own interests in research on individual differences, even while a student at Leipzig. His research in reaction times won him the doctorate there. For a few years after that he pursued his interest in the measurement of abilities with Francis Galton [1822-1911].

Cattell's most productive years were during his chairmanship of the department of psychology at Columbia University. There he worked with E. L. Thorndike [1874-1949] devising and improving mental tests until he was dismissed for publicly demanding that conscientious objectors be exempt from mandatory military service in World War I.

His departure from the academic scene did not lessen Cattell's interest in achieving recognition of the new psychology by the brotherhood of scientific scholars. His interest in publication dates back to 1894, when he and Mark Baldwin teamed up to create another voice for psychology besides Hall's *American Journal of Psychology* (founded 1887). Together they established *The Psychological Review*. Having been elected to the prestigious American Association for the Advancement of Science, Cattell set out to achieve wider recognition for psychology within the scientific community. He took over and revamped *Science*, established *The Scientific Monthly* and edited *American Men of Science*. He rounded out his venture into the field of publication with several other useful sources of information for those engaged in the promotion of scientific research.

In addition to his original contribution to the field of mental testing and his editorial effort to have psychology accepted in the highest scientific circles, Cattell also anticipated the wave of the future: the emergence of psychology as a profession. In 1921 he organized the Psychological Corporation to supply test materials and more sophisticated equipment that psychologists would find useful either in clinical practice or in the laboratory.

EDWARD BRADFORD TITCHENER [1867-1927]

Edward Bradford Titchener was one of the students from Great Britain who were attracted to Wundt's laboratory as the way to become a part of the exciting prospect of establishing a scientific approach to the study of mind. Returning to Oxford, he found little interest in the new discipline and accepted a position at Cornell University in New York State. One of the most loyal of Wundt's students, he translated three editions of the master's *Principles* as they came off the press. At Cornell he set about upgrading the laboratory already established there by Frank Angell in 1891. He engendered lively interest in psychology in his students, and succeeded in training an impressive number of doctoral students who later made significant contributions to the advancement of the new discipline. He was active also in establishing the American Psychological Association, and continued to defend Structuralism against the prevailing Functionalism that held the interest of the majority of American psychologists. As indicated earlier, he became actively involved in the controversy over imageless thought, maintaining that no meaning can exist without images to support it. Indeed, much of the value of Titchener's contribution to the youthful discipline was in providing restraint on the uncritical enthusiasm that greeted it on every side.

This enthusiasm was short-lived. One of the characteristics of Functionalism was its extended front. In its effort to be practical and make psychology serve the needs of all, psychology had come to include many diverse interests. The result was a fragmentation of the field of psychology into movements or schools. Among these schools, Behaviorism was not the first to appear, but it was the one destined to change radically the direction of psychology in America.

JOHN B. WATSON [1878-1958] AND BEHAVIORISM

Among the pressures that prepared the way for the shift in focus of psychology in America away from the analysis of consciousness to the study of behavior were the growing dissatisfaction with highly theoretical debates (like the one over imageless thought), and the growing interest in the study of animal behavior. Pioneers in the study of animal behavior were George Romanes [1858-1894] and Lloyd Morgan [1852-1936]. They took the position that animal behavior, later known as comparative psychology, was an area well worth studying in its own right. Moreover, it provided opportunities for investigation without the subjectivism involved in introspection. So the term "behavior" was not new to psychology when, in 1913, John Watson issued his famous manifesto. This appeared in the *Psychological Review* under the title, "Psychology as the Behaviorist Views It". The shift of interest from mind and conscious states to response or behavior that Watson heralded was to create a new definition of psychology.

There was not too much unusual about Watson's academic career before he launched the movement that was destined to change radically the direction of psychology in this country. He had come to the University of Chicago in 1900 to study under John Dewey, but became interested in psychology through the Functionalist development that James Rowland Angell [1869-1949] and Harvey Carr [1873-1954] were upholding at the University of Chicago, in contrast to the brand of Functionalism that Robert Sessions Woodworth [1869-1962] and James McKeen Cattell were promoting at Columbia. After taking his degree there, he taught for a few years. In 1908 he received the appointment to a full professorship at Johns Hopkins University. At Johns Hopkins he inherited an animal laboratory previously run by Cattell, and pursued researches in animal learning and behavior. Here he also began the studies in the conditioning of fear in children which gained him considerable renown.

The first translation into English of the work of Ivan Pavlov [1849-1936] on the conditioning of the salivary reflex in the dog appeared in 1927, but his Nobel Prize winning demonstration of the conditioned salivary reflex (Pavlov 1904) was well known throughout the European and American learned communities. Watson, however, had relied more on Bekhterev in his making of conditioning what would appear to be a quite objective and mechanical explanation of all learning, and with this idea his project of a new psychology based on the conditioned reflex began to take shape (Watson 1915: 143):

While recognizing the importance to all psychological students of Pawlow's [sic] work on secretion reflexes, our own work has centered around the conditioned motor reflex of Bechterew [sic], since we find for this method an immediate and widespread usefulness.

. . . The *conditioned motor reflex*, while familiar in a general way to everyone, has not, so far as I know [in contrast to the conditioned secretion reflex work of Pavlov], engaged the attention of American investigators. This is not surprising in view of the fact that all of the researches have appeared in Russian and in periodicals which are not accessible at present to American students. At least we have not been able to obtain access to a single research publication. The German and French translations of Bechterew's "Objective Psychology" give the method only in the barest outline. Bechterew's summary was the only guide we had in our work at Hopkins.

Watson's emphasis on observable behavior, rather than on consciousness and sensory changes, thus, already evident in his paper of 1913, here begins to find the method appropriate to its implementation, a method consonant with his idea of eliminating consciousness altogether from the concerns of psychology. Watson took this step in *Behavior: An Introduction to Comparative Psychology*, which appeared in 1914, and he affirmed it again in 1919 with *Psychology from the Standpoint of a Behaviorist*. The third edition of this last work, published in 1929, Misiak and Sexton (1966: 329) consider "the best presentation of the system".

Behaviorism as the focus of the new psychology aroused immediate interest, and Watson's sharp critique of all mentalistic concepts as outmoded and meaningless assured the movement of the strong support of the media. Among American psychologists the reaction was mixed. Abroad,

Watsonian Behaviorism never caught on. Even Pavlov, who may have been flattered by the attention given to his work on conditioning, never showed the slightest interest in Watson or the movement. In evaluating the impact of Behaviorism on the field of psychology, one must remember that psychology in America was already moving away from preoccupation with mind and mental states in the direction of behavior. What Watson's bold declaration did was to turn this movement into a new definition of psychology in terms of behavior, rather than in terms of mind or consciousness. For those, like Robert Sessions Woodworth (1918, 1938), who (along with a number of reputable psychologists) could not accept Watson's radical denial of consciousness, the term "behavior" included activities of the mind as well as muscular and glandular responses. It should be mentioned in passing that although radical Behaviorism professes to do away with all mentalistic concepts, it did not do away with Associationism. In fact the conditioned reflex depends entirely on association to explain the shift of a reflex response away from the natural stimulus to an artificial one. As a result of the shift of emphasis that Watson brought about, for many years, the reply of most psychologists in America to the question: "Are you a behaviorist?" would be: "Certainly, what else is psychology about? But I am not a Watsonian behaviorist."

COMPETING SCHOOLS

For twenty years, after Watson's attempt to redefine the field and method of psychology, competing schools or movements continued the splintering of the field, and a number of loyalties developed. Robert Sessions Woodworth, mentioned above in conjunction with Cattell as a solid contributor to the advance of psychology in this country, published a brief exposition of the tenets of these competing schools of psychological thought under the title *Contemporary Schools of Psychology*. Bearing the copyright date of 1931, this book provides a valuable contemporary assessment of the fragmented state of psychology in America during the 1920's (Woodworth 1931: 3):

> The past thirty years have been remarkably productive of new movements in psychology, with the result that we now see the curious phenomenon of schools differing radically from one another in their ideas as to what psychology should be doing and how it should go to work. These schools remind one of schools of philosophy, and are scarcely to be paralleled at present in the other natural sciences. Perhaps their existence in contemporary psychology is a sign of the youth of our science and of the vast number of unexplored possibilities that we have still to examine, as well as of our recent departure from the parental household of philosophy. How important any one of them is can scarcely be told till they have had more time to develop. Meanwhile, they are certainly interesting to any one who wants to obtain suggestive ideas.[13] They are

---

[13] In his later revised edition of this work (1948: 3-4), Woodworth gives this further characterization of the leading ideas: "Unknown territory obviously calls for exploration in all directions. For the research psychologist the unknown territory is that apparently familiar ground which we call human activity or more precisely the activity of the human individual, with some reference also to man's humbler animal cousins. Some of our explorers are fascinated by one, some by another of the many phases of individual

contemporary schools in that all have arisen recently, while none as yet shows any signs of early death.

In this work, thus, Woodworth points out that these schools or systems represent different areas of interest, but what they had in common, as Woodworth later summarized (1948: 4), was the belief that their particular approach would ultimately prove to be the "key to a unified understanding of human activity as a whole". This belief, held in common by competing protagonists, lent a polemic character to this period of American Psychology. Murchison [1887-1961] considered these differences so great that he took from them the very title for his two collections, respectively, the *Psychologies of 1925* and the *Psychologies of 1930*.

Here is Woodworth's listing, with a rough date of origin (or at least of rejuvenation in scientific guise) of the then-competing schools: Structuralism (1879), Functionalism

---

activity; and the schools can to a certain extent be distinguished simply by the activity which they prefer to investigate. More than that, each school believes that hidden in its own field is the true key to a unified understanding of human activity as a whole. For one school the illuminating fact is that man perceives the environment; for another, that he learns by experience; for another, that he feels and desires; and for another, that he acts by use of his muscles and so does something in the world. It may be that desire is the key to action, that perception is the key to desire, that learning is the key to perception. With one kind of human activity chosen as the central fact, a system of methods and concepts can be organized and a comprehensive theory worked out to the satisfaction of at least one school of thought. The majority of psychologists maintain a rather skeptical attitude toward these ambitious undertakings, but still find the schools stimulating and suggestive. Each school explores intensively in its chosen direction and makes concrete discoveries which enlarge the boundaries of the known territory of psychology. Meanwhile each school has to be watched, since its claims are sometimes excessive."

(1898), Associationism (1898), Psychoanalysis (1900), Person-alistic and Organismic Psychology (1900), Purposivism or "Hormic Psychology" (1908), Behaviorism (1912), and Gestalt (1912). We are already familiar with several of these. Struc-turalism was a name given to Wundt's system by his disciple, Titchener. Functionalism, as we have noted, was a general characteristic of the broad American approach to psychology. Associationism was the basic doctrine accepted in some form by most of the schools, except Gestalt, and the focus of the Associationist doctrine came to be the studies of stimulus and response (S-R Bond), as Behaviorism became dominant in America. Psychoanalysis in America goes back to Freud's appearance at Clark University in 1909 at G. Stanley Hall's invitation. Although developed as a form of psychiatry, the dynamic approach to behavior of psychoanal-ysis and its emphasis on the unconscious appealed to psychologists. Personalistic and organismic psychologies were an attempt to make psychology more responsive to personal concerns. Personality was not yet accepted as a legitimate topic in psychology. Purposivism or Hormic Psychology was largely the child of William McDougall [1871-1938] with his doctrine of multiple instincts. Behavior-ism was the most boisterous of all the schools or systems.

GESTALT PSYCHOLOGY

It remains to say a word about Gestalt. Gestalt psychology became an active force in American psychology in the 1920s. As we have noted, it was introduced in Europe by Alexis Meinong and Christian Ehrenfels [1859-1932] with the concept of "Gestaltqualität"—the quality of wholeness or form which is present in perceived meanings over and above the sensory data involved. By 1912, Max Wertheimer's demonstration of the phi-phenomenon had clarified the concept of Gestalt, and gave the movement its distinctive name.

As we saw in Chapter 4, the demonstration of this phenomenon had grown out of the work that Wertheimer and his colleagues had been doing at the University of Berlin. The phi-phenomenon is the phenomenon of apparent movement which is experienced every time we go to the cinema. It involves showing a sequence of pictures that have been taken of an object in motion. The movie camera takes a sequence of still shots of a moving object, and when these pictures are shown at a speed above the flicker threshold the viewer has a clear impression of smooth movement.

Wertheimer did not have a movie camera or projector. He used a disk with a slot that was rotated in front of a paper disk that had a series of straight lines alternating between the horizontal plane and a position elevated at an angle of about 30 degrees from it. When the wheel was rotated and the alternate lines exposed in rapid succession at the slot, the viewer has the distinct impression of the line at an angle moving towards the horizontal. The rotation might be in either direction, but the perceived movement is unmistakable. The point made by Wertheimer and his fellow workers is that something is perceived in this operation that was not provided by the sensory input, which input is nothing more than a sequence of motionless lines flashed on the retina, but the result is an unmistakable perception of movement. In other words, there is not a one-to-one relationship between the sensory input and the perception to which it gives rise. The perceived or apparent movement therefore, involves something more than the addition of simple sensory impression held together by spatial and temporal association.

This additional factor they called a Gestalt, the organization of these distinct sensory impressions into a meaningful whole. Obviously this Gestalt quality is not provided by the external senses and must come from some kind of organization within the central nervous system.

Max Wertheimer, Kurt Koffka, Wolfgang Köhler and Kurt Lewin, the original group of Gestalt psychologists discussed above in Chapter 4, mounted a strong attack on both Behaviorism and Structuralism, since both presented an atomic approach to psychology, reducing complex wholes to their irreducible elements. And both rely on Associationism to account for the manner in which these units become assimilated into meaningful wholes or patterns. Wertheimer's group immediately set about formulating a complete psychology around the Gestalt explanation of perception. Word of this new psychology came to this country in the early 1920s, having been delayed by the interruption of communication between Germany and America by World War I. Here it met with strenuous opposition, by reason of its incompatibility with Associationism (a basic assumption, as we have seen, of all the schools, except psychoanalytic and Hormic approaches). Toward the end of the decade and early in the 1930s, the four proponents of Gestalt, as we saw, came to the United States to escape from Hitler's pressure, and accepted positions on the faculties of several colleges and universities. They were a distinguished group, and they kept Gestalt ideas alive, even though their original plans to remake psychology in terms of the laws of perception gradually faded away. Their holistic approach to psychology, however, continued to attract followers, and has continued to make its presence felt, particularly in the field of counseling and therapy. The Gestalt critique of Behaviorism had a sobering effect on the original enthusiasm with which Watson's manifesto had been greeted. In this connection, it is one of those strange turns of history that Max Wertheimer published his demonstration of the phi-phenomenon in 1912 in Germany, the year before Watson announced his Behaviorist manifesto. The closing of the borders and the outbreak of World War I did much to prevent word of Wertheimer's breakthrough from attracting attention among psychologists in this country until early in the 1920s, and it waited for the coming of the expatriates from Germany to this country towards the end of that decade and later to make Gestalt a lively topic in psychological circles.

EDWARD L. THORNDIKE [1874-1949] AND LEARNING THEORY

In the late 1920s and 1930s psychology in America became absorbed in theory and research in learning, trying to determine a basic pattern or paradigm which all learning follows. This interest in basic research in learning in departments of psychology coincided with the efforts of Edward L. Thorndike at Columbia University College of Education to make educational psychology a genuinely experimental discipline. Since the search was for the basic pattern that all learning follows, it was natural to study learning or conditioning in a relatively simple animal. Watson's introduction of Bekhterev's investigation of the conditioned motor reflex seemed to provide a thoroughly experimental approach to learning.

Thorndike and Watson, as we will see more at length in Chapters 8 and 10, had supplied psychology with an objec-

tive method for research in learning, subsequently mathema-
tized by Hull (summarized in Hull 1943, 1951). The model
they provided was taken up and transformed by B. F.
Skinner [1904-1990] in the 1930s under the banner of "Neobehaviorism". The neobehaviorist model was distinguished
by its de-emphasis of stimulus-response bonds as theoretical
constructs in favor of emphasizing the role of reinforcement
as experimentally observable (a shift in emphasis, by the
way, which had the effect of invalidating Thorndike's
theoretical "law of effect"—cf. p. 158 below). Emphasis on
rats and mazes as providing the paradigm focus for experimental analysis of behavior remained the constant foundation
of behaviorism and neobehaviorism alike.

It was thus that the Norway rat got into the psychological
laboratory, replacing the polished brass resonators and the
Hipp Chronoscope that had adorned the original laboratories
in an earlier era. With this reference to the manner in which
research in learning became a high priority in American
psychology toward the end of the 1920s, we close this
discussion of the first period of American Psychology, and so
prepare for the next chapter to observe the line of development that psychology took in other countries.

Chapter 6

EXPANSIONS IN EUROPE

We have noted that experimental psychology was begun in Germany with Wundt's laboratory in Leipzig, and was enthusiastically received in America. In the European universities, the situation was quite different. Instead of the rush to establish and equip separate departments of psychology, the move was rather to assimilate the new psychology into related disciplines. The result was a broadening of psychology with emphasis on clinical psychology that American psychology was slow to recognize and encourage.

In England, the older universities of Oxford and Cambridge were slow to admit the new psychology into their well established program of studies. This is why Titchener and Mc-Dougall came to America and made important contributions to psychology in this country. All this is rather surprising when we recall that it was Locke, Hume, and the Mills of the British School of Empiricism who were responsible for turning philosophy in the direction of the analysis of human experience, and that it was Alexander Bain who coined the term "psychophysical parallelism" that found wide acceptance among the founders of experimental psychology. Everywhere in Europe there was resistance to the separation of psychology from the parent field of philosophy.

In Great Britain, the new psychology was slow to catch on. Oxford and Cambridge led the resistance, refusing to allow the new science a place in their curriculum. In spite of this foot-dragging behavior, some important developments owe their origin to British sources. As we have seen, Darwin's evolutionary doctrine carried over into American Functionalism. In his studies of the inheritance of intelligence, Francis Galton [1822-1911] attempted to trace the influence of heredity on human intelligence in researches that appeared in the work entitled *Hereditary Genius* (Galton 1869). This was just ten years after the publication of Darwin's *Origin of Species*. Galton's work on tests of human ability and the application of sophisticated statistical methods for analyzing them attracted the youthful Cattell from an instructorship at the University of Pennsylvania to work with Galton. Together Galton and Cattell pioneered the study of individual differences that caught the interest of Alfred Binet [1857-1911], who transformed the method of assessing human intelligence by introducing the concept of mental age with the first test of children's intelligence in 1905 (Binet and Simon 1905, 1911).

This initial interest in developing methods for measuring human intelligence was continued by Charles Spearman [1863-1945], whose *General Intelligence* (1904) aroused great interest abroad and engaged the efforts of brilliant statistical theorists in the attempt to derive the nature of intelligence from the analysis of test data. This refined use of quantitative methods combined psychology with mathematics in a manner that Herbart had never conceived of and Wundt had barely opened up with his study of just noticeable differences and reaction time measurement. It is probably the greatest contribution of English workers to the expansion of psychology into areas little dreamed of by the founders.

As far back as the demonstration of the one-way-law of nerve conduction by Charles Bell [1774-1842] in 1811, English researchers have been active in neurology and areas of physiology important to psychology. Again, we are moving far beyond the experimental physiology of Johannes Müller into behavioral studies that involve the operation of the nervous system as a whole. In recent years this interest in the medical aspects of psychology has resulted in close cooperation with the medical profession in the development of some of the most advanced programs of treatment for the mentally ill.

British psychologists also did much to open up the field of animal psychology, or comparative psychology, as it is now called. In this area C. Lloyd Morgan was a leader who saw that subhuman attempts at problem solving are worthy of study quite apart from any presumed parallel with human intelligence. This approach marked a new era in study of animal behavior and put an end to the anecdotal approach, which was chiefly interested in searching animal behavior for instances of human-like intelligence. Lloyd Morgan's caution against drawing quick parallels between human problem solving and that of subhuman animals was expressed in a simple statement that has since been known as "Morgan's Canon" (1894: 53):

> In no case may we interpret an action as the outcome of the exercise of a higher psychical faculty, if it can be interpreted as the outcome of the exercise of one which stands lower in the psychological scale.

This is an application of "Ockham's razor", and is sound enough if not pressed too far, in which case it leads to the denial of differences that actually exist, as has happened in the attempt to account for human language as merely an advanced form of communication evolved from the signs used by lower animals.

As the study of individual differences opened up by Francis Galton added an interesting area to the expanding field of psychology, so did the work of Lloyd Morgan and his associates contribute much to the area of comparative psychology. This work provided the title and a solid base for John B. Watson's Behaviorism and contributed to the search for a single paradigm of all learning that set the stage for the extensive research program on theories of learning that occupied center stage in American psychology through the late 1920s into the 1950s. These are some of the ways in which psychology in England contributed to the growth of the discipline in spite of the fact that it had a very slow start there.

FRANCE, SWITZERLAND, BELGIUM

The French reaction to the new psychology was quite different from what we have noted in England. The response to the opening of Wundt's laboratory in Leipzig was quick and positive, with no opposition from philosophy, except from Henri Bergson [1859-1941]. In fact the recognized leader of psychology in France, Theodule Ribot [1839-1916] turned from philosophy to psychology. He studied psychology both in Germany and England and was a strong supporter of Associationism. Although he was never interested in setting up a psychological laboratory, he taught the new subject at both the Sorbonne and the College de France, and he wrote extensively on problems of psychopathology. Ribot was joined by Alfred Binet and Pierre Janet [1859-1947], who with him represented the early interests of French psychology. The fields of interest and greatest contribution in France have been psychopathology, study of mental retardation, and mental measurement. France led the way in the effort to establish more humane methods of dealing with people suffering from mental disorder. When Phillipe Pinel [1745-1826] was named director of the first hospital for mentally disturbed patients, the first thing he did was to demand that the shackles and restraints be removed from the inmates. This was followed by the effort to understand the nature of the bizarre behavior of the patients housed in the asylum. Sometime later, Jean-Martin Charcot [1825-1893], already a world renowned neurologist, took charge of the Salpetrière, Napoleon's munitions warehouse converted into a mental hospital, where he began his clinical demonstrations. He was especially interested in hysteria and had begun his studies of hypnosis. At the outset he was convinced that hypnosis was effective only with the hysteroid patient and this precipitated a heated debate between him and a doctor in general practice, Ambroise-Auguste Liébeault [1823-1904], who was using hypnosis successfully in relieving the pain of his clients. Liébeault and Hyppolyte Bernheim [1840-1919], a neurologist who joined him later, were convinced that hypnosis is induced by suggestion and is not dependent on any weakness or neuroticism on the part of the patient.

Undoubtedly Charcot had a great influence on Sigmund Freud in the evolution of psychoanalysis. Moved by world-wide interest in Charcot's work in distinguishing between true pathology of the nervous system and the various ways in which the symptoms of the neurotic can mimic the signs of true neuropathology, as well as by his interest in hypnosis, Freud managed a small stipend that would permit him to spend several months in Paris, attending Charcot's clinic in the year 1885-1886. There is a strong probability that even Freud's conviction that the neuroses are caused by repression of the sexual drive (libido) was suggested by remarks of the eminent French neurologist. The date of Freud's first publication, *Studies in Hysteria*, was 1895, shortly after his work with Charcot.

The French interest in psychopathology extended to the field of mental retardation. At the end of the eighteenth century Jean Itard [1775-1838] was called on to examine a boy who had been abandoned and had grown up in the woods. After working with him for a while, Itard concluded that he was a hopeless imbecile and gave up on him. Edouard Séguin [1812-1880] became interested in the boy and was able to achieve a degree of improvement with him. As a result, Séguin devoted his life to work with retardates and developed the first test of their ability. This was the beginning of the movement to treat the mentally retarded as persons deserving humane treatment and an opportunity to learn at least some basic skills.

Another French contribution to psychology that has opened up a vast field of research and has achieved a permanent place in psychology is the work of Alfred Binet, who was mentioned earlier as a pioneer in French psychology. For some years Binet had been working with children of lower ability, designing tests that would accurately measure their potential. In 1904 he was assigned by the French Government to devise a testing program that would enable the education department to assign pupils to programs appropriate to their abilities. Out of this came his first test of children's intelligence. This was a test of general intelligence or all around ability, rather than a test of any specific capacity. Cattell and Galton had used measurements of sensory threshold, reaction time and attention span in the hope that the average of these abilities would reveal the general level of ability of the person. Binet had the advantage of knowing that these tests of separate functions had little or no correlation with the ability to do well in school. In place of these, he devised a set of tasks or problems that ranged from following simple directions and making change to noting similarities and differences between abstract terms. In addition to substituting the concept of general intelligence for psychophysical measurements, he introduced the concept of mental age to quantify his results. Mental age is the level of performance of a child in terms of the average performance of children within her/his age group.

With these concepts—general intelligence and mental age and the method of obtaining empirical evidence to establish them—the testing movement was launched, and the study of individual differences became a permanent chapter of psychology. In 1916, within five years of Binet's untimely death, Lewis Madison Terman [1877-1956] at Stanford had published the Stanford-Binet Intelligence Scale, the first intelligence test for children, while the terms M.A. ("mental age" or level of functioning) and I.Q. ("intelligence quotient") became household words in English speaking countries.

Before leaving France and its extension of psychology into

Archives de Psychologie

PUBLIÉES PAR

Th. Flournoy
Prof. extr.

Ed. Claparède
Privat-Docent

à la Faculté des Sciences de l'Université de Genève

TOME PREMIER

Avec 57 figures

V 1

GENÈVE
CH. EGGIMANN ET Cie EDITEURS
PARIS : FÉLIX ALCAN — LEIPZIG : JOH.-AMBR. BARTH
LONDRES : WILLIAMS ET NORGATE
1902

Often reported in the literature as "founded in 1901", this title page from the first volume suggests rather 1902 as the correct date for the founding.

the fields of mental disorder, the unconscious states and the measurement of intelligence, we shall include a brief reference to psychology in the French speaking part of Switzerland. A live interest in psychology surfaced there late in the last century. Théodore Flournoy [1854-1920] established the first laboratory in Geneva in 1892, after having attended Wundt's lectures in Leipzig. With his student, Edouard Claparède [1873-1940], he founded the *Archives de Psychologie* in 1902 (see illustration opposite). Claparède was especially interested in child study, and his successor in the chair of psychology, Jean Piaget [1896-1980], has drawn world wide attention by his ingenious methods of studying children's approach to reasoning. Piaget came to psychology by way of logic and biology. His interest in psychology was focused on the logical processes of children as they attempted to solve everyday problems in their environment. He devised some ingenious problems to test the development of the child's approach to logical reasoning. He viewed the growth of perception and reasoning of the child as going through three rather uniform stages: sensory-motor, concrete operations, and formal operations. The stage of formal operations represents the adult level of logical reasoning.

Another French speaking country that was active in the first period of experimental psychology was Belgium, particularly at the University of Louvain. These beginnings will receive attention in Chapter 8.

As we conclude the story of the beginnings of psychology in France, Switzerland, and Belgium, one cannot fail to note how much the subject matter of psychology has been broadened by the inclusion of medical psychology and the areas of psychopathology, retardation and hypnosis, as well as the introduction of a sound method of measuring general intelligence. Such a broadening of the field of experimental psychology had taken the discipline well beyond the analysis of the conscious processes, the goal that Wundt had set for the new psychology.

Interest in the new psychology surfaced very early in Italy, as evidenced by the appearance of *La psychologia come scienza positiva*, published by Roberto Ardigò [1828-1920] in 1870, four years before Wundt's *Principles* appeared. This introduction of experimental psychology provoked the ire of the philosophical establishment, which was predominantly much under the control of Hegelian Idealism. In spite of opposition, psychological laboratories were established at the universities of Turin and Rome before the end of the century, and their work was sufficient to attract the Fifth International Congress of Psychology to Rome in 1905. Even so, academic psychology did not achieve a very high profile in Italy. But Francesco de Sarlo [1864-1937], a devoted student of Brentano and a surgeon and philosopher as well, established a laboratory in Florence in 1903. Because of his broad interest in medical psychology, he did much to liberate psychology from the narrow positivistic framework set by its founders. Another person who brought the new psychology from the laboratories of Wundt and Külpe was Federico Kiesow [1858-1940]. He taught Gemelli and Ponzo, whose contribution will receive attention in Chapter 7.

An interesting and original approach to the problem of relating features of the physical constitution to personality characteristics was made by Angelo Mosso [1846-1910] and Cesare Lombroso [1835-1909] in the laboratory of Turin.

Mosso devised the instrument for measuring muscular effort and Lombroso attracted worldwide attention by his *L'Uomo Delinquente* (*The Delinquent Man*, 1876), in which he made the attempt to link the tendency towards criminality with certain physical features of criminals. Although his work can hardly be regarded as successful, it was the background of a number of attempts to correlate physical features with personality traits, as later seen in the work of Spranger (1913), Kretschmer (1921), and Sheldon and associates (1940, 1942).

According to Misiak and Sexton (1966: 247), even before Pinel and Charcot were reforming the treatment of the insane in Paris, Chiarugi [1759-1820] had introduced more humane methods of dealing with the patients housed in the mental hospital in Rome. In Italy, as in France, both psychiatry and psychology benefitted from the early interest of psychologists in mental illness. This interest not only broadened the field of psychology, but it served to create a more favorable climate of exchange between the two new disciplines of psychology and psychiatry.

Here as elsewhere, interest in the new psychology caused educators to take a new look at pedagogy and the traditional approach to teaching that seemed remote from the insights into child development that psychology was establishing. The recognition that learning is a growth process that changes with the physical maturation led to some extensive radical reforms in teaching methods. It was a time when radical reforms of the educational programs were in the air. In the vanguard of these reformers was Maria Montessori [1870-1952], who came to the problems of learning from training in medicine and hands-on experience in working with retardates. Out of this background she developed the method of teaching that bears her name. The method is based on the child's ability to learn in an environment rich in interesting objects, and the function of the teacher is to be on hand to answer questions and to see that each child is engaged in some activity of his/her own choice. Originally intended for the preschool child, the method was found effective with older children also. The Montessori method is known and highly regarded in many countries to this day.

Russia

Interest in the new psychology appeared very early in Russia. Ivan M. Sechenov [1829-1905] studied experimental physiology at the University of Berlin. It will be recalled that it was here in Johannes Müller's laboratory in experimental physiology that Wilhelm Wundt conceived of the idea of experimental psychology, based on Müller's physiological model. From Müller's distinguished student, DuBois-Reymond, Sechenov learned to measure the bioelectrical phenomena that accompany stimulation of a nerve. Returning to Russia, he brought with him also a strong antivitalism bias and the goal of reducing all conscious activities to electrical sources with the aim ultimately of offering a mechanical explanation of all mental functions.

With this orientation Sechenov dominated the first years of experimental psychology in Russia, and set its boundaries entirely within the field of physiology. In the same year that the first volume of Wundt's *Principles of Physiological Psychology* appeared (1873), Sechenov published an article, "Who Must Investigate the Problems of Psychology and How?", which appeared in his volume of *Psychological Studies* (see illustration opposite) along with a reprint of his 1863 classic, *Reflexes of the Brain*. There could be no doubt about the an-

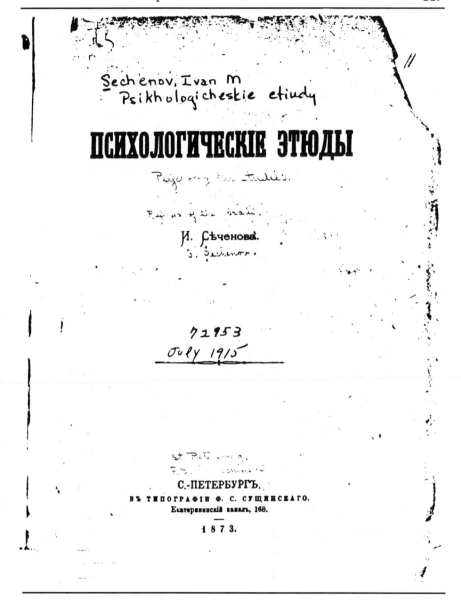

Photocopy of the title page of the title page of the 1873 publication of Sechenov's "Psychological Studies", from the only copy in the United States, held by the Goddard Library of Clark University in Worcester, MA.

swer: an unequivocal, "only the physiologist". Even sensation as a conscious process Sechenov subordinated to reflex action, in this radically anticipating the later Russian influence that, through Bekhterev's work (1907-1910), sprung up in America under the banner of "Behaviorism", as we saw in the last chapter (Sechenov 1873: 391):

> The conscious and reasonable mental activity of man is based on the same nervous mechanisms as the motor effects of lower nervous processes, where the middle phase, or sensation, regulates the movement to the benefit of the organism.

It was in just this way that Sechenov distinguished the new science from the philosophical psychologies of old (ibid. 341):

> When the greatest thinkers of the past compared the physical and mental life of man, they usually found not affinities, but only great differences. . . . And it was quite natural for them to do so, for in those days physiology did not exist, and the phenomena of the body had not yet been sufficiently analysed to make the resemblance between some of them and psychical activities noticeable.
>
> Things are different nowadays:—*physiology possesses a number of data that establish the affinity of psychical phenomena to those purely somatic acts which are called the nervous processes of the body.*

Ten years earlier he had published a controversial work under the title, *Reflexes of the Brain* (Sechenov 1863). Much of his work was based on the reflex, and this was the legacy of his influence on his Nobel Prize winning junior colleague, Ivan P. Pavlov [1849-1936].[14] Because the reflex offered an entirely objective approach to psychological phenomena, it became the trademark of the first phase of psychology in Russia.

Easily the Russian best known among psychologists is the physiologist, Ivan P. Pavlov, the originator of the conditioned reflex and winner of the Nobel Prize in 1904 for work on the physiology of digestion. Pavlov received his training in the medical school of the Military Academy, but his interests were in physiological research. For this he was indebted to Sechenov, whose devotion to physiological psychology he shared. His early researches were on the glandular reflexes that are involved in the digestion of food. He preferred this system of reflexes because of its remoteness from direct conscious control. And, since the salivary reflex is more easily subjected to quantitative measurement, he chose it for the study of conditioning that won for him the Nobel Prize.

Vladimir M. Bekheterev [1857-1927] was another Russian psychologist who attempted to make psychology completely objective. After initial training in medicine at the Military Academy in Petersburg, he spent some time with DuBois-Reymond in Berlin and also visited Charcot's clinic in Paris. He spent a short time in Wundt's laboratory at Leipzig and manifested some interest in the introspective method, but later abandoned it because of its lack of objectivity. Returning

---

[14] Although Pavlov took his M.D. from the University of St. Petersburg in 1883, almost five years before Sechenov left that faculty for the University of Moscow, and—like everyone else in Russian physiology—was importantly influenced by Sechenov's views, he does not seem to have directly studied under Sechenov.

to Russia, he was assigned to the position of head of psychiatry at the University of Kazan. There he became interested in medical psychology, and established a laboratory to study the psychophysiological factors in mental disorders. Misiak and Sexton (1966: 225) call him the pioneer in objective experimental psychology in Russia. In 1904 he wrote an article on the subject matter of objective psychology which he later expanded in book form and published as *Objective Psychology* (1907-1910). Apparently this work and its introduction to the conditioned reflex of Pavlov inspired John Watson's "behaviorist manifesto", which appeared in 1913. Although the conditioned reflex is the centerpiece of Behaviorism, and in spite of Pavlov's insistence on a completely objective psychology, it is strange that he never showed the slightest interest in Watson's work.

After 1917 and the Communist takeover in Russia, there were several attempts to shape psychology according to the Communist Party line. Psychological laboratories were established in philosophy departments of the universities, but the first independent center for training and research in psychology was established in Moscow in 1911 by G. I. Chelpanov [1862-1936]. He had been trained under Wundt and, according to Luria (a.1977: 23), was a staunch defender of the method of introspection. Chelpanov and introspection ran afoul of the party line, and he was displaced by Konstantin N. Kornilov [1879-1957], who attempted to set psychology to the rhythms of dialectical materialism. His movement received the name "reactology", because it attempted to show how a wide range of human behaviors respond to socioeconomic factors. In a sense it was a group psychology which emphasizes the dependence of the individual on the group. Kornilov managed to maintain his leadership in psychology until 1930, when the publication of Lenin's *Philosophical Notebooks* shifted the emphasis in Soviet psychology to the ability of the human being to change the environment rather than merely to react to it. Still in charge of the Psychological Institute, Kornilov was largely responsible for bringing to Moscow some bright young psychologists who were able to turn Russian psychology around and rescue it both from the subjectivism of introspection and from the limited vision of the physiologists.

The three persons most involved in setting a new direction for psychology in Russia were Lev Semyanovich Vygotsky [1896-1934], Alesandro R. Luria [1902-1977], and Alexi N. Leontiev [1903-1979]. Of these Vygotsky was clearly the leader, as Luria so generously affirms (a.1977: 38):

> It is no exaggeration to say that Vygotsky was a genius. Through more than five decades in science I have never again met a person who even approached his clearness of mind, his ability to lay bare the essential structure of complex problems, his breadth of knowledge in many fields, and his ability to foresee the future development of his science.

When Vygotsky came to Moscow in 1925 to join Kornilov's psychology research team, he was familiar with the major contributions to psychology in Western Europe and America, and he felt the same growing disillusionment with the new psychology that many felt had failed to live up to its promise of fifty years before. This conviction was shared by his fellow workers at the institute, Luria and Leontiev. The three teamed up to rescue psychology from the irreconcilable dilemma between the subjectivism and antiscientific method of the Introspectionists and the reductivism of the Reflexologists. Neither of these had the means to deal with the higher cognitive processes. Vygotsky and the other members of the troika were familiar with the Gestalt critique of both the Pavlovian reduction of all behavior to the reflex and the Introspectionist attempt to reduce all higher conscious states to their constituent sensory elements. But the Moscow group felt that the Gestalt approach had not gotten much beyond pointing out the defects of its opponents. Vygotsky had an abiding interest in developing an approach to the higher cognitive processes based on reliable experimental data. This goal animated him and his collaborators to engage in research related to thought processes. Language comes immediately to mind as an area of human behavior that involves higher thought processes. Hence much of his research was devoted to the study of the manner in which the child learns to speak. He was familiar with Piaget's ingenious experiments with children, and he adapted some of Piaget's methods in his work with mentally defective children and with ethnic groups in relatively isolated Soviet Republics. He was not comfortable with Piaget's relatively fixed stages in the development of logical thought, and he was convinced that the development of logical thinking depends very much on the development of speech. Speech brings in a cultural factor from the environment to bear on the maturation of internal structures. Learning the meaning of the spoken word and the use of language to obtain what the child wants depend on the child's relationship with the mother or mother figure. This cultural factor external to the child is what makes communication by true language unique to the human species. In Vygotsky's view, there is no way to explain human language simply as a more elaborate development of communication among subhuman species. For him, thought and speech are something as natural to the human being as flying is to the bird and swimming to the fish. But thought and speech do not develop entirely from within. They depend on interaction with other human beings as well. This means that there is a cultural contribution to the child's learning to talk. Vygotsky's view of the uniqueness of human language was not merely a theoretical assumption, but grew out of his extensive researches with children and mental defectives. This view is obviously quite at odds with the elaborate efforts to train subhuman animals to speak that have preoccupied some psychologists in America.

The originality and genius of Vygotsky's contribution to the understanding of thought and language is seen in the combining of symbol and tool in the efforts of the child to solve a problem that is beyond his capacity at a particular stage of his development. The possibility of the child's use of language symbols as tools was something that neither Köhler in his demonstration of the use of tools by his chimps, nor Piaget with his explanation of egocentric speech by children, had suspected. Vygotsky (1930: 28) states his position in a very succinct manner:

> To summarize what has been said thus far in this section: The specifically human capacity for language enables children to provide for auxiliary tools in the solution of difficult tasks, to overcome impulsive action, to plan a solution to a problem prior to its execution, and to master their own behavior. Signs and words serve children first and foremost as a means of social contact with other people. The cognitive and communicative functions of language become the basis

of a new and superior form of activity in children, distinguishing them from animals.

This statement clarifies the manner in which Vygotsky sees children using the beginnings of language as a tool to accomplish tasks. The summary also suggests why the term "socio-historical" has been applied to his linguistic system.

In spite of the fact that Vygotsky was a convinced follower of Marx and considered his own socio-historical view of language to be an example of dialectical materialism at its best, the work of his co-workers was strongly curtailed shortly after his death in 1934. However, Luria and some of the others transferred their work to the study of the effects of brain injury on the higher thought processes. They were able to demonstrate that localization of thought processes does not become established until relatively late in the child's development, and always retains some possibility of shifting as a result of trauma or brain surgery. Since their work was now in the field of neurology, they suffered no government interference, while adding further empirical evidence in support of their view of the constant interaction of speech and thought.

Amazingly, psychology in the Soviet Union has flourished and has acquired international stature since 1950 in spite of the order to purge itself of foreign and "bourgeois" contamination and to concentrate on Pavlov's program. More than anything else this seems to be result of the new direction given to Soviet Psychology by the Vygotsky, Luria and Leontiev troika. Vygotsky's imprint on psychology in the Soviet Union is best seen in the positions of influence occupied by his disciples (Cole 1978).

In a later chapter it will be interesting and instructive to compare some of the work of Vygotsky's followers with the work in cognitive psychology carried out by Jerome Bruner, Noam Chomsky, Howard Gardner and others in the United States.

SUMMARY OBSERVATIONS

As we conclude this brief review of the beginnings of psychology in foreign countries, we note how much the field of psychology has been broadened by the inclusion of medical psychology, with its interest in mental disorder, hypnosis, mental retardation, and the introduction of mental testing. In comparing the evolution of psychology in Europe with developments in America, we note much less attachment to the laboratory abroad and closer connections with the medical profession and with other areas of applied knowledge than was true during the same period in this country. Already, in the development of these specialized areas of applied psychology, we see a hint of the emergence of clinical psychology as a discipline related to medicine but able to justify its own independent existence.

Chapter 7

ARISTOTELIAN INFLUENCE ON THE NEW PSYCHOLOGY

In the last three chapters we have followed the mainstream of the development of psychology as it tried to achieve acceptance as a scientific discipline. The new psychology was, as Wundt contended, quite independent of the prevailing post-Kantian metaphysics, but from the beginning it was under the strong influence of Associationism and mechanistic Positivism. On the periphery of this line of development, while intensely interested in it, were intellectual movements that had little effect on psychology in its formative stages, particularly in America, but which were destined to exert more and more influence as psychology moved out of the halls of academia and began to deal in depth with the real problems of real people in the areas of clinical and counseling psychology.

For one thing, there was a revival of scholarly interest in Aristotle during the second half of the nineteenth century that resulted in the excellent critical editions of the Aristotelian Corpus: the Berlin edition of the Greek text (Bekker Ed. 1831-1870) and the Oxford edition of a translation into English (Ross Ed. 1928-1952). These made the original works of Aristotle available in vernacular translations and aroused some interest. We have called attention to Franz Brentano, whose *Psychology from an Empirical Standpoint* appeared in 1874, as one of those who approached the new psychology from an Aristotelian viewpoint. Coming on the scene the same year in which the publication of Wundt's *Principles of Physiological Psychology* was completed, Brentano's work took a position quite at odds with the sensationalist bias of the man who more than anyone else set the direction of the new psychology. As we have noted, Brentano's "act psychology" was based on Aristotle's theory of cognition, whereas Wundt's "psychology of content" was soon absorbed by the Associationism of the British Empiricists, Locke and Hume. Wundt's work was received enthusiastically and did much to launch the new psychology; Brentano's contribution was ignored by Wundt's followers. Not until forty years later was it revisited in the form of Gestalt psychology.

A much more vigorous and significant revival and development of Aristotle's psychology came from another source. This was the revival of the Aristotelo-Thomistic synthesis at the University of Louvain and elsewhere at centers in Italy and Spain. In the middle of the nineteenth century there were signs of renewed interest in Scholastic philosophy and the desire to recapture a synthesis of Scholastic thought. This interest was more advanced in the Iberian Peninsula because of the continuity its major university centers had maintained with the medieval university traditions established in northern Europe during the high Middle Ages—a continuity reinforced by the economic and political isolation of Iberia from Central Europe as a result of the Reformation, the secession of the Low Countries, and the tension between the monarchies of England and Spain.

This renewed interest in the Scholastic past was brought to focus and given definitive form by the Encyclical, *Aeterni Patris*, of Pope Leo XIII (1879). Pope Leo had been a long time student and admirer of Thomas Aquinas, the great light of the 13th Century, whose contribution we noted in Chapter 2. In his encyclical, Pope Leo extolled the breadth and depth of the great doctor's wisdom and advocated a return of Catholic thinkers to this rich heritage. He also insisted that St. Thomas be reinstated as the philosophical mentor and guide in Catholic centers of higher learning.

Since, as we also saw in Chapter 2, St. Thomas' life was devoted to setting forth the doctrines of Christian faith within a basically Aristotelian framework, the revival of Thomism entailed at the same time a return to Aristotle, in effect an Aristotelian renascence.

THE WORK OF MERCIER AT LOUVAIN

What is of particular interest to the psychologist is the fact that this forceful reintroduction of Aristotle's psychology into Western thought coincided so closely in time with the launching of the new psychology. In the year 1882, the young Desiré Mercier [1851-1926] was given the assignment of establishing the Institute Philosophique within the University of Louvain, for the purpose of reviving and maintaining an authentic expression of Thomistic philosophy on that campus. For Mercier the revival of the philosophy of St. Thomas did not mean devoting one's time to another commentary on the thirteenth century master. Rather, it meant the application of the wisdom of St. Thomas to the problems of contemporary science. Mercier found in the new psychology the opening he was looking for. After spending some time with Wundt at Leipzig he returned to establish a psychological laboratory at Louvain, and began a series of lectures on physiological psychology. The laboratory was opened in 1892, not many years after Wundt had succeeded in setting up his laboratory in Leipzig. Under the able direction of Armand Thiery and Albert Michotte [1881-1965], the laboratory at Louvain soon gained international recognition.

We get some notion of the great regard that Mercier felt for the new psychology from his haste to familiarize himself with the work of Wundt and his return to equip a similar laboratory at Louvain at a time when the term "psychophysics" was beginning to give way to the term "physiological psychology" to distinguish scientific psychology from the older "rational psychology". The following statement (cited by Misiak and Staudt 1954: 34-35), dating from 1891, early in Mercier's career at Louvain, sums up very well the defense of his own interest in the new psychology, an attitude that he would like his students at the Institute to share:

> Psychology is undergoing today a transformation from which we would be blameworthy to remain aloof . . . Here is a young, contemporary science, which is in itself neither spiritualistic nor materialistic. If we do not take part in it, the psychology of the future will develop without us, and there is every reason to believe, against us. . . . We must prepare workers who will produce their own works, original experiments, which

no one can overlook without ceasing to be familiar with the science.

Mercier's publications are extensive and varied. Unfortunately, his active promotion of psychology was cut short by his appointment as Archbishop of Malines, the Primatial See of Belgium, in 1906, a position in which he taught the world the effectiveness of non-violent opposition to the German invaders in World War I. As a result of this grave responsibility his writings in psychology were ended prematurely. In addition to numerous journal articles, he wrote two books that have gone through a number of editions: *Psychology* (1894), and *The Origins of Contemporary Psychology* (1897).

The *Origins* is a very valuable commentary on the background of experimental psychology by a person who was on the scene when the new psychology was launched and who had great hopes for its future. There is no better authority on the strong Cartesian influence on experimental psychology when it was opening its first laboratories. Mercier's exposition of the strange combination of idealism and positivism is valuable for anyone who is puzzled by the fact that it took nearly two generations of psychologists to discover that it is the human person, rather than the mind (either conscious or unconscious), that is the true subject of psychological study. In the *Origins*, Mercier very convincingly traces the powerful influence that Descartes' complete opposition between soul and body had exercised on the beginnings of scientific psychology. Likewise, Descartes' totally mechanistic concept of the body, as we saw in Chapter 3 above, prepared the way for the positivistic orientation that began to surface very early in American psychology. Sensing the unsound direction in which the new psychology was heading, Mercier turned to the psychology of Aristotle for the basis of the union of soul and body, a conception without which psychology becomes either totally mentalistic or an extension of physics. He was convinced that Aristotle provided the best philosophical base for the understanding of the intimate union of mind and body that makes psychology ring true as the study of the human person in action, a conviction summed up in his assertion (1897: 338) that "The Aristotelian philosophy lends itself better than any other to the interpretation of the facts of experimental psychology."

Mercier sees in Aristotle's definition of the human being as a "rational animal" a formula that combines the highest aspirations of reason with the lowest level of organic functions in a psychosomatic unity that we call the human person. The evident fact of the interaction of soul upon body and body upon soul is a given in his approach to the new psychology. His resistance to both an exaggerated spiritualism and to the opposite extreme, the reduction of psychology to biology, is evident in his approach to the psychological laboratory. The psychosomatic unity of the human person is the starting point for meaningful analysis of human experience and behavior. Psychophysical parallelism is not. Mercier was convinced that all mental activity is conditioned and supported by the biological organism in which it takes place. This conviction is reaffirmed by his complete confidence in Aristotle's approach to psychology, a confidence in support of which, in a lecture delivered before the Royal Belgian Academy around the turn of the 20th century, Mercier referred to Wundt's own remarks on "animism" in the 4th edition of his *Grundzüge* (1893: II 633) as supporting the view that the Aristotelian doctrine of the soul squares better with the results of experimental psychology than either dualism or materialism.[14]

This approval of Aristotle on Mercier's part is further reflected in the following passage from the final chapter of his book tracing the *Origins of Contemporary Psychology* (Mercier 1897: 339):

> But if, with Aristotle and all the teachers of the School, we admit that man is a composite substance made up of matter and an immaterial soul, that his higher functions are really dependent upon his lower functions, that not one of his inward acts is without its physical correlative, not one of his thoughts without its representation, not one of his volitions without sensible

---

[14] Mercier 1900: 449: "'Les résultats de mes travaux, dit Wundt, ne cadrent ni avec l'hypothèse matérialiste ni avec le dualisme platonicien ou cartésien; seul l'animisme aristotélicien, qui rattache la psychologie à la biologie, se dégage, comme conclusion métaphysique plausible, de la psychologie expérimentale' (*Grundzüge der phys. Psych.*, II, 4ᵉ Aufl., Cap. 23, S. 633)."

Thus Mercier. We obtained a copy of the 1893 4th edition of the *Grundzüge* by interlibrary loan from Loyola University of Chicago, and were unable to verify the citation. Comparison of Wundt's actual statements in the text in question, unless indeed there are variant versions of the edition in question, suggest that Mercier was summarizing three sections of Wundt's 1893 text—the two sections ("Materialism" and "Spiritualism") preceding and the section on "Animism"—in his French address. But if that is the case, why does the French text of Mercier, a notoriously careful thinker and a student of Wundt, present the remarks as a direct citation?—unless this be an illustration of "the rather off-hand manner which is customary among French authors", according to Maritain (1958: xviii), "on the matter of quotations", in which case we can only hope that the customs have since changed for the better (as indeed scholarship demands).

emotion, at once the concrete phenomenon presented to consciousness gets the note of a combination which is both psychological and physiological. It depends both upon conscious introspection and upon biological and physiological observation. In short, we have a clear indication of the raison d'etre of a science of psycho-physiology.

Not all those who joined enthusiastically in the revival of Thomistic philosophy were as ready as Cardinal Mercier to accept the new psychology. In some quarters it would seem that the revival of Thomism was an opportunity to revel in historical research into the achievements of the Scholasticism of the thirteenth century, rather than a challenge to apply the wisdom of St. Thomas to the problems of the twentieth. Generally in Thomistic circles, the new psychology would be suspect because of its secular and mechanistic orientation, and the fact that it had substituted the mind and conscious-ness for the richer and more meaningful Aristotelian concept of the soul as the vital and unifying principle of living organisms. This caused many schools under Catholic auspic-es to look upon experimental psychology with suspicion, because of its extravagant claims and its deterministic bias (a negative attitude was not allayed when Freudianism first began to move from psychiatry into psychology). Others, again, imitated Oxford and Cambridge in resisting the establishment of scientific psychology as an academic Department independent of the Department of Philosophy.[15]

---

[15] Notre Dame University, for example, today has a strong program leading to the doctorate in psychology, but this program was not inaugurated until 1969. The review in this chapter is confined to the pioneers and first generation of experimental psychology.

Nonetheless, a viable return to Aristotle that began as an effort to clear up the extant texts in the preparation of reliable vernacular translations was given great impetus and a contemporary voice even in intellectual circles interested in the new psychology as a result of the renaissance of Thomism. This was because Thomism is automatically a revival of Aristotle, as we have seen in the discussion of psychology in the Middle Ages; and this revival extended to psychology in its modern development as well.

At the beginning of this chapter we noted that we are dealing with movements on the periphery, rather than in the mainstream of psychology in America, and that their influence in this country came at a later stage in the evolution of psychology. The contribution of this return to the Aristotelo-Thomistic synthesis fostered by Mercier at Louvain and later taken up in colleges and universities under Catholic auspices is not to be found in the extent or prominence of the research results but in the new look at psychology that it involved. The return to Aristotle's psychology demanded that psychology focus on the living organism and from there proceed to investigate consciousness and mind. In a word, it was to demand a biological approach to psychology, rather than have psychology begin with the upper storey of vital function, consciousness itself. All this is well epitomized by the contrast that was made in an earlier chapter between Descartes' definition of the soul as mind or conscious principle, and Aristotle's definition of soul as principle of all vital functions. Unfortunately, the first generation of psychologists were not prepared to move out from the Cartesian view of mind and regarded any reference to the soul as an attempt to introduce spiritualism and religious tradition into what they wished to be a purely scientific enterprise. As a matter of fact, Mercier and those who subscribed to the

Aristotelian view of soul were concerned with soul simply as the unifying and vivifying principle of a living organism, rather than with its religious and supernatural potential. Three centuries of dualism and religious controversy had well-obscured the fact that, on Aristotle's conception, the soul is by definition no more supernatural than the foot, a point that remains obscured in mainstream psychology to this day.[16] Hence those who championed an Aristotelian view in

---

[16] Even to this day, the reason most frequently alleged for rejecting the soul—namely, that consideration of the soul involves one in supernatural-ism—is as entrenched as it is ill-conceived. As soon as psychology begins to take into consideration the whole person, from cells and tissues to hopes and fears, the theoretical necessity of some such notion as Aristotle called soul and its explanatory superiority to modern dualism becomes, in the context of contemporary scientific knowledge of the organism, overwhelmingly apparent, as may be made clear by citing the following contrast of "Aristotelian Unity vs. Psychophysical Parallelism" drawn in my earlier introductory textbook (Gannon 1959: 22):

It will be recalled that Descartes equated the soul with thought and limited its functions to conscious acts. Aristotle equates it with all the functions of protoplasm. According to the Greek philosopher, the primary activity of the soul is not sensation, thought, or feeling. The first function of the soul is to make real and actual an organism that otherwise would be only potential. Since nutrition is the absolutely necessary requisite if the organism is to survive, we may say that the fundamental manifestation of the soul is that of the nutritive functions. Inseparably linked up with nutritive activities are the other properties of protoplasm: respiration, reproduction, and irritability. No matter how high one goes in the scale of organisms, the most important thing is the metabolism that keeps the organism alive. All other operations follow upon this. The secondary position of consciousness with respect to the integrity of the organism is illustrated by the periodic interrup-tions of consciousness by sleep, during which time the body continues to carry on all the necessary metabolic functions unaided by conscious control. A much more striking example of the same thing is provided

this regard were bound to find themselves somewhat outside of the mainstream.

THE CATHOLIC UNIVERSITY OF AMERICA

Another university that showed great interest in the work of Wundt and the laboratory at Leipzig during its early years was the Catholic University of America. In an excellent chapter on Edward A. Pace [1861-1938], Misiak and Staudt (1954: 66-83) detail the manner in which this pioneer of psychology among Catholics in the United States went abroad to study philosophy and took his degree in experimental psychology under Wundt in 1891. On his return to Washington he immediately set about introducing the new psychology, first with courses in experimental psychology within the school of philosophy, and later by equipping a laboratory, among the first to be established in this country. Pace was a charter member of the American Psychological Association and, like Hall and Cattell, he lost no opportunity to promote the new science of psychology. We noted in connection with Cardinal Mercier that the new psychology was suspect among Catholic theologians and philosophers. Pace was well aware of this, and repeatedly pointed out how important it was for Catholics to get over their fears and become familiar with the developments in this field that had so much to offer.

---

by those cases of severe infection or brain injury in which consciousness is suspended for days while the organism mobilizes all its energy to resist the threat of dissolution. Consciousness is important, and it makes possible some of the highest manifestations of life; but consciousness depends upon life, not life upon consciousness."

The continuation and expansion of Pace's pioneer work at the Catholic University was insured by a chance meeting between him and a young student for the Paulist Congregation shortly before 1900. The young Paulist was Thomas Verner Moore [1877-1969], who responded enthusiastically to Pace's presentation of the possibilities of the new science of psychology. Later he consulted Pace about preparation for a career in psychology and was advised to pursue a rigorous course in mathematics, physics, chemistry and biology. He enrolled in the graduate program at the Catholic University, completed his studies for the doctorate and did a dissertation under Pace. He received his Ph.D. in 1903, and shortly thereafter went to Germany to study psychology in the laboratories of Wundt and Külpe. A bout with tuberculosis interrupted his program, and he was forced to return to the United States, where he spent three years as Newman chaplain at the University of California, Berkeley. During this time he continued his studies of physiology and chemistry. With health restored he returned to Washington where he began his career as a member of the psychology faculty of the Catholic University. But his training was not yet finished. Shortly after he began his teaching career in psychology, he visited Witmer's child clinic in Philadelphia and decided to introduce a similar project in conjunction with the psychology department of the Catholic University. In preparation for this, he took up medicine at Georgetown and completed his medical training at Johns Hopkins, extending it into the field of psychiatry under Adolph Meyer, who was the guiding light of the mental hygiene movement in America.

By this time the United States was moving towards World War I and psychologists and psychiatrists were in great demand. Moore took a commission in the Medical Corps and served both at home and abroad. It was during this service that he came into contact with psychoanalysis. He found Freud's clinical insights helpful in dealing with some shell shocked victims of the war. Out of this experience came *Dynamic Psychology* (1924), the first serious attempt to sort out the strengths and weaknesses of psychoanalysis by a Catholic author. All this is prelude to his career as head of the psychology department at the Catholic University for twenty-five years. It goes far to account for the early clinical interest of his department, even as he improved the faculty and insisted on a rigorously scientific program for degree candidates.

Three things may be said to characterize Moore's leadership as head of the department of psychology. First, he actively promoted psychology, and a noteworthy portion of his writing was aimed at breaking down the prejudice against experimental psychology in Catholic colleges and universities. Second, he introduced Charles Spearman's [1863-1945] factorial study of intelligence and made original contributions to the multiple factor analysis of intelligence. Third, he was a pioneer in combining clinical experience with academic training in the preparation of psychologists. This was in the early 1920s, when, as we shall see in the next chapter, clinical psychology was little more than a name, and psychology departments in this country were not yet prepared to think of the professional possibilities of psychology.

Dr. Moore's interest in the clinical aspects of psychology stemmed in part from his training and experience in psychiatry and also from a profound concern to bring the findings of psychological research to bear on both children and adults suffering from retardation or mental disorder. This interest is reflected in the fact that direct clinical experience was a part of the regular course leading to the doctorate from the beginning of Moore's chairmanship. It is also evident in the fact that the journal that he established in 1930 as the publication medium of the Department was named *Studies in Psychology and Psychiatry*. Later on, with the aid of Rockefeller funds, he expanded the Department of Psychology into the Department of Psychology and Psychiatry (an innovation abandoned later in the Department's history). In all of these innovations, the aim was to integrate clinical training with a solid rigorous training in general psychology. This was in the late 1920s and early 1930s, when psychology departments in many universities were not prepared to incorporate training in clinical subjects with the traditional degree requirements, but forced those interested in a career in clinical psychology to seek their clinical experience in a mental hospital, as we will have occasion to see in discussing Shakow's experience in Chapter 9. At the Boulder Conference in 1948, this combination of a strong academic course and the opportunity for hands-on clinical experience became the standard of training of the clinical psychologist.

In addition to professional and educational activity, Moore, a profoundly spiritual man, was concerned with the integration of psychology with authentic religious experience. To this end he wrote several books, the most notable of which is *The Life of Man with God* (1956). For his spiritual writings, his personal life equipped him in an unique way. His own lived experience took him from the Paulist priesthood, through formation in Benedictine spirituality, to the final years spent in a Carthusian hermitage. In the course of his extended period as head of the department of psychology, Moore produced a number of journal articles and several books on psychology. Among the books, two stand out for their depth and comprehensiveness: *Cognitive Psychology* (1939) and *The Nature and Treatment of Mental Disorders* (1943); while a third, *Dynamic Psychology* (1924), stands out for its balanced exposition of the early Freud. The last mentioned title is a good example of Moore's efforts to remove the barriers to the acceptance of depth psychology among Catholic students and writers.

This early interest in medical psychology and psychiatry on the part of Moore made it easy for the Catholic University to receive approval by the American Psychological Association for its doctoral program when the great surge of interest in clinical psychology occurred following World War II. The leadership of the Catholic University in giving a clinical direction to psychology was followed by several other institutions under Catholic auspices. We shall give brief attention to three of these.

The three institutions that will be considered next are foundations of the Society of Jesus in this country, each of which has made significant contributions to the development of psychology in America. This review is not an attempt to establish credit for priority, but rather to trace in broad outline the manner in which psychology achieved the respected place it now holds in each of these institutions. Moving from east to west the universities are: Fordham of New York, Loyola of Chicago, and St. Louis University.

FORDHAM UNIVERSITY

The gradual emergence of experimental psychology from philosophy at Fordham University and other schools under Catholic auspices followed much the same pattern that we have noted in the emergence of psychology as an independent discipline at the Catholic University of America. Misiak and Staudt (1954: 244) gives no hint of an undergraduate department with a recognized major at Fordham until 1930.

At the time of publication Misiak was recently retired from the faculty of Fordham. Undoubtedly various courses in the new discipline had been introduced into the curriculum well before this date.

Fordham was somewhat unique in that Walter G. Summers, S.J. [1889-1938], was already in the process of constructing and developing a lie detector when he took up his work as head of a graduate department. His instrument, undoubtedly the forerunner of the polygraph, depended on the careful measurement of a single bodily reaction to emotional stress, viz., the galvanic skin reflex (GSR). Research was soon extended into the areas of learning, child study, visual discrimination and individual differences. Training in clinical psychology later became a strong component of the psychology department to meet the growing demand after World War II.

In addition to the research projects of graduate students, two faculty members have achieved national recognition. These are Henryk Misiak for his scholarly work in the history of psychology (with Virginia Staudt Sexton 1954, 1966); and Anne Anastasi [1908-] for her comprehensive introduction to individual differences (1937). She also had the distinction of serving as president of the American Psychological Association in 1972. William Bier, S.J., also deserves mention for his work on instruments for use in selecting candidates for the religious life and in helping Catholics in psychology to get in touch with one another by establishing the American Catholic Psychological Association. This was in no way an effort to set up a rival to the APA, but an effort rather to encourage Catholics to become more actively involved in that association and in other professional organizations as well. The American Catholic Psychological Association also provided needed support for the teachers in Catholic institutions where some prejudice against the new psychology still existed. The group was later assimilated as a division of the APA.

LOYOLA UNIVERSITY, CHICAGO

According to Wauck (1979), the beginnings of special courses in psychology go back to 1910 with a course labeled Physiological Psychology, offered particularly for students preparing to teach. Soon other courses in psychology were provided for students going into some phase of social work. One of the first child clinics was established by William Healy [1869-1963] in 1910. It had been established to deal with the problems of delinquent youth of the Chicago area. This was a very early opportunity for students to observe a clinical program in operation at one of its earliest sites. A sympathetic interest in Healy's program seems to have moved the faculty of Loyola to introduce courses in abnormal psychology, social pathology and child study. So when the department of psychology was established at Loyola University in 1927 by George H. Mahowald [?-1966], clinical topics were a part of its offerings.

All of these circumstances favored the launching of a graduate program in psychology that would include clinical experience. The assignment of Charles I. Doyle, S.J., to Loyola University in 1933 was the impetus that was needed. Father Charles Doyle had done graduate work in theology and had served on the staff of *America*, the enlightened organ of the Society of Jesus in this country. Coming with the first doctoral degree in psychology from St. Louis University, he took over the chairmanship of the department at Loyola with a clear idea of the direction it should take and the organizational skills needed to translate his vision into reality in the expansive Chicago setting.

Although Doyle retained an abiding interest in the analysis of the higher cognitive powers as a result of his training under Hubert Gruender, S.J., he readily saw the advantage to psychology of providing psychological training to the professions of education, medicine, and social work. This put Loyola in an excellent position to move into the clinical and counseling areas, as these entered upon an era of great expansion following World War II. When the department developed its program of training in clinical psychology, it did not withdraw interest in the more academic experimental fields, such as sensory perception, cognition and learning.

Several faculty at Loyola authored books that received considerable notice in the field: Magda Arnold (1960, 1970), Charles Curran (1969) and Eugene Kennedy (1975).

St. Louis University

Another university under Jesuit auspices in this country that took the new psychology seriously from very early was St. Louis University. The beginnings of psychology there can be traced to a course in experimental psychology included in the offerings in philosophy at the early date of 1891, while the formal establishment of a department took place in 1925 (Misiak 1954: 258). But during this period Hubert Gruender, S.J., published one of the early introductions to the new psychology in English (Gruender 1920). He had discussed the will from an empirical point of view even earlier (Gruender 1911). Raphael McCarthy, S.J., was assigned to the newly established department in 1927. Coming from London

University, where he had studied with Aveling, he was interested in extending the role of psychology beyond the classroom and the laboratory. His books, written for the wider lay public, emphasize the importance of psychology for an understanding of the self and show an awareness of the mental hygiene movement that had been triggered by Clifford Beers' *A Mind that Found Itself* (1908). The titles of McCarthy's popular studies indicate the broadening scope of psychology in anticipation of the movement in the direction of clinical psychology: *Training the Adolescent* (1934) and *Safeguarding Mental health* (1937). It appears, however, that the department which he had headed was not prepared to move in this direction until much later. A recent communication from the current chairman, James H. Korn, indicates that the clinical program did not receive approval until 1960.

THE UNIVERSITY OF THE SACRED HEART (MILAN)

Another example of the new psychology developing under the stabilizing influence of Neo-Thomism is seen in the opening of a department of psychology simultaneously with the birth of the new Catholic University of the Sacred Heart in Milan in 1924. As was the case with Mercier's leadership in establishing the Institute Philosophique of Louvain, it was largely through the vision and energetic leadership of one man that the resistance to the new psychology was broken down in Catholic circles of Italy. This fascinating man was Agostino Gemelli [1878-1959].

Unlike Mercier in Belgium and Pace in America, Gemelli came to psychology from a completely medical and scientific background. Misiak (1954: 128) remarks that the boy Gemelli showed precocious interest in the origins of life by writing on the results of his observations of the plant life on the shores of the nearby lakes of his native Lombardy. After receiving the medical degree he continued cellular researches with Camillo Golgi [1843-1926], who developed the method of cell staining that permits the course of a myelinated nerve fiber to be traced from the cell body of its origin to its peripheral terminations. But histological research did not satisfy Gemelli's desire to learn more about the mystery of life itself. Although he read deeply, the materialistic orientation of the biological sciences left him dissatisfied. During this period he became actively interested in socialist ideologies and fell in with the agnosticism and the revolt against papal authority that were bound up with the *Resorgimento*. At the time when he should have been settling into a career, he was restless and dissatisfied with the materialistic answers of the Positivism provided by his associates in the scientific field. Further reading of the masters of science only convinced him that they did not have the answers he was looking for. Coming into contact with young intellectuals who found no incompatibility between the Catholic faith and the earnest pursuit of learning, he turned his life around, joined the Franciscan Order, and was ordained a priest in 1906.

Up to this point there is little evidence of any interest in psychology, other than his realization of the need to study the whole organism as well as the single cell. For the next four years he combined biological studies and philosophy at various universities, receiving a doctorate in philosophy from Louvain in 1911. The evidence that his contact with the neo-scholastic movement at Louvain was a strong influence inclining him to experimental psychology is clear from these words from his autobiography (Gemelli 1952: 97-98):

Its line of thought, following the fundamental thesis of Scholasticism, emphasized the evaluation of scientific discoveries, and I undertook to exhibit the basic facts, particularly those achieved by the biological sciences. Perhaps it was this work which led me to take a special interest in the progress of experimental psychology, so that from the first I urged my philosophical collaborators on the *Revista* [*di filosofia neoscolastica*] to attempt to evaluate the results of experimental research in the field of psychology, and to reconsider and assess such results from the point of view of philosophy and in philosophical terms.

In the same connection two paragraphs later he adds:

Now I would like to show how, while inquiring into philosophical problems and without neglecting my histological research, I became interested in psychology and came finally to live it and to devote to it all my scientific effort.

Gemelli turned to Federico Kiesow [1858-1940], whose laboratory had achieved considerable recognition, for basic training in experimental psychology. He was introduced to Oswald Külpe by Kiesow and spent some time with Külpe working on the higher cognitive processes. During the same period he made the acquaintance of Emil Kraepelin [1856-1926], a pioneer in psychiatry, who developed the first diagnostic categories of the mental disorders. This added psychiatric experience to his medical background and probably contributed to his decision to take a broad and comprehensive approach to psychology. The involvement of the whole organism in emotion drew his interest and he took up the work of Charles Sherrington [1857-1952] to refute the Lange-James theory of emotion that was attracting attention in the first decade of the 20th century. This interest in emotion and his strong conviction of the unity of the human organism in all its reactions led him quite naturally to the study of personality.

This brings us up to the year 1915 and the entrance of Italy into World War I. Joining the army, Gemelli was commissioned at once and set to work on developing the testing and training program for airplane pilots. But his work as chaplain and organizer of psychiatric services were equally important. With all these demands on his time, he never failed to keep up his writing. After the end of the War Gemelli became intensely interested in the problem of mental retardation and spent some time working with mentally handicapped children at St. Vincent's Institute in Milan. But he had long been interested in getting a Catholic University for Italy started. The opportunity came with the establishment of the University of the Sacred Heart by Pope Benedict XV in 1921. Gemelli was already well known at the Ambrosian library, which at that time was under the direction of Achille Ratti, who was soon to succeed Benedict XV as Pope Pius XI. Gemelli was named the first rector of the new Catholic University.

This was an auspicious moment for psychology. Like G. Stanley Hall at Clark University a quarter of a century before, Gemelli lost no time in equipping a laboratory and establishing a department of psychology with the rector of the university as its head. Under a chairman who combined great interest and facility in writing with hands-on experience in a number of areas of psychological interest and a background rich in the biological sciences, the new department was assured of success. Its history has been that of productivity in a wide variety of areas of psychological interest. Researches extend from detailed work in linguistics and psychoacoustics to a critique of the Gestalt view of perception and the attempt to arrive at a sound explanation of the psychoses. At a meeting of the APA shortly after the close of World War II, Gordon Allport reported on a tour of the laboratories still functioning in Europe. In this report Allport stated that Gemelli's laboratory was the most productive he had found.

In 1965 I myself had a brief visit with Professor Leonardo Ancona in his office as chairman of the department of psychology of Sacred Heart University. At that time it came as a surprise to learn that the university numbered 24,000 in its various schools, almost equally divided between male and female. It came as a greater surprise to learn that at that time the university did not grant the doctoral degree in psychology. Instead, it supplied psychological training and appropriate certification for a wide range of specialties and professions.

OTTAWA, MONTREAL, AND LAVAL UNIVERSITIES

In evaluating the impact of the Aristotelo-Thomistic Synthesis on the development of psychology, these three Canadian universities deserve mention. The acceptance of the new psychology in the schools under Catholic auspices in Canada was delayed almost a full generation after its acceptance in Belgium, Italy and the United States. The interest of the Catholic centers of learning in Canada was more in the direction of clinical psychology, and, as we have seen, clinical psychology did not take the shape that we now know until the late 1930s. Hence the Canadian Catholic universities had little contact with the first experimental laboratories, unlike the American and European Universities we have discussed. However, when they did begin to emphasize psychology, their approach was very similar to that of the institutions we have been examining. In other words, their approach reflects the Aristotelian spirit and orientation of the Thomistic Revival and the openness to experimental psychology advocated by Cardinal Mercier at Louvain, Monsignor Pace at the Catholic University of America, and Agostino Gemelli at the University of the Sacred Heart in Milan.

SUMMARY

This chapter began with a brief sketch of the revival of Aristotle begun in Germany by the scholars at Berlin University and extended and given dynamic impetus by the renaissance of Thomistic thought initiated by Cardinal Desiré Mercier at Louvain in 1889. In the earlier chapters, we have tried to trace the beginnings of psychology in typical university settings in this country and abroad. In introducing this chapter we noted that the psychological activities engaged in by these schools under Catholic auspices have not been a part of the mainstream of the development of psychology as a scientific discipline in America. But the representatives of the Aristotelo-Thomistic approach to psychology have continued to be interested observers of psychology as it went through the convulsions of the 1920s, ready to enter into meaningful research whenever psychology can release itself from some of its extreme postures.

In its beginnings the orientation of academic psychology was narrowly mentalistic. One need only recall Wundt's definition of the new psychology as "the analysis of the conscious processes". As it progressed, academic psychology seemed to get further and further away from serious engagement with the real problems of real people. The whole movement of Watsonian Behaviorism and Neobehaviorism's frustrating attempt to establish a single paradigm of learning were so remote from a meaningful approach to the basic problems of human existence that it seemed almost a waste of time to engage in dialogue about them.

In America the failure of psychology to live up to the promises of its beginnings and the mechanistic Positivism of John Watson's Behaviorist manifesto brought psychology to an impasse. It was becoming clear that this was the end of the road for psychology unless it could come up with a program that would address the real problems of human existence. Even the language of psychology had become foreign to those who looked for more help with the problems of living. It was only after the radical shift of interest from mind, whether conscious or unconscious, to the person and the self in clinical psychology that psychology began to speak in phrases that seemed to bear resemblance to the language of the Aristotelo-Thomistic synthesis.

This shift was well begun before World War II but pushed to the fore with the upsurge of clinical and counseling interest in the post war years. Within the last twenty-five years, the revived interest in the cognitive functions and the appearance of a new science of mind have also indicated the inadequacy of Positivism and the need to find a better formula for human nature than psychophysical parallelism.

The Aristotelo-Thomistic approach to psychology is grounded in biology. From the basic properties of the organism, it proceeds through the various levels of function to intelligence and volition. Its basic psychological position may be summed up in the following statements:

1. The human being is a psychosomatic unit. Mental states affect the way the body functions and subtle bodily changes influence mood and thought.
2. The emotions are an integral and very important aspect of behavior. They cannot be dismissed as irrelevant on the ground that they are not rational.
3. Only in virtue of an overall unifying principle can the diverse functions of the human person work together for the welfare of the total organism. Psychology is not concerned with possible supernatural functions of this unifying principle. Whether this principle of unity be called the soul is irrelevant, but its contribution must not be confined to consciousness.
4. The functions of intelligence and reason and their expression in true language cannot be explained in terms of matter alone.
5. The study of personality is not complete without the recognition that the subject has the capacity to make some choices, and these choices make a palpable difference in the subject's life. To speak of the politics of human freedom or of human rights without accepting this principle is contradictory.

All of these statements are grounded in basic human experience. They are neither difficult to accept nor do they place any restrictions on experimental psychology. In fact they provide the broad base for scientific progress that was lacking in the launching of psychology. The number of "new psychologies" in the first century of psychology as a science suggest that such a doctrine of the human person might have saved psychology some of its embarrassments.

The response (in Slife Ed. 1990) to the work of Daniel Robinson on Aristotle (mentioned in our discussion of

Aristotle in Chapter 1 and in our discussion of psychology in the middle ages in chapter 2) I take as a hopeful sign, in the contemporary situation of psychology, of contributions yet to be made in the search for a broader, more humanistic, and conceptually integrated approach within the discipline, such as is reflected in the article by Kimble (1989) under the title "Psychology from the Standpoint of a Generalist".

Chapter 8

APPLIED PSYCHOLOGY IN AMERICA

We concluded the survey of the beginnings of experimental psychology in America roughly in the year 1930 on the note of fragmentation, as the new psychology became divided into schools or movements. These movements were so diverse that one author (Murchison) entitled his reviews of the American scene *Psychologies of 1925* and *Psychologies of 1930*, respectively. It is to the credit of the new and struggling discipline that it did not bog down in polemics concerning the direction that psychology should take. While psychology departments were still in some confusion, psychology was moving into the marketplace.

While the theoretical study of psychology and improvements in methods of research were actively pursued in university departments, the new psychology was rapidly

155

moving into the market place. It is to the beginnings of psychology as a profession that we now direct our attention. At this point it is significant to recall that those students who had gone to Leipzig to learn the then-new psychology in Wundt's laboratory did not agree with his insistence that psychology should confine itself to the research laboratory, but insisted that it should seek practical applications as well. From the beginning, one of the characteristics of American Functionalism was its pragmatic outlook, its interest in developing practical applications of psychology to the problems of everyday living. Before going into the various applications of psychology that have expanded psychology as a profession, it might be well to note the amazing growth experienced by the discipline as we approach the one hundredth anniversary of the founding of the American Psychological Association. Recall that the APA was founded under the leadership of G. Stanley Hall in 1892, with a charter membership of 26. By 1930 it boasted 1100 members. By 1973 the number had grown to 35,000, due in large measure to the upsurge of professional psychology, especially in the clinical and counseling areas. Up to the present, the numbers show little sign of leveling off, with the APA reporting 50,000 members in 1985, and 96,632 members in 1988. The members are divided among 44 divisions, and an additional 5,000 members of the association who do not belong to any division, bringing the total of those engaged in some phase of psychology to more than 100,000.

The breakdown of these figures indicates how much the development of psychology as a profession contributed to this growth. It is time now to consider how, after some rather tentative and uncertain beginnings, the areas of applied psychology achieved professional recognition and swelled the numbers, so that professionals now outnumber the psychologists in teaching and research by a large margin.

EDUCATIONAL PSYCHOLOGY

The first area to seek the help of the new psychology was education and the field of human learning. It would be a mistake, however, to consider changes in educational philosophy and practice to be merely the application of insights discovered by psychology to problems of the classroom. Historically the situation is much more complicated than this. The new psychology and what has come to be known as educational psychology have had a parallel development. We noted in chapter 4 that Johann Friederich Herbart [1776-1841] had written on the subject of experimental psychology well before Wundt thought of opening the Leipzig laboratory. In 1824 Herbart published a work whose title emphasized that the new science of psychology should be grounded in mathematics and metaphysics, but he had no interest in experimental data to support his theory. Rather he turned his interest toward pedagogy, following J. H. Pestalozzi [1746-1827], the Swiss educational reformer, who was revamping classroom practice in terms of the needs of the developing child. Pestalozzi was not a psychologist, but he was very interested in obtaining experimental support for his changes in classroom practice. All of this led naturally to a great increase of emphasis on psychology in the training of new teachers. Thus, almost without knowing it, psychology was being applied to an important area of training, and educational psychology became its first professional field. This extension of scientific methods into the field of education placed great emphasis on experiments in learning and opened up a new field of theory making and testing. It was this combination of interest in learning and in a thoroughly experimental approach to psychology that made E. L. Thorndike a leader in the development of learning theory in America.

The combination of Watson's demonstration of conditioning in small children and Thorndike's experimental approach to learning and his critique of the doctrine of faculty training gave high priority to theory and research in learning in many psychology departments, even as it gained for the rat colony a comfortable place in academia. This focus on basic research in learning was prompted by E. L. Thorndike's doctrine of "connectionism"[18] and his controversial "law of effect". The "law of effect" simply asserts that what results in a satisfying state of the organism gets stamped in and becomes a permanent part of the organism's response repertoire. Likewise a response that fails to give satisfaction gets stamped out. This "law" and the "law of exercise" (which simply extends the law of effect to cover the role of repetition and practice, i.e., habit formation) became the pillars on which Stimulus-Response bond theories of learning were based. Learning theories developed around the effort to prove or disprove them as the paradigm of all learning. This

---

[18] In Thorndike's work, the term "connectionism" referred to the association of particular responses with specific stimulus situations through trial-and-error learning, and, more generally, between various "bits of knowledge" or "discrete ideas". In contemporary cognitive science, the term "connectionism" has been reintroduced, but now to designate the link between mind and brain, the hypothesis, that is, that consciousness must be embodied, and that the brain by its very material and physiological nature is the locus of that embodiment. Here again, as in behaviorism earlier, it is Sechenov's ghost that is the unacknowledged mentor: see the discussion in Chapter 4 above.

is an example of basic research in learning that preoccupied many departments between 1930 and 1960.

From his days at Harvard under William James, Thorndike had shown great interest in studies of animal intelligence. It was the behavior of animals in a puzzle box, rather than in a maze, that caught his attention in particular. Out of this interest came his reduction of all learning to the trial-and-error formula.

Thorndike did not engage in research based on maze running rodents, but he was concerned in reducing the process of human learning to its lowest common denominator. His position of leadership in the field of educational psychology made Teachers' College at Columbia University a powerful influence in creating the academic space for a scientific approach to educational psychology as a special application of general psychology. From the late 1920s through the 1950s, the development of theories of learning and methods of testing them was a major interest of the mainstream of psychology in the United States.

This interest of education in turning to psychology for help was even more apparent abroad. Binet, the French psychologist, initiated the mental testing movement in trying to develop a test that would separate the slow learners from the children of normal intelligence in order to improve the educational climate for both. Both Piaget [1896-1980] and Maria Montessori [1870-1952] tried to ground their educational methods on careful psychological observations of the child's readiness to learn, rather than on traditional methods of instruction that depended heavily on rote memory.

Noting that educational psychology has a history of its own, we turn now to areas of psychology in which the applications of psychology are not so obvious as in learning. The first to draw our attention are industrial and clinical psychology, which began about the same time. We shall take up the role of psychology in industry first, because its development did not encounter the sort of opposition that has dogged the course of clinical psychology.

There is something ironic about the fact that the application of psychology to industrial pursuits was opened up by Hugo Münsterberg [1863-1916], whom William James had imported from Wundt's laboratory to teach experimental psychology at Harvard after James had left the field for philosophy. In more than 200 articles and at least one book, *Psychology and Industrial Efficiency* (1913), Münsterberg explored the benefits to industry that psychology had to offer. But it was Walter Dill Scott [1869-1955] who gave industrial psychology its start with a work entitled *The Theory of Advertising* (1903). This was at the outset of his career as professor of psychology at Northwestern University, a position he had accepted on his return from Leipzig with a doctorate in the new psychology under Wundt. Scott pursued this interest in the applications of psychology to business and industry during his years in the psychology department and later on as president of Northwestern University. He was instrumental also in introducing the new psychology to the Carnegie Institute, where he spent two years on leave from Northwestern, just prior to World War I. At the Institute he worked with Walter V. Bingham [1880-1952], broadening the scope of industrial psychology while gaining acceptance for it as a valued application of psychology in the field of commerce and industry. Throughout this period membership in the American Psychological Association was heavily weighted with academic psychologists, who were concerned about the acceptance of psychology by the scientific community and felt that industrial psychology was a concession to popular demand just when academic research efforts were beginning to command favorable attention by representatives of the hard sciences. This opposition from the representatives of academic psychology may seem strange in view of the practical and pragmatic character of functional psychology, as the new discipline took root in American soil. But both industrial and clinical psychology had to make their way in the face of this critical attitude on the part of those who were engaged in teaching and research. To counter this grudging acceptance by the APA, which was then firmly in the hands of the representatives of pure science, the Association for Applied Psychology was established in 1937 with its own journal, *The Journal of Consulting Psychology*.

The rapid growth of industrial and clinical psychology, not to mention a number of related fields, succeeded in changing the climate of resistance among academicians to the application of psychology to practical ends. In the reorganization of the APA in 1945, industrial and clinical psychology were brought into the parent association and the divisional structure was established. Throughout the course of its growth, industrial psychology drew upon the data accumulating in other fields of psychology, and especially in clinical psychology that was experiencing considerable growth during the period immediately preceding World War II. After the War, all of the applied areas expanded at an unprecedented rate. By 1985 the amazing membership total of 50,000 had been reached.

At the same time, programs for the training of candidates for the various specializations were being shaped to fit the needs of expanding industries, and attention was given to standards for the certification of persons entering the field. To this end the American Board of Examiners in Professional Psychology (ABEPP) was established in 1947. By 1963 industrial psychology accounted for more than 12% of the membership in the APA, and clinical psychology could claim an imposing 37% of the total roster of members. Today persons trained in industrial psychology will be found in personnel departments of many industries, where their concern is often with labor relations and employee assistance programs. They are also in demand as members of various consulting teams.

CLINICAL PSYCHOLOGY: BEGINNINGS

Clinical psychology today belies its humble beginnings. What began with little more than a program for carefully testing young children in the laboratory established by Lightner Witmer [1867-1956] at the University of Pennsylvania has given rise to at least four divisions of the APA and now accounts for some 12,000 members who hold divisional classification and many more who are doing clinical work but are unclassified.

Lightner Witmer established the first child clinic in 1896 as a part of the recently established psychological laboratory (Hilgard 1987). This child clinic and his later hospital school soon became the pattern for psychology departments at such places as Yale, Iowa, The Catholic University of America, and elsewhere. Witmer had been brought into the field of applied psychology by the request of a school teacher for help with a child suffering from a learning disability. The clinical approach began with a careful evaluation of the child. In the beginning, clinical attention centered around carefully testing the child's abilities. The mental testing movement was just beginning to gather momentum at the time. It soon became clear, however, that children who were having difficulty in school often had problems of a physiological nature as well. Noting this, Witmer established a hospital school in which he hoped to offer appropriate training for persons interested in child psychology. This was probably one of the first attempts in the United States to bring psychology and medicine closer together in a cooperative enterprise for the total health of the client.

Even in this modest effort to combine the new science of psychology with the established profession of medicine, some of the tensions surfaced that were to create major hurdles for clinical psychology in later years. At the same time that psychology departments in major universities were establishing hospital-related child clinics, some psychiatrists in charge of mental hospitals were turning to psychologists and establishing psychological laboratories for research in mental illness. Among the psychiatrists who contributed significantly to the growth and development of clinical psychology was Adolf Meyer [1866-1950], who brought psychologists on board to conduct research in mental illness when he was in charge of Worcester State Hospital. In his work with the mentally ill, he developed his eclectic psychobiological theory and brought it into psychiatry during his tenure as professor of psychiatry at Johns Hopkins University. In this he anticipated in some respects the holistic concept of mental and physical illness that much later would provide the common ground between clinical psychology and behavioral medicine.

Even during the decade between 1910 and 1920, while clinical psychology was largely preoccupied with testing, two factors converged to hasten its recognition as a profession. The first of these was the appearance in 1916 of *The Measure-*

ment of Intelligence by Lewis Madison Terman. In this work Terman described his thorough revision and standardization of the French Simon-Binet tests, utilizing the concept of mental age as the unit of measurement.

This successful breakthrough in the measurement of intelligence revived Cattell's original interest in individual differences and set off a flurry of group tests of intelligence, including the Alfa and Beta tests adopted by the United States Army for use in selecting young men for appropriate lines of service in World War I. The development of these tests enabled the army to employ the term "selective service" in place of the ugly word "draft". The work of psychologists in developing the Alpha and Beta tests for the United States Army gave wide visibility to psychology as a profession. One of the casualties of this development is that James McKeen Cattell, the first psychologist to show interest in the measurement of individual differences, lost his professorship at Columbia University because of his pacifist stance and his objection to having psychologists being brought in to serve the American war effort.

Although the new discipline of psychology would continue to be dominated by persons engaged in teaching and research for some time yet, another unmistakable step toward its development as a profession is noted in a resolution by the APA in 1915 requiring some criterion of competence in mental testing by those who administered or interpreted mental tests. This was the beginning of a long series of efforts to police the field of clinical psychology on the way to establishing for it public standards as part of the psychology profession.

Because of the later influence of psychoanalysis on the development of clinical psychology, it is important to say a word about the influence of Sigmund Freud. We have noted in an earlier chapter that the period of the 1920s was marked by the fractionation of psychology and the proliferation of a number of schools or movements. One of these, according to a contemporary, Robert Sessions Woodworth, was psychoanalysis.

It will be recalled that Sigmund Freud had visited this country in 1909 at the invitation of G. Stanley Hall, President of Clark University. But it must be remembered that Freud was a medical doctor who held academic psychology in very low esteem. Early in his career he turned his attention to neuroses, and from his clinical observations of neurotic clients he gradually formulated his theory and gave it the name "psychoanalysis". Some American psychiatrists in World War I familiarized themselves with Freud's techniques and used them successfully in dealing with "shell shocked" soldiers returning from the front with a variety of neurotic symptoms.

In academic circles, however, those who formed the psychoanalytic movement were largely concerned with the Freudian view of the unconscious and the inner conflicts resulting from the efforts of the ego to strike a workable balance between the insatiable demands of the id and the unreasonable strictures of the superego. The fact that Freud himself was more interested in elaborating theory than in testing his theories by research made psychoanalysis a somewhat unwelcome intruder into academia until a much later date. It was only after research in personality had achieved acceptance, and projective personality tests had become well known, that Freud's basic psychological concepts were seriously integrated into psychology departments.

Psychoanalysis and Freudian dynamics was the new psychology in America after World War I, and such words as "id" and "superego", "oedipus complex" and "libido", became a part of the sophisticated vocabulary in the 1920s and 1930s, but it is difficult to estimate the impact of Freudian dynamics on psychology in this country. Although his theories are full of observations and interpretations that are basically psychological, the fact that Freud regarded the activities of consciousness as a facade that hides what is really going on within the person, and that he was somewhat disdainful of psychological research, probably had the effect of keeping psychoanalysis at a distance from psychological laboratories.

It must be remembered also that Freud was a medical doctor, and that psychoanalysis is basically a branch or modality of treatment that was still struggling for acceptance in the medical profession. As a result, psychoanalytic theory and practice was taught in special institutes originally headed up by someone who had been analyzed by Freud himself or by one of his inner circle. Although psychoanalysis was growing in popular appeal and was hailed as the new psychology in the early 1930s, it was rather slow to gain a place in the psychology curriculum of universities. Courses in abnormal psychology were introduced, and these often became forums for the discussion of Freudian concepts. Terms like "defence reactions", "oedipus complex" and "neurotic behavior" became topics for discussion in the classroom, but psychotherapy was not a part of the curriculum. This had to wait until personality had been accepted as a legitimate area of psychological research. Even when psychology departments in universities began to develop programs in clinical psychology, training in the techniques of psychoanalytic therapy was not a part of the curriculum. The student wishing to learn psychoanalytic techniques had to undergo psychoanalysis with someone outside the university faculty.

After World War II, the Veterans Administration, driven by the great need for psychologists with clinical training, engaged in a crash program to train clinical psychologists. At this point the full impact of psychoanalytic theory came into prominence in the universities. By this time Freud's theories had undergone considerable revision by Alfred Adler [1870-1937], who took up permanent residence in this country in 1932, and even more by Karen Horney [1885-1952], Erich Fromm [1900-1980] and Harry Stack Sullivan [1892-1949]. These neo-Freudians broadened psychoanalysis beyond the landlocked dynamics of the ego, the id, and the superego. They emphasized social factors that have a profound effect on the developing person.

Karen Horney's *The Neurotic Personality of Our Time* (1937) became extremely popular and illustrates this extension of psychoanalysis well beyond the limits proposed by Freud. About the same time Gordon W. Allport [1897-1967] and Henry A. Murray [1893-1988] opened the in-depth study of personality and broadened the scope of academic psychology by showing the research possibilities created by the various tests of personality that had been devised over the course of the years. Allport co-authored a test of values (Allport and Vernon 1931), and Murray with Morgan (Morgan and Murray 1935) contributed the *Thematic Apperception Test*. The *Rorschach Ink Blot Test*, so-called after the Swiss psychiatrist Hermann Rorschach [1844-1922], had been known and variously used in this country since 1921 (Rorschach 1921). The first version of the *Minnesota Multi-phasic Personality Inventory* (MMPI) made its appearance in 1943 (Hathaway and McKinley 1943).

All of these tests provided inviting research topics and helped to achieve a secure position for clinical psychology in departments throughout the country. The close connection between the developments of clinical psychology and personality and their relatively late admission into the psychology curriculum in American universities must seem very strange to an outsider. If the basic subject matter of psychology is not the human person, what then is psychology about?

A partial explanation may be found in the overemphasis on conscious states and learning and the acceptance of Associationism and Determinism as the givens when the scientific study of psychology began in the late nineteenth century. There was also the conflicting situation between those who were unwilling to discard consciousness in the study of human behavior and the radical Behaviorists who wanted to base everything on the reflex. (The situation was not altogether different from the crisis in psychology that Vygotsky encountered in Moscow in 1925.)

While it is true that the functional orientation of American Psychology from the beginning made room for the consideration of behavior problems and abnormal mental states, the clinical study of the person and the beginnings of psychotherapy were delayed by the predominance of academicians in the membership of the APA. There was also the fact that the medical profession was undergoing a shift towards a greater dependence on biology and chemistry as the basis for diagnosing and treating disease. As a result, physicians found little room for psychological factors in their approach to clients.

The situation in Western Europe was quite different. The tension between clinical psychology and academic psychology, on one hand, and between clinical psychology and psychiatry on the other was never apparent abroad. In France and Italy, as we have seen, the new psychology was often taken up by medical doctors and its clinical applications to mental disorders were highly valued. Shakow [1901-1981], who wrote the best early basic history of clinical psychology, speculates (1969: 225) on "what might have happened [in the United States] if instead of this laboratory approach, the French tradition of the hospital had become dominant, and experimental psychology had taken its start from experience there". But in this country these tensions, present from the beginning, tended to grow as the numbers of clinically trained persons increased rapidly in response to the training programs sponsored by the Veterans Administration.

The growth of clinical psychology as a profession was enhanced by the organization of the American Association of Applied Psychologists in 1937. This association was organized by the combined efforts of industrial and clinical psychologists who did not feel that the APA was sufficiently sensitive to their need for some method of certifying the competence of those entering the fields of clinical and industrial psychology. The recognition of the growing strength of the American Association of Applied Psychologists caused the Council of the APA to work with the leaders of APA to combine the two organizations into a single association. This was accomplished with a single set of by-laws in 1945. At the same time a committee was set up to look into appropriate training for clinical psychologists. Guidelines were drawn up for graduate programs for the training of clinical psychologists in 1947, and the American Board of Examiners in Professional Psychology was incorporated. This Board sets standards for the certification of graduate training programs, and awards a prestigious certification to individual psychologists who meet specific criteria demonstrating competence in clinical work.

CONCLUSION

We may conclude this chapter on the efforts of psychology to gain recognition as a profession with an additional note on the growing need to address the problem of professional ethics. As long as the chief concern of psychology was to gain recognition as a scientific discipline, there was little need to give attention to ethical concerns beyond the code of the scientific community concerning honesty in reporting data and respect for the claims of originality in research. But as psychology expanded as a profession and began to intervene in the lives of people, the need for sound ethical principles became imperative. To this end the Association formed a committee which was commissioned to draw up a code of ethics for the Association. In 1953 the first code of ethics was approved by the Council and published. Since then several revisions have appeared, indicating the increasing concern for the image of the profession of psychology as psychologists become more involved in areas of public and private morality.

With this evidence of concern about the responsible conduct of all those who claimed to be psychologists, one may say that psychology is established both as a science and as a profession. One may also note that this belated development in America of the clinical applications of psychology had the salutary side-effect of compelling the ivory-tower experimental psychology to broaden the scope of its concern to something much more approximating the totality of the human person. The next chapter will trace the factors that contributed to the explosion of clinical and counseling psychology in the wake of World War II.

Chapter 9

CLINICAL AND COUNSELING PSYCHOLOGY ASCENDANT: THE AGE OF THE PSYCHOTHERAPIES

The modest beginnings of clinical psychology, its reluctant acceptance by established departments of psychology, and its explosive development following World War II have been briefly indicated in the preceding chapter as a significant dimension of the development of psychology as a profession. The story of the emergence of clinical psychology as a profession needs further elaboration, both because of its intrinsic interest and because of its part in shaping the image of psychology in the later years of this century. In addition, some time must be given to a consideration of Counseling Psychology, a spin-off from the clinical stem. This chapter will cover the growth of these disciplines that have so altered the face of psychology and expanded its reach into areas far beyond the narrow limits set by Wundt. The most important

171

changes that contributed to the unpredictable growth of clinical and counseling psychology occurred between 1935 and 1960.

In discussing the forces that helped clinical psychology to emerge from a child clinic attached to a philosophy department or a laboratory attached to a mental hospital to a dominant position in the APA, it is important to know the obstacles that stood in the way of this advance. There were two sources of difficulty. One came from the departments of psychology geared to a rigorous program of research. The other came from the medical specialty, Psychiatry. Experimental psychology, focusing on behavior, rather than on the subjective states of feeling and emotion, was ill-prepared to deal with the disturbed individual in a clinical setting. Moreover, there was the difficulty of accommodating training in therapy within the psychological curriculum. Prior to World War II, because of their greater numbers, the balance of power in psychology was in the hands of the academics. If it were not for the great need for clinicians and counselors in the post war period, clinical psychology would have developed much more gradually.

The opposition on the part of psychiatrists originally seemed to be a matter of concern for the patient and for the danger of allowing anyone but a physician to engage in any kind of therapeutic intervention with a client. As the numbers of certified clinical psychologists increased, the conflict with psychiatry often seemed to center around reimbursement for services. Reimbursement became a matter for legislation and civil rights once entitlement claims and third party payers entered the picture.

Pressure on clinical psychology from both academics and psychiatrists has not gone away, but it is not as intractable as it was forty years ago. Moreover, psychiatrists and clinical psychologists sometimes work together as a clinical team of professionals no longer concerned about status. The client is free to chose between several options, to some extent determined by state regulations. There is somatic therapy, provided by a psychiatrist (psychotropic drugs, electroshock therapy or psychosurgery); psychotherapy, which may be provided by a certified clinical psychologist, a certified counseling psychologist, a psychiatric nurse or a psychiatric social worker; or therapy by someone certified in a related specialty.

The tensions that clinical psychology experienced with experimental psychology on one hand and with psychiatry on the other retarded the development of clinical psychology, but at the same time contributed to its growth toward a suitably independent maturity. In the next chapter we shall note how clinical psychology has helped to shape the image of psychology as we approach the end of the century.

Before taking up the important changes in American psychology that opened the way for the robust entry of clinical psychology into the field, one should point out that clinical and counseling psychology had a somewhat parallel development, and that many of the same forces and many of the same persons contributed to both divisions. In order to avoid the confusion that comes from the repetition of names and movements, it seems better to concentrate on clinical psychology and postpone the mention of counseling until a convenient point later on.

If we compare the climate of American psychology in the early 1930s with that of 1896, when Lightner Witmer opened the first psychological clinic in Philadelphia, we note some very significant differences that prepared the way for the clinical approach to the study of human behavior. For one thing, *person* is emerging in American psychology as the true focus of the discipline. Shakow (1964) gives Freud much the credit for this, but Hilgard (1987: 306) points out that the early interest of Morton Prince [1854-1929] in multiple personality and in the psychogenic origin of neurotic disturbances makes him one of the pioneers in the dynamic approach to mental disorders. His founding of the *Journal of Abnormal Psychology* (1906) helped to gain academic respectability for the study of the problems of disturbed people.

The shift of interest of psychology from the theoretical framework of a mind-body dualism to a unifying concept of the person was a major step in removing the opposition to the admission of clinical psychology into the mainstream. Gordon W. Allport deserves great credit for his groundbreaking work in this area, entitled *Personality: A Psychological Interpretation* (1937). His ability to discuss problems of the ego, the self and the person in acceptable psychological terms and his insistence on the necessity of studying the person in all his/her uniqueness was like a breath of fresh air to people who had become accustomed to think of psychology in terms of abstract and intricate learning theories based on the S-R bond concept. Personality was a lifelong interest of Gordon Allport. This interest extended to all areas of human relations, and his influence in establishing social psychology in psychology departments throughout the country was substantial, as his works on prejudice and group morale testify. As we saw at the end of Chapter 4, Allport gives credit to the structuralists of the Gestalt tradition, whom he met in Germany, for reinforcing his conviction that the time had come to give personality and interpersonal relations a central place in the study of psychology (Allport 1967). He also used his influence to place voluntary exiles from Hitler's Germany in university positions in this country. Among these were leading exponents of Gestalt Psychology in Germany. Max Wertheimer [1880-1943], who had put new life into the Gestalt movement by his demonstration of the phi-phenomenon, mentioned earlier, came to New York in 1933 to join the faculty of the New School for Social Research. Kurt Koffka [1886-1941] introduced Gestalt Psychology at Smith College and Wolfgang Köhler, who was well known to psychologists in America because of his *Mentality of Apes* (1917), became head of the department at Swarthmore College and continued to gain support for Gestalt Psychology by his research and writings. But of all the Gestaltists exiled from Germany, it was Kurt Lewin who had the greatest influence in establishing social psychology as an integral part of the curriculum in psychology. As one looks back on the situation immediately before our entrance into the second world war, and the blow that Hitler struck to civilized society, it is easy to see how ready psychology departments were to welcome the study of personality and social psychology. All of these factors prepared the way for the great surge forward of clinical and counseling psychology that took place immediately following World War II.

Henry A. Murray is another person who significantly advanced the cause of clinical psychology by bringing his experience with psychoanalysis in a clinical setting to Harvard and engaging in an impressive research project on motivation. Out of this came the *Thematic Apperception Test* (TAT) (Morgan and Murray 1935).

This emphasis on the person in academic psychology was reinforced by Carl R. Rogers [1902-1987]. His client-centered therapy was introduced in 1942 by the book, *Counseling and Psychotherapy*. His non-directive approach to therapy—with the therapist standing back to create an atmosphere in which the person could solve his or her own problem—caught on immediately and became the new therapy for a time. Rogers, trained in psychoanalysis, had become disenchanted with psychoanalysis as a therapeutic method because of its failure to achieve positive results with children. Others, including Murray, had criticized psychoanalysis theoretically for its psychic determinism and its overweighting of the sex drive to account for human motivation. Rogers had the advantage of having tried psychoanalysis in two child clinics in which he had been a therapist and found it did not work. Probing the unconscious for insight into the deep causes of deviant behavior had little to offer for the needed behavior change. Instead, Rogers' client-centered or non-directive approach helps the client to explore his/her own feelings and attitudes by assuming a non-judgmental manner. The therapeutic goal is to enable the client to achieve deeper insight into the self and into the motivations that are determining his/her life. Rogers, with Socrates, assumes that having acquired this self knowledge, the client will make the appropriate change of behavior.

Rogers' client-centered therapy had wide appeal and provoked lengthy discussions of the relative merits of directive and non-directive approaches to therapy. This helped to gain status for clinical psychology in departments of psychology. In addition, Carl Rogers took an active role in developing the program for the appropriate training of therapists. In the 1930s the candidate wishing to prepare to engage in psychotherapy found very little sympathy within university departments. A suitable program leading to the Ph.D. with a major in clinical psychology did not exist, and departments of psychology were reluctant to engage in a program that would require the costly supervision of students engaging in therapy. At the same time, the resistance to psychotherapy in the hands of anyone not having a medical degree became more vocal. Carl Rogers presents a good example of the dual sources of opposition to clinical psychology prior to World War II. Before the end of the war and for a short time afterwards, counseling was thought of in connection with vocational guidance in a school setting. Counseling involving a psychotherapeutic engagement with adults was unknown. Rogers encountered the opposition of the medical profession when he was being considered for the directorship of the new community Child Guidance Center in Rochester, New York. Later on, his problems with the experimentally oriented department of psychology at the University of Wisconsin illustrate the problems of clinical psychology in a university setting (Rogers 1967). Even the post war changes did not lessen the tension between experimental and clinical psychology at many universities. Conflicts with the Department of Psychology at the University of Wisconsin over the selection and training of future clinicians had much to do with Rogers' decision to transfer to the Western Behavioral Sciences Institute at La Jolla, California, in 1964.

The problem of securing adequate training for the person who wishes to become a clinical psychologist is an ongoing one. To understand the progress that has been made since the 1920s, it is necessary to recall that clinical psychology grew out of the child guidance clinics that had become a part of many universities as adjuncts to the psychology departments. The basic role of the psychologist in a child guidance clinic was that of test expert, a psychometrician. Therapy was not a part of the job description. By the 1920s psychology departments were well prepared to supply training in test construction, administration and evaluation, but when it came to preparation of students to engage in psychotherapy, they were neither ready nor favorably disposed. This pretty well describes the situation until the Veterans Administration put out its desperate call for counselors and clinical psychologists and offered attractive grants to pay for their training. Prior to the inauguration of the Veterans Administration program, if the candidate for clinical training could not be persuaded to remain in the safer waters of experimental psychology, the only option was to seek employment in the psychological laboratory of a mental hospital (e.g., David Shakow accepted a position as psychologist at Worcester State Hospital in 1921) or to undergo analysis privately with an approved psychoanalyst. Not a few opted for both.

The first move of the psychologist seeking training in psychotherapy was to find employment in a mental hospital. The candidate had to pursue this clinical experience on his/her own. It was in no way tied in with the candidate's pursuit of a degree in psychology. Shakow (1969) describes himself as one of those whose interest was drawn to psychology by an early contact with psychoanalysis that seemed to open the way to the kind of psychology that interested him, viz., the study of the whole person. There was no provision for this kind of combination of clinical experience with graduate study in psychology when he entered Harvard in 1921. He mentions the commissioning of the first Committee on Standards for Training Clinical Psychologists in 1930 by the APA (Shakow 1969: 5). He also notes that the first tentative effort to establish a curriculum for clinical psychologists was made by Columbia University in 1936. In response to the request for more psychologists trained in counseling and psychotherapy by the Veterans Administration and its attractive grant program to support students in clinical training, the APA reactivated the Committee on Training in Clinical Psychology in 1947 (Misiak and Sexton 1966: 183). This was followed by a series of high-level conferences called to develop suitable training programs at the graduate level and to establish a uniform procedure for certifying competent clinicians. A Committee on Graduate Internship in Psychology met at Vineland in 1944. The work of this committee was continued and extended by a series of conferences: the Boulder Conference (1949), the Stanford Conference on Psychologists' Careers in Mental Health (1955), the Estes Park Conference on Training for Research (1958), the Miami Conference on Graduate Study in Psychology (1958), the Greystone Conference on the Professional Preparation of Clinical Psychologists (1964).

Most of these conferences aimed at standardization without stereotyping training programs. Their recommendations were based on the principle that a clinical psychologist must first of all be a psychologist. This was the first official recognition of clinical psychology as a full fledged member of the psychological household. The Committee encouraged flexibility and recommended the development of innovative programs with the goal of improving clinical practice. All of these conferences emphasized the importance of combining a full year of carefully supervised internship in a clinical setting with a sound academic program leading to the doctoral degree in clinical psychology. As these programs were implemented, they eliminated the hit and miss system that had prevailed before the war, but they did not relieve the tensions between the experimentalist and the clinician in university departments.

In this effort to describe the struggles of clinical psychology to achieve acceptance as a legitimate area of psychological concern, the discussion, thus far, has been confined to problems within the academic and professional areas of psychology and psychiatry. The period that we have been describing also saw the birth of a movement that pointed up the need for clinical psychology in communities throughout the country. This was the mental health movement. Even without the crash program precipitated by World War II, this movement would have created the need for a significant increase in the number of psychologists prepared to offer counseling and therapy in private or community sponsored clinical settings. In 1908 Clifford Beers [1876-1943] published *A Mind that Found Itself*. By demonstrating that mental illness is not a hopeless condition, and that something can be done to improve the lives of those who have been diagnosed as mentally ill, the book and its author launched a national movement to raise the consciousness of the public concerning the neglect of persons confined to mental hospitals and the stigma attached to mental illness. Beers formed The National Committee on Mental Hygiene and campaigned vigorously for more humane treatment of persons suffering from mental disorders.

Beers attracted the favorable attention of important people like William James and was able to secure the active support of Adolf Meyer [1866-1950], the distinguished psychiatrist and head of the department at Johns Hopkins. In fact, it was Adolf Meyer who gave the name "mental hygiene" to the movement. This title suggested concern for prevention of mental illness as well as more humane care of the victims. After some serious internal conflicts, the national Committee on Mental Hygiene evolved into the National Association for Mental Health, which continues the effort to remove the stigma of mental illness and to support research into its causes.

The mental hygiene movement was fortunate to have Adolf Meyer as its professional leader in its early days. Well in advance of his time, Adolf Meyer had a holistic approach to mental disorder that has been called "psychobiological" for want of a better name. For him, mental illness was not something that happened to the mind alone, but to the whole person. This broader view of mental disturbance suggested that mental illness might to some extent be self induced, or at least that, with proper guidance, the client could do something about it. As child guidance centers attached to the psychology departments of universities gave way to the formation of community mental health centers prepared to offer counseling and psychotherapy to an adult population, the widespread need for counselors and therapists with sound psychological training grew proportionately. This could not have happened without a profound change of attitude on the part of the general public towards mental disorders, a change that was brought about chiefly by the mental health movement.

It should be noted in passing that during the same pre-War period the problem of "lay analysis," i.e., the propriety of persons without medical training engaging in therapy, was being discussed both within psychoanalytic associations and in the medical profession.

COUNSELING PSYCHOLOGY

Early in this chapter we called attention to the close relationship that has always existed between clinical and counseling psychology and noted that the factors that have affected the growth of one have had a similar effect on the other.[19]

---

[19] Illustrative of this is the connection between clinical psychology and school psychology as part of the background to the emergence of counseling psychology. As we saw in Chapter 8, clinical psychology owes its beginnings to Lightner Witmer's child clinic, established in conjunction with the psychological laboratory of Pennsylvania University in 1896. The connection of child clinics with the school system was present from the start, and the emphasis on psychological testing is very evident in children's clinics. Clinical psychology began to take shape when clinics were extended to include adult clients, under pressure from the mental hygiene movement. Under similar pressure from John Dewey and the advocates of education for living in a democracy, psychologists working in child clinics were encouraged to move into the area of vocational guidance and to become specialists in the use of various special aptitude tests to assist students in the choice of careers. For the psychologist working in conjunction with schools, the emphasis was on various tests and their interpretation. This gave rise to a special department of the school system, as counseling became heavily weighted in the direction of vocational guidance, and the work of psychologists working in the school system became more and more that of a person who specialized in measurement—in other words, a psychometrician.

To be cast in the role of a psychometrician seemed unduly stereotyped and restrictive to persons who had passed the demanding requirements to obtain a degree in psychology. So there was a move toward counseling functions that reached well beyond the limits of the evaluation of school achievement and career guidance. Moreover, in individual counseling concerning school achievement, the guidance counselor often encountered problems of a personal and emotional character that were well beyond the scope of the school guidance program. Having to refer these students to clinical psychologists or psychiatrists caused some guidance counselors to think of the broader aspects of personal counseling in a more therapeutic setting than the school system could provide.

During the 1930s all the changes that had favored the development of clinical psychology opened the way for personal counseling by an approved psychologist. By this time a variety of therapies, based on the dynamics of Freud and Jung, were being introduced into training programs for counselors, while Alfred Adler, Karen Horney, Eric Fromm and Harry Stack Sullivan were broadening the base of psychoanalytic therapy by insisting on the importance of the role of the social environment in adjustment. As we noted

Granting this overlap and close parallel between them, it is not surprising that considerable confusion about these two fields of applied psychology exists. Nevertheless, there is sufficient difference in the historical background and the training programs of these two disciplines to warrant treating them separately. Hilgard (1987: 629) has summed up the situation in a manner that prepares the way for the consideration of counseling psychology:

> Over the years a distinction gradually developed between clinical psychology, which addressed the problems of mental and emotional difficulties on the uncertain boundary between psychology and psychiatry, and counseling and counseling psychology, which dealt with difficulties encountered in the course of trying to succeed in school and, on the positive side, vocational guidance, acquiring appropriate skills in social participation and general preparation for life

---

above, the influence of Gordon Allport and Henry Murray in shifting the focus of psychology from the study of mind to the study of the whole person helped to break down prejudice among psychological purists against admitting clinical and counseling psychology programs to full status in university departments. A short sentence by Gordon Allport (1940: 11), based on a sweeping survey of the literature, tersely sums up the end of an era in academic psychology: "The mind-body problem, never solved, has been declared popularly null and void."

The time was right for Carl Rogers to receive a favorable hearing for his non-directive approach to counseling and to suggest that counseling and psychotherapy belong together (Rogers 1942). It is the capacity to engage in psychotherapy that distinguished the counseling psychologist from others who may engage in other kinds of counseling and guidance.

All of these factors contributed to create space for psychologists specially trained in a counseling role, i.e., trained in helping people to deal with personal problems that did not incapacitate them or require hospitalization.

more on the borders between psychology and education than between psychology and psychiatry. The
techniques are overlapping ones, and such distinctions
readily become blurred. Most simply put, the clinical
psychologist grew out of what was learned in mental
hospitals (and commonly served internships there),
while the counseling psychology grew out of what was
learned in the efforts to individualize instruction.

All that was needed for the emergence of counseling
psychology as new profession within the field was the establishment of a suitable training program and provision for
certification that would insure the identity of counseling
psychology as distinct from its clinical counterpart. Shoben
(1956) dates the official beginning of counseling psychology
with the Northwestern Conference in 1951. At this conference
the difference in the training of clinical and counseling
psychologists was set forth. In addition to the requirements
for a doctoral degree in a program approved by APA, both
would require a year of supervised training in an appropriate
facility. For the clinician, this would be in a hospital for the
mentally disturbed, while for the counselor the supervised
training would be a community mental health center or
counseling centers located in colleges or universities. The
image of counseling psychology was more clearly delineated
by the foundation of its own journal, the *Journal of Counseling*,
in 1954.

Counseling psychology evolved out of a mixture of
traditions—vocational guidance, mental measurements, and
psychotherapy. Originally located solely in educational
settings, its primary focus was assisting individuals to find
appropriate occupations. The enormous growth of the mental
measurement movement during and after World War I

provided the vocational counselor with the tools to measure individual differences in minute detail. Testing and later developments in trait and factor psychology added a scientific credibility to the work of vocation guidance counselors and established the respectability this work needed for full status in academic institutions. By the late 1930s and 1940s the psychotherapy movement added a third influence to the emergence of counseling psychology. While the psychotherapy movement was due in part to the increasing awareness of Freud's ideas, it was, as mentioned earlier in this chapter, the work of Carl Rogers that brought psychotherapy into mainstream psychology training programs. Rogers' work tapped the American values of optimism, pragmatism, and self-determination. His shift of emphasis from psychopathology to growth and development became the central focus of counseling psychology.

As counseling psychology evolved it overlapped clinical psychology. Counseling psychologists increasingly practiced psychotherapy with diverse populations and without the exclusive reference to occupational concerns. Training programs in counseling psychology, while retaining an interest in the role of occupation in peoples lives, increasingly incorporated coursework in clinical issues and topics.

Despite this overlap, theoretical distinctions between clinical and counseling psychology remained. First, counseling psychology endorsed an educational rather than a clinical and remedial or medical model. Clients (not patients) were viewed as intact individuals who were seeking assistance in coping with life stresses. Clients were taught new coping strategies and behaviors. The focus was not on overcoming deficits, but rather on accessing existing resources. Second, counseling psychology utilized a developmental model. Calling on the work of developmental theorists such as Erik

Erikson, William Stern, Gordon Allport, and others, counseling psychologists sought to remove blocks to normal growth and encourage completion of stage-appropriate tasks. Finally, counseling psychology advocated preventive as well as remedial approaches to development.

As in the case of clinical psychology, the recognition and acceptance of counseling was assured overnight by the Veterans Administration as it introduced a crash program to make up for the shortage of clinically trained personnel to meet the needs of the veterans returning from World War II. In fact, the Veterans Administration established the Office of the Assistant Administrator for Vocational Administration and Education to provide career counseling and vocational guidance to help veterans avail themselves of the educational benefits available to them in preparation for their return to civilian life. For the first few years after World War II, many of the counselors were former educators and persons equipped to administer and evaluate tests and to do vocational guidance. However, as the post war pressure diminished, the approved training program in counseling psychology began to take effect and the profession of counseling psychology gradually took the shape that the recommendations of the Northwestern Conference had set forth.

THE HUMANISTIC EMPHASIS

Particularly after the end of the War, counseling and clinical psychologists found themselves in the midst of the battle of the psychotherapies, as various modifications of the dynamic theories of Freud and Jung were evolved, existentialist and Gestalt-based theories were introduced, and the advantages of directive vs. non-directive methods were debated. Out of this situation a new movement emerged, so-called "Humanistic Psychology". It grew out of the dissatisfaction with both

Behaviorism and Psychoanalysis as basic psychological theories and movements. Its chief proponent was Abraham Maslow [1908-1970] but it drew strong support from Rollo May [1909-], Carl Rogers, and others. Humanistic psychology reinforced the shift in emphasis from the treatment of neuroticism and maladjustment to a positive view of the human potential. Maslow felt that psychology had concentrated too much on the negative aspects of human behavior, on maladjustment and neuroticism. He maintained that psychology should concentrate on helping people to recognize the peak experiences in their lives and exploit them.

Humanistic Psychology has attracted a number of people from outside the field of psychology, and as a result it is difficult to state just what it stands for. We will return to this problem in Chapter 11. For now it is enough to note that one of the effects of the humanistic emphasis on counseling psychology has been to enhance group counseling and the development of self-improvement programs. In the last chapter there will be an opportunity to explore the total effect of this movement and of the various psychotherapies on the general direction of psychology as it moves into the twenty-first century.

Chapter 10

THE AGE OF THEORY AND SYSTEMS:

UNDERCURRENTS

The twenty years between 1930 and 1950 have become known as the age of theory and systems. This is because the mainstream of American psychology was preoccupied with basic research in learning theories. By this time Behaviorism had been shored up by logical positivism and became known as Neobehaviorism, with B. F. Skinner as its spokesman of choice. The interest in learning theory dates back to E. L. Thorndike and his "connectionism" with his so-called law of effect, as we saw in Chapter 8. In the extensive research on learning theory undertaken by the Neobehaviorists, debate ranged over various explanations of the manner in which stimulus and response become connected, but there was never any question of the universality of Associationism as an adequate explanation of cognitive activity. Only the attempt by Edward Chace Tolman [1886-1959] to introduce cognitive maps and some Gestalt planning into the rat's repertoire stood out as a partial exception (Tolman 1932).

There were, however, developments of great significance for psychology going on quite independently of the rather exclusive area of theory and basic research on learning. These developments had been going forward during the period in which Clinical Psychology was taking form, but instead of being concerned with therapy they were striving for recognition as a part of academic psychology. These areas are: Personality, Social Psychology and Biological or Physiological Psychology. These topics of interest in the development of psychology were mentioned but not sufficiently reviewed in the last chapter, because they belong to experimental psychology rather than to the clinical applications of the discipline which formed the subject matter of that chapter.

PERSONALITY

We have already noted that personality was not a part of the new psychology during the first half century of its existence. When the first discussion of personality as a scientific enterprise was published in America (G. Allport 1937), Neobehaviorists and S-R Bond advocates found it hard to accept. The inclusion of personality as an important part of the psychological curriculum is due especially to two men, Gordon Allport and Carl Rogers. Rogers' client-centered therapy placed the person in a central position, and the resulting self-psychology brought personality into sharper focus. The excitement and interest created by his emphasis on the self advanced the study of personality, while workers in the field of counseling debated the relative merits of directive and non-directive methods of counseling. At the same time, studies like *The Nature of Prejudice* (G. Allport 1954) and *Personality and Social Encounter, Selected Essays* (Allport 1960) placed the person in its natural setting—in interaction with other persons. In addition, Gordon Allport early emphasized the value of the personalized and idiographic approach to personality, as contrasted with the nomothetic orientation that was so deeply rooted in the scientific method. By this time, as we noted in the closing pages of our last chapter, psychophysical parallelism and the mind-body problem had all but disappeared.

As indicated in the last chapter, instruments for assessing personality came on the scene and opened up the possibility of interesting comparisons among subjects. They also gave rise to debates over the relative merits of projective and non-projective tests. *The Rorschach Ink-Blot Test* appeared in 1921 but was little used until the 1940s (Rorschach 1921/1942). Morgan and Murray's *Thematic Apperception Test* (TAT) appeared in 1935 as the instrument used in his in-depth study reported as *Explorations in Personality* (Murray 1938). The *Minnesota Multiphasic Personality Inventory* (MMPI) appeared in 1943 and almost immediately generated a whole family of research projects. In the background of this interest in the study of personality was the increased emphasis on the ego among the non-orthodox interpreters of Freud, notably Jung, Adler, Horney, and Sullivan. The work of Erik Erikson [1902-] on the problem of identity and the passage through adolescence to maturity added depth to personality studies (Erikson 1963). When the humanistic movement began to gain momentum, it profited from this widespread interest in personality, while at the same time contributing to the importance of the topic in the psychology curriculum. As final evidence of the permanent place of personality in psychology, extensive discussions of theories of personality had reached the textbook stage and began to appear in the titles of books, such as: Hall and Lindzey, *Theories of Personality* (1957).

SOCIAL PSYCHOLOGY

Social Psychology has never been too remote from the mainstream of experimental psychology since Wilhelm Wundt published his ten volume *Völkerpsychologie*, which he completed in 1920 (see gloss on Reference entry). Today this work would probably be classified as cultural anthropology, but it surely indicates that the founder of experimental psychology was well aware of the mutual interaction of cultural factors and individual behavior. He just did not believe that an experimental approach was suitable for studying social phenomena. At the same time, the book *Völkerpsychologie* indicates that the author's psychological interests were not confined to the introspections of the laboratory. The indication that there is place for social psychology in the overlap between sociology and psychology was uniquely manifested in the simultaneous appearance in 1908 of two books containing the term "social psychology" in their titles. One of these books was by a sociologist, E. A. Ross [1866-1951] and the other by a psychologist, William McDougall [1871-1938]. Even though McDougall came to Harvard in 1920 with a reputation in psychology already established in England, his *Introduction to Social Psychology* (1908) did not signal the beginnings of genuine interest in social psychology in an era dominated by Behaviorism, when the optimistic future predicted for the conditioned reflex had caught the imagination of the younger American psychologists. Interest in social psychology among psychologists was stimulated especially by the work of a group of French pioneers in sociology whose writings had aroused international interest towards the end of the last century.

Auguste Comte [1798-1857] gave sociology its name and at the same time its positivistic approach. He pointed the way to the objective study of the manner in which people interact, withholding value judgments of their behavior. Comte's work was followed by several books by French authors in the field of social behavior. The titles of these works show the authors' awareness of the manner in which psychological factors are involved in social issues. Gabriel Tarde [1843-1904] published *The Laws of Imitation* in 1890. This was followed by Gustave Le Bon's [1841-1931] study of *The Crowd* in 1895, and Emile Durkheim's [1858-1917] *Suicide: A Study in Sociology* in 1897. Hilgard (1987: 575) notes that Durkheim was in correspondence with Wundt and had spent some time in the laboratory at Leipzig, so he was well aware of the beginnings of experimental psychology as well as of Wundt's views of the inappropriateness of experimental studies of social behavior.

To some extent the advance of social psychology as a special area within the broad field of psychology was delayed by McDougall's tenacious defense of his doctrine of instincts (hormic psychology) in the day when the vanguard of psychologists in this country were confident that all behavior change could ultimately be explained by the maze-running rat. As Tolman put it in his address to the American Psychological Association (Tolman 1937: 364):

I believe that everything important in psychology . . . can be investigated in essence through the continued experimental and theoretical analysis of the determiners of rat behavior at a choice-point in a maze.

Thus social psychology got off to a slow start, in spite of the fact that F. H. Allport [1890-1978] did much to establish social psychology in the curriculum of psychology departments with his notable *Social Psychology* (Allport 1924), while the Murphys (Gardner Murphy [1895-1979] and Lois B. Murphy [1902-]) added emphasis with their *Experimental Social Psychology* in 1931. Even though the subject of attitude would assume an important place later on, the demonstration by Louis L. Thurstone [1887-1955] of an equal-interval scale for measuring attitudes (Thurstone 1928) was not followed up. This slow emergence of social psychology as an important and widely recognized area within the field of psychology is in marked contrast with its explosive development beginning sometime in the 1940s. Many of the same forces that had contributed to the rise of personality study were at work to create the demand for a better understanding of the manner in which social forces play upon the human person throughout life. Indeed, Gordon Allport, the man who did much to revitalize psychology by introducing the study of personality, is regarded as one of the founders of social psychology. But among those recognized for their special contribution to the rise of social psychology, Kurt Lewin has left the deepest impression on the discipline (see esp. Lewin 1936). The youngest of the Gestalt psychologists who came to this country to escape Nazi pressure and possibly extinction, Kurt Lewin brought with him an interest in group dynamics that gave new vitality to social studies. He used the analogy of a physical field of force and viewed the person as living in psychological space acting and being acted upon by the group of which he/she is a part. This imagery and Lewin's dynamic approach put new life into social psychology at a time when the influence of the group on the individual was coming to the fore on the international scene and the Nazi phenomenon was a palpable threat. The importance of social factors in social psychology is well brought out in Gordon Allport's definition of social psychology (1967a: 41): "An attempt to understand and explain how thought, feeling and behavior of individuals are influenced by the actual, imagined or implied presence of others".

Among those who promoted the cause of social psychology as an important element of the psychology curriculum was Theodore M. Newcomb [1903-1984]. The title of an early publication (1943) indicates how central to social psychology his interests ran: *Personality and Social Change: Attitude and Social Formation in a Student Community.* He was invited to Michigan University to establish there one of the first doctoral programs in social psychology. As he continued to study and write on social topics, he was active also in organizations that devoted themselves to social issues. Newcomb was one of the organizers of the Society for the Psychological Study of Social Issues, and later served as its president. In 1981 Theodore Newcomb was the recipient of the Gold Medal Award of the American Psychological Association. This recognition was at the same time a tribute to him for, and the public recognition of, the prestige that social psychology had achieved among his peers.

As social psychology gained in prestige and acceptance, a number of psychologists contributed to its advancement. Some of these contributions are cited as freely by sociologists as by psychologists, which is another indication of the extensive overlap of these two fields. Among the frequently cited investigations are works by Theodor Adorno [1903-] et al. (1950). Solomon E. Asch [1907-] is frequently cited for his writings on social psychology and especially for his investigations of group pressure (Asch 1956). John Dollard [1900-1980,] working with Neal E. Miller [1909-], Leonard W. Doob

[1909-], Hobart O. Mowrer [1907-], Robert R. Sears [1908-], Clellan S. Ford [1909-] and Carol I. Hovland [1912-], formed a team for some time at the Yale Institute of Human Relations. Out of their efforts to combine Hull's theoretical attempt (1943, 1951) to measure the comparative strength of drives with the psychoanalytic theory came the concept of social learning (Miller and Dollard 1941), to which Bandura and Walters made significant contributions twenty-two years later (Bandura and Walters 1963).

The revival of the study of instinct in the 1950s added an interdisciplinary dimension to social psychology. McDougall had emphasized instinct in his *Introduction to Social Psychology* (1908). In fact, it was the debate with John Watson (McDougall 1924, 1929; Watson and McDougall 1929) and the exaggerated claims for the conditioned reflex that drove instinct out of the field for a quarter of a century. The concept of instinct was reintroduced into the psychological vocabulary in this country by the work of the European ethologists, under the title "species typical behavior". The work on imprinting by Konrad Lorenz [1903-] became known in this country around 1950. Wasman's careful studies of ants and bees had aroused interest earlier (1897, 1899). Among the most striking of the later ethological works was that of von Frisch (1950) in his very careful field observations on the manner in which the bee locates sources of nectar and communicates this information to the hive. Some very interesting examples of instinctive behavior in birds were also reported.

To students brought up in the belief that all behavioral change could be accounted for by conditioning, the climate in this country was not very congenial to the study of instinct, even under a different name. Ethology triggered some heated debates and probably helped to break the grip of S-R bond thinking on American psychology at a time when the field of social psychology was expanding. Social issues were very much to the fore, and attracted the interest of psychologists during the period of social unrest and dislocation following World War II. In addition to the SSPSI (Society for Social Psychology and Social Issues) and the Yale Institute for Human Relations, a Department of Social Relations was established in 1946 at the University of Michigan. Social psychology gained in prestige and support from all these efforts and experienced continued growth during the 1950s, but this euphoria could not be sustained, and the discipline went into a period self-questioning and uncertainty in the 1960s. Unsettling questions concerning the need for tightening the methods of obtaining data and concerns about the relations between experimental and applied areas of social psychology arose. Fortunately, these problems were resolved sufficiently to avoid any serious setback to the discipline, and the permanent position of social psychology in departments was not endangered.

BIOLOGICAL PSYCHOLOGY

Psychology has come a long distance since the term "physiological psychology" was encountered in the first textbook on the new psychology (Wundt 1873). The term was used by Wilhelm Wundt to make sure that no one would confuse the experimental psychology which he was presenting with the "rational psychology" that had long been a chapter in philosophy. In the background of those beginnings of scientific psychology, without the then relatively recent findings on the nervous system—such as the one-way-law, the speed of the nerve impulse, and the law of specific nerve energies—the new psychology could not have gotten off the ground. Problems of the transmission of the nerve impulse and the biochemical changes that take place at the synapse have continued to be investigated by neuroanatomists and neurologists, with only casual concern on the part of psychologists. In fact, during the period of active research on learning theory, learning theorists were warned to avoid speculation about the neural mechanisms involved in their particular theories. To engage in such speculation was regarded as "neurologizing", an activity better left to the neurologist. Thus, the great majority of psychologists avoided the area of the nervous system, and physiological psychology was not considered to be a significant element in programs leading to the Ph.D. in psychology.

The one area of physiological psychology that continued to haunt psychologists, however, was the problem of brain localization. To what extent are conscious functions allocated to particular sites in the brain? And what is the possibility of these functions shifting their location or being absorbed by another region (equipotentiality)?

This problem first surfaced in the modern era under the name of *phrenology*. This is the preposterous doctrine that the strength or weakness of specific mental abilities can be accurately gauged by carefully studying the contour of the cranium. It rose out of the commonly accepted doctrine of mental faculties that had been developed especially by the Scottish empirical philosopher, Thomas Reid [1710-1796], whom we encountered in Chapter 3. Reid's "faculties" were the desiccated remnants of the "powers of the soul" that Aristotle and Thomas Aquinas had used to account for the distinguishable operations of a dynamic and inquisitive mind. By the time phrenology came along, the doctrine of faculties, as it was presented in standard textbooks, identified these powers with compartments of the brain. Early in the nineteenth century, Franz Gall [1758-1828] and Johann Kaspar Spurzheim [1776-1832] proposed that the relative strength or weakness of these faculties could be accurately discerned by studying the contours of the skull (Gall and Spurzheim 1810-1819). This involved the assumption that the more highly developed faculties would require a greater amount of brain mass in this region and this would cause an elevation of the skull at that point.

This exaggerated claim was immediately challenged by the French brain anatomist, Pierre Flourens [1794-1867], and the debate over brain localization was on. It has continued into this century, setting the stage for extensive use of extirpation methods to explore the brain. In extirpation experiments, the effect of brain lesions on the capacity to learn and on retention of motor habits have kept psychology in closer touch with this area of physiological research than with studies of the nerve impulse or the sense organs. Indeed, studies of brain localization have put physiological psychology at the cutting edge of neuroscience and the "new science of mind".

In discussing the beginnings of the new psychology in Russia in Chapter 6, we noted the attempt by Sechenov and Pavlov to reduce psychology to physiology, and it is somewhat amazing that Watson's Behaviorism, which had borrowed the conditioned reflex from the work of the Russians, nevertheless did nothing to develop physiological psychology. It was Karl S. Lashley [1890-1958], who had learned ablation techniques from S. I. Franz [1874-1933], that kept psychology in touch with physiology during the 1920s and later. Lashley's work stands out as classic, not only because it was the first attempt to observe the effects of brain extirpation on the learning and the retention of learned behavior in the Norway rat, but also because of the unexpected results obtained (Lashley 1929). Having conditioned rats to run a maze in the standard fashion, Lashley delicately severed various nerve pathways in the brain of the rat without disturbing other areas. After recovery the rats were returned to the maze and the amount of learning loss was carefully measured. He found that in terms of learning loss, the precise area of the cortical insult seemed to make little difference. He found that the decrement of learning was roughly proportional to the total amount of brain tissue that had been disturbed. These results ran in direct opposition to the prevailing theory of conditioning, which held that the effects of conditioning or learning involve changes in the nerve pathways and connections[20] that were exercised during the learning activity and are retained in these synapses and pathways. This is a peripheral theory of learning in contrast to central theories that hold that learning depends on the central organ, the brain.

In terms of the brain localization controversy, Lashley's experiment would seem to argue convincingly against any position of extreme localization of functions in the brain and in favor of mass action. The differences, however, between the human brain and the brain of the rat are sufficient to render such broad conclusions suspect, in the absence of parallel data based on the primate brain. The results of Lashley's demonstration probably contributed to the neglect of physiological psychology during the 1930s, the period of preoccupation with learning theory.

Hilgard (1987: 427) has this account of the decline of interest in physiological psychology at this point in time:

---

[20] Whence Thorndike's theory of learning took the name, "connectionism". See footnote 18, p. 158 above.

During the years approximately 1930 to 1950, theoretical psychology was preoccupied with the behavioral aspects of learning, and prominent theorists felt justified in avoiding speculations about the neural basis of learning. These included Thorndike, who had earlier been sure about the changes in synaptic resistance, Guthrie, Hull, Skinner, Tolman and others. They couched their theories in terms of input and output, with the brain as a 'black box' where unknown things went on, although in some instances, intervening variables were inferred without reference to their neurological conditions. Pavlov's cerebral physiology was rejected, although his findings on the behavioral aspects of the conditioned reflex were very prominent.

In other words, the effects of conditioning were assumed to take place in the synapses of the peripheral nervous system, rather than in its center, the brain.

For whatever reasons, a dormant period of physiological psychology ensued after Lashley's work. In addition to Carl Lashley, three men are largely responsible for revival of interest in physiological psychology. They accomplished this breakthrough by reviving the problem of brain localization and boldly setting out to study the relation of the brain to behavior in spite of the brain's forbidding complexity. These were Donald O. Hebb [1904-1985], David Krech [1909-1977] and Karl H. Pribram [1909-]. All three had worked with Lashley at one time or other and apparently drew some of their enthusiasm for brain study from him. At the same time, they all were convinced that there is more involved in learning than the formation of S-R bonds. In other words, they all took a "centrist" orientation, believing that learning cannot be accounted for merely in associative bonds formed in the peripheral nervous system, but that the brain, the center, is involved even in the simplest kinds of learning. The time for renewed interest in the brain was ripe also because of the declining acceptance of the reductionist assumptions of neobehaviorism.

By this time the Yerkes primate laboratory had been established at Orange Gables, Florida. This permitted ablation experiments to be carried out on various classes of monkeys, with opportunities to study the effects of cortical ablation on brains closer to the human brain in biological sequence. Harry Harlow's [1905-1981] chimpanzee colony at the University of Wisconsin made the cognitive and affective behavior of chimps available for closer study. At the same time, a revival of interest in Köhler's [1887-1967] *Mentality of Apes* had suggested the value of Gestalt approach to the understanding of intelligent behavior. All of these factors combined to gain a wider audience for Hebb's *Organization of Behavior* (1949) and Pribram's theoretical and experimental approaches to brain localization considered against the background of evolution of brain structures (Roe and Simpson 1958). Krech's work moved more in the direction of neurochemistry, which was also making great strides in the 1950s. All of these investigations enhanced the position of physiological psychology, even among those psychologists who were fearful of translating psychological problems into neurological terms.

The long debate over brain localization reached a temporary recess with the acceptance of the fact that higher thought processes are not sharply localized in well defined areas, as is the case with primary sensory and motor functions. Those more complex functions depend on the involvement of other parts, but retain special dependence on roughly defined areas. The possibility of one part of the brain substituting for another is still somewhat unclear, but the difference between a youthful and an aging brain has been well documented in this regard. Any suggestion of equipotentiality has been abandoned. Maturation and aging have an important role in the whole process of localization of functions in the brain. The pioneering work of Karl Pribram and his associates has great promise for the future, as the PETT (Positron-Emission Transaxial Tomography) and CAT (Computerized Axial Tomography) scans yield functional as well as anatomical data. Once a method for studying the manner in which the layers of the cortex relate to one another in performing complex operations has been developed, we may gain valuable insight into creativity and goal directed behavior. This is clearly an agenda for the next century that will have great bearing on psychology.

It was not only the study of the brain that was yielding interesting results and modifying outgrown views of the activity of the nervous system during the years between 1930 and 1960. Early in this century Charles E. Sherrington [1857-1952] had published a classic on the operation of the nervous system (Sherrington 1906). His studies on nerve transmission convinced him that the passage of the impulse from one neuron to an adjacent one is an electrochemical phenomenon, not fully explained in terms of electrical phenomena alone. His point was contested by two other workers, E. D. Adrian [1889-1977] and J. C. Eccles [1903-], but the dispute was eventually resolved in favor of Sherrington's hunch. Today, chemical neurotransmitters and inhibitors can be purchased in the local pharmacy. Even more significant than the problem of neurotransmitters was a better understanding of the propagation of the impulse along a nerve fiber. The study of this impulse, together with the minute electrical potential that accompanies it, has led to the development of the electroencephalogram (EEG) or brain wave, an important diagnostic sign.

This period was fruitful also in clarifying how the ear distinguishes pitch (Békésy 1947) and in supplying valuable information on the manner in which the brain responds to shapes and to the on-off signals from the retina (Hubel and Wiesel 1968). Some of those working in cognitive studies found this understanding of sensory functions a very helpful approach to higher level functions.

We may bring to a close this section on developments in biological psychology with a brief note about the split-brain research of M. S. Gazzaniga and R. W. Sperry [1913-], which merited the Nobel award in 1983. These workers had severed the main commissure that connects the two hemispheres of the brain to relieve a subject of seizures. This made possible observation of the effect of the stimulation of one hemisphere alone and led to the conclusion that, in spite of the fact that the two hemispheres of the same brain are mirror images of each other, they do not have quite identical functions (Gazzaniga, Bogen and Sperry 1962). This has led to the designation of logical, linguistic and mathematical functions as "right brain" functions, while spatial and artistic creativity have come to be designated as "left brain" activities. Much more evidence will be needed before these generalizations can be shown to hold true in all individuals. In accepting the Nobel prize, Roger Sperry was at pains to point out that these hemispheric differences do not in any way undermine the unity of consciousness that is a property of the person, rather than of the brain alone.

A final observation that can be of great help in understanding ourselves is in order, as we leave the area of biological psychology and the fascinating problem of the localization of areas of the brain. Relying on data from the evolution of the human brain, Paul D. MacLean [1913-] has given us the term "the triune brain" to indicate the hierarchical organization of the human brain with three levels of function (MacLean 1973). He uses the terms "reptilian", "paleomammalian" and "mammalian" to suggest the behavioral level of these three evolutionary divisions of the brain. His treatment of the limbic lobe in connection with the emotions is particularly helpful background for a psychology of the emotions.

With this we conclude the discussion of the three areas of psychology that made significant advances between 1930 and 1960. Developments in all of these areas helped to create a demand that psychology take a new look at what it means to be human. From this background emerged a widespread movement referred to as humanistic psychology.

A CENTURY OF PSYCHOLOGY

Among the signs of the maturity of psychology that we have called attention to was the publication of the first code of ethics in 1953. This was followed by several revisions, as psychology became more conscious of its obligations to the general public. Aware also of the approaching centenary of the discipline, the Policy and Planning Board decided to commission an in-depth study of the state of the discipline as a basis for future planning.

When the Policy and Planning Board of the American Psychological Association launched this monumental research project, they looked out on a vast field of scientific theory and research, the abandoned positions of earlier schools, and the opening up of new areas of interest. They had reason for modest gratification over the phenomenal increase in membership in the various divisions of the APA and the higher regard for psychology by the general public, not to mention the increasing demand for persons trained in psychology for a variety of services. Psychology had achieved all this in the three quarters of a century that had elapsed since Wundt opened the first laboratory. At the same time, there was also reason for concern, since much of the research that had accumulated seemed disconnected and remote from the real problems of living. To date psychologists had not found ways of investigating the emotions, or addressing problems that are important in the conduct of daily living. All this seemed to indicate that the time was right to engage in an in-depth study of psychology as the best basis for decisions regarding its future.

In their annual report to the APA for 1951-52 published in the *American Psychologist* (1952: 563), The Policy and Planning Board made it clear that they had made "a special effort to organize a comprehensive study of psychology as profession and as science, as education and as practice". When the National Science Foundation indicated an interest in an evaluation of the science of psychology and was favorably disposed to grant funding, the Policy and Planning Board decided (ibid.: 264): "a) that since the National Science Foundation appeared ready to sponsor immediately a study focused upon psychology as a science, it would be desirable to submit a proposal to the Foundation for the support of such a study; b) that a supplementary study concerned with psychological practice, supported by other foundations, might be developed later as a means of studying the profession as a whole". Whatever concern there may have been about the exceedingly rapid growth of the profession of psychology, the study was limited to the study of psychology as a science.

With the full sanction and considerable financial assistance of The National Science Foundation, the study was launched in 1952. The study as a whole was conceived under two distinct aspects. "Project B", placed under the direction of Kenneth Clark [1914-], was devoted to matters of psychological personnel and training. "Project A", by far the larger part of the study, dealt with substantive questions about psychology as a scientific discipline, bearing accordingly the general title of *Psychology: A Study of a Science*. The study of Project A was itself conceived as two studies, "Study I. Conceptual and Systematic", and "Study II. Empirical Substructure and Relations with Other Sciences", both placed under the editorial leadership of Sigmund Koch [1917-]. Accepting the challenge of overall editor, he appraised the situation as being "the first time in [psychology's] history" that the discipline shows itself "ready or almost ready to assess its goals and instrumentalities with primary reference to its own indigenous problems" (Koch 1959b: 783).

Study I of Project A, *Psychology: A Study of a Science*, took three volumes and seven years to complete (Koch 1959, 1959a, 1959b), while Study II of Project A took an additional three volumes and four years (Koch 1962, 1963, 1963a). A projected seventh volume, to have been published by Koch as a "Postscript to the Study", Koch himself was unable to bring himself to release, although he had a version ready as early as autumn of 1964, according to his remarks to John Deely in a conversation the evening of June 6, 1990. (The themes of this volume, hence, are to be found only in the scattered form of Koch's later articles). The study of Project B under Clark's editorship surveyed the work of psychologists, their interests, graduate and undergraduate programs in psychology departments, and the caliber of students entering the field. The results of the Project B study were published in 1957 under the title *America's Psychologists* (Clark 1957).

The initial proposal for these studies as a whole included both the science and the profession of psychology, but the involvement of the National Science Foundation made it necessary to limit the study to psychology as a science. This exclusion of the study of Clinical and Counseling Psychology seriously limited the value of the enterprise as the basis for planning for the future. If the goal of the Policy and Planning Board in launching the study had been to provide a tidy summary of what psychology had accomplished in its first century and to indicate strengths to be exploited and weaknesses to be eliminated, it was sorely disappointing. As the title of Project A, the major part of the study *Psychology: A Study of Science*, indicates, the investigation took the shape of a look at the manner in which a relatively young science emerges. This limited scope also prevented it from giving any indication of the revolutionary changes that were taking place even as the study was being conducted.

With the completion of the three volumes of Study I of Project A, which comprised the most basic part of the study, the effect was to bring the Age of Theory and Systems to an end. Commenting in an epilogue to the third volume, the senior editor, Koch, had this to say (1959b: 783, Koch's own emphases):

> *It can in summary be said that the results of Study I set up a vast attrition against virtually all elements of the Age of Theory code.* . . . No one is prepared to retreat one jot from the objectives and disciplines of scientific inquiry, but most are inclined to re-examine reigning stereo-

types about the *character* of such objectives and disciplines. There is a longing, bred on perception of the limits of recent history and nourished by boredom, for psychology to embrace—by whatever means may prove feasible—problems over which it is possible to feel intellectual passion. The more adventurous ranges of our illimitable subject matter, so effectively repressed or bypassed during recent decades, are no longer proscribed.

For the first time in its history, psychology seems ready—or almost ready—to assess its goals and instrumentalities with primary reference to its own indigenous problems. It seems ready to think contextually, freely, and creatively about its own refractory subject matter, and to work its way free from a dependence on simplistic theories of correct scientific conduct. The day of role playing as a route to reassurance may be drawing to a close. If our science cannot, in terms of attainment, feel secure, it is at least the case that the dance of respectability, as called from the wings by some fashionable theory of proper science, is no longer a dependable source of security.

. . . .

The institutionalization of each new field of science in the early modern period was a *fait accompli* of an emerging substructure in the tissue of scientific knowledge. Sciences won their way to independence, and ultimately institutional status, by achieving enough knowledge to become sciences. But, at the time of *its* inception, *psychology was unique in the extent to which its institutionalization preceded its content and its methods preceded its problems.* If there are keys to history, this statement is surely a key to the brief history of our science. Never had a group of thinkers been given so sharply specified an invitation to create. Never had inquiring men been so harried by social need, cultural optimism, extrinsic prescription, the advance scheduling of ways and means, the shining success story of the older sciences.

. . . few who fairly look at the brief history of our science could agree that the *balance* between extrinsically defined tradition and creative innovation—prescription and production—has for any sizeable period been optimal. From the earliest days of the experimental pioneers, man's stipulation that psychology be adequate to *science* outweighed his commitment that it be adequate to man. From the beginning, some pooled image of the *form* of science was dominant: respectability held more glamor than insight, caution than curiosity, feasibility than fidelity or fruitfulness. A curious consequence—even in the early days when such trends were qualified by youth—was the ever-widening estrangement between the scientific makers of human science and the humanistic explorers of the content of man.

This comment was re-echoed and reinforced by this same author, Sigmund Koch, almost a quarter of a century after the completed publication of *Psychology: A Study of a Science*. He expressed his serious reservations about the scientific status of the discipline thus (Koch 1985: 93):

My position suggests that the noncohesiveness of psychology finally be acknowledged by replacing it with some such locution as 'the psychological studies'. The psychological studies, if they are really to address the historically constituted objectives of psychological thought, must range over an immense and disorderly spectrum of human activity and experience. If significant knowledge is the desideratum, problems must be approached with humility, methods must be contextual and flexible, and anticipations of synoptic breakthrough held in check. . . . Characteristically, psychological events—as I have implied throughout the discussion of antinomality—are multiply determined, ambiguous in their human meaning, polymorphous, contextually environed or embedded in complex and vaguely bounded ways, and evanescent and labile in the extreme. This entails some obvious constraints upon the task of the inquirer and limits upon the knowledge that can be unearthed.

Chapter 11

PSYCHOLOGY ON THE EVE
OF THE TWENTY-FIRST CENTURY

Strong winds of change were blowing across the psychological landscape as America emerged from World War II. It would be impossible for psychology to remain the same in the face of the dramatic developments in personality, social, and physiological psychology that we have been examining in the foregoing chapter, to say nothing of the great surge of Clinical and Counseling psychology as a result of the postwar demand for therapists.

HUMANISTIC PSYCHOLOGY

The professional psychologists were changing the image of psychology and beginning to be counted in making decisions that would set directions that psychology should take for the future. The "person" was brought back to the center of psychology, and served to bring a number of new viewpoints into focus. Carl Rogers' client-centered counseling and Gordon Allport's vindication of a scientific approach to the study of personality provided excellent rallying points for advocates of change. At the same time, psychoanalytic therapies shifted their emphasis away from the unconscious to the ego and the self. Phenomenology and Existentialism added their critique of Behaviorism, and introduced psychologists to the concepts of non-being, being-in-the-world, and becoming. A number of psychologists saw American psychology as controlled by prevailing traditions: Psychoanalysis and Behaviorism. They decided that it was time to break this hold, and designated themselves The Third Force. Sutich has caught the deep resentment the psychological establishment felt at the time by psychologists who wished to see psychology freed from the limited perspective of learning theories dominated by positivistic behaviorism (Sutich and Vich 1969: 4):

. . . So overwhelming was the predominance of behaviorism that any publishable material outside its scope was typically met with ridicule or even worse. Only the behavioristic perspective and similar approaches were considered 'scientific'. There was, however, a grudging acceptance of psychoanalysis among some editors of official psychology periodicals who thought that it had made a significant but 'unscientific' contribution. Condescending tolerance is not an unfair description of the behaviorists' attitude toward psychoanalysis.

Worst of all was the ostracism and the obvious avoidance of third force psychologists by their behavioristically oriented colleagues and associates. To be a humanistically oriented psychologist in the decade following the end of the Second World War was to be virtually a professional outlaw.

Members of the Third Force took a position opposed to orthodox psychoanalysis and behaviorism on the ground that both denied the capacity for choice that is the mark of the human person. For Psychoanalysis this determination comes from within, indeed, but from forces hidden in the unconscious; for the Behaviorists, ultimately determination comes from without, since they hold that behavior is controlled by the environment.

The critics of the state of American psychology in 1950 drew strong support, not only from the well established client-centered counseling of Carl Rogers and the person-oriented psychology of Gordon Allport, but also from therapists who had been influenced by Phenomenology and Existentialism. Among these is Rollo May who, though trained in psychoanalysis, had become disenchanted with its ineffectiveness in therapy. His work on existentialist therapy was one of the first to appear. May had become acquainted with the work of Søren Kierkegaard [1813-1855] on death anxiety (Kierkegaard 1844), and was spurred to produce his own major study on anxiety, *The Meaning of Anxiety* (May 1950, 1977). Sometime later he edited a book that brought together a number of papers presenting an existentialist approach to therapy (May 1961). This, together with his rich background in the humanistic orientation of psychology, made him the leading exponent of existential psychology in America. However sound the goal of ridding American psychology of the deterministic shackles of Psychoanalysis and Behaviorism, the Third Force needed a more meaningful title. This was provided by Abraham Maslow, who succeeded in amalgamating the positive and negative forces under the banner of "Humanistic Psychology". Abraham Maslow was truly a remarkable and gifted person. Sometime in the 1940s, working with Bela Mittelmann on the dynamics of mental retardation, Maslow became convinced that too much time was being spent on analyzing abnormal states of the client and not enough time on the search for positive, happy experiences of the individual. Out of this came his *Motivation and Personality* (Maslow 1954). This book proposed a hierarchy of human needs, from the lowest need for food and shelter to those that he called "peak" experiences. The book was an immediate success, and did much to assure his leadership in a movement that caught the interest of people from a great variety of backgrounds who wished to see psychology become more involved in basically human concerns, rather than with neobehaviorist theories and systems. The initial enthusiasm was sufficient to launch several journals within a few years. The first of these, *The Journal of Humanistic Psychology*, appeared in 1961 under the editorship of Anthony J. Sutich.

Sutich's statement of the reason for choosing the name for the journal tells us something about the emphasis that this movement placed on making psychology truly human (Sutich and Vich 1969: 8-9):

'Humanistic' was selected for the title of *The Journal of Humanistic Psychology* because it was expected that in the long run, the positive, affirming, explicit value commitments of psychologists with this orientation would restore 'humanistic' to its original positive emphasis. Secondly, the various points of view represented by humanistic psychology—that is, phenomenology, certain versions of existentialism, self-theory, the experiential therapies and personality systems, many of the intrinsically based psychological theories of culture, and so on—shared a common concern about man and his potentialities. Third, the term, 'humanistic' helped fill the need for an encompassing perspective that would combine the various positions and give them a general direction.

Of interest also is Maslow's formulation of Humanistic Psychology adopted as the operative definition for the new journal by Sutich, the journal's editor (quoted from Sutich and Vich 1969: 7):

The Journal of Humanistic Psychology is being founded by a group of psychologists and professional men and women from other fields who are interested in those human capacities and potentialities that have no systematic place either in positivistic or behavioristic theory or in classical psychoanalytic theory, e.g., creativity, love, self, growth organism, basic needs gratification, self-actualization, higher values, ego-transcendence, objectivity, autonomy, identity, responsibility, psychological health, etc. This approach can also be characterized by the writings of Goldstein, Fromm, Horney, Rogers, Maslow, Allport, Angyal, Bühler, Moustakas, etc., as well as by certain aspects of the writings of Jung, Adler and the psychoanalytic ego-psychologists.

This statement, with slight modification, was used as the statement of purpose by the Association of Humanistic Psychology when it was formed in 1963. These quotations give some notion of the diversity of people and the wide range of approaches to psychology loosely held together under the caption "Humanistic Psychology". Under the influence of Carl Rogers and Abraham Maslow enough interest was generated in the human potential, growth and self-transcendence to launch *The Journal of Transpersonal Psychology* in 1974. This journal opened the movement to the meditative practices of the East and the doctrines of Zen. This brings Humanistic Psychology to the borderline of parapsychology and altered states of consciousness, with a strong drift towards mysticism.

It can be seen from this brief review that the humanistic movement drew its verve and vitality from extremely varied sources, many of them outside the field of psychology. Not all of them were concerned about how all this related to mainstream psychology. For some years the Association of Humanistic Psychology held its annual meeting just following the convention of the APA. After a period of some misunderstanding, the Association for Humanistic Psychology became a Division of the American Psychological Association.

Given the diversity of backgrounds and interests of those who subscribed to the humanistic movement, it would have been impossible for the movement to maintain a unified structure for long. The splintering was accelerated by the death in 1970 of Abraham Maslow, its charismatic leader. Since then the relations of Humanistic Psychology with the mainstream is largely the responsibility of members of Division 32.

Even as the humanistic movement was at its peak, another novel and unpredictable chapter in experimental psychology was being quietly written. This is in an area quite remote from humanistic psychology, yet as closely related to the human potential as anything that Maslow or May had projected. So at odds with the tradition of academic psychology was this dramatic breakthrough that it has received the title "The Cognitive Revolution".

COGNITIVE PSYCHOLOGY

Not a few observers of the history of psychology view the return of interest in cognitive functions as a revolution. In the context of John Watson's total rejection of consciousness in favor of behavior, the revival of interest in creative thought and cognitive operations unquestionably amounts to a revolution. But in the context of this review of the manner in which psychology took shape over the years, the revival of cognitive psychology indicates that psychology has come full circle since the founding of Wundt's laboratory in 1879. It will be recalled that Wundt's method of choice for psychology was exclusively the introspective analysis of conscious states while they are in progress. But what makes the changes of the 1950s and 1960s revolutionary is the fact that the cognitive revival brought together a number of independent disciplines quite remote from psychology, and focused their attention on the way the mind works, rather than the on the conclusions it arrives at. This enterprise revived some of the oldest questions in philosophy, like the possibility of innate knowledge, what constitutes empirical proof and the origin of true language. Psychology was only one of these disciplines, rather than the convener and organizer of the interdisciplinary enterprise that has remade the face of psychology. In terms of the interest in consciousness and cognitive operations, psychology has indeed come full circle.

If there is any one insight that made the investigation of cognition unique and productive beginning in the 1950s, it was the shift from problem solving to information processing. Newell (1985: 393-4) summarizes the situation very well:

> The great cluster of events that occurs in the second half of the 1950s, below the line (of problem solving) signifies the shift to an information-processing viewpoint—the start of a revolution in cognition. It can be seen in the variety of different strands—Broadbent, Milaler, Bruner-Goodenow-Austin, Chomsky, Tanner-Swets, and so on. All were generated out of a rapidly shifting conceptual base growing out of the development of communications and computer technology, plus the mathematics of systems, as in game theory and operations research. The confluence of these strands, each distinct in many ways—*their unity in diversity*, to use a well worn phrase—produced a conceptual explosion.

The revolution was carried out in a series of high-level symposia and in close collaborative work of teams of bright people usually within university settings. Several foundations fostered the work by grants and special allocations of funds. Sources as different as the Bell Laboratories, the Harvard Center for Cognitive Studies, and the work in developing feedback mechanisms to guide ballistics at MIT, figured in and were combined in a cooperative effort to penetrate the secrets of cognition.

An attempt to record the names of all of those thinkers whose suggestions or ideas contributed to the cognitive revolution, to say nothing of the proper apportioning of credit, is well beyond the scope of this review. Fortunately, the developments and those responsible for them are well recorded in books and journal articles of the period. An excellent summary may be found in Ernest Hilgard (1987), and a more detailed evaluation with special attention to the background of modern philosophy has been done by Howard Gardner (1985). Psychologists can claim a major share in this immense collaborative effort, but they were not the major conveners of the crucial symposia in which the basic ideas were nurtured, nor did they open up the investigation of the manner in which the mind receives and processes its information. To convey some idea of the scope and diversity of disciplines that contributed to the revival of interest in the human mind at the midpoint of this century, it will be informative to note the source of contributions that proved crucial in this enterprise.

We have noted that the major insight that triggered the cognitive revolution was the shift from problem solving strategies to information processing. At this point the computer and with it the renewed interest in the logic of mathematics provided just the kind of support needed to keep up the momentum of the revolution. In all of the stages in the development of the computer, the logical operations of the human mind were a constant point of immediate reference. The binary system itself is derived from one of the first lessons in logic. Books on thinking became a part of the computer student's library, and technology merged more and more with psychology. In the development of the microchip, with its amazing capability for memory, the goal shifted to the fascinating possibilities of artificial and simulated intelligence. One of those at the cutting edge of simulated intelligence was Herbert A. Simon [1916-]. With A. Newell [1927-], he published one of the early works on the simulation of cognitive processes (Simon and Newell 1958).

Reference to the computer brings us the involvement of mathematicians in the cognitive revolution. In fact, Alan Turing [1912-1954], a gifted mathematician, developed a conceptual prototype of the computer that bears his name (see Herken 1988). But the contribution of mathematics to the whole cognitive revival goes back even to the work of Alfred North Whitehead [1861-1947] and Bertrand Russell [1872-1970] in the attempt to derive the basic laws of logic from mathematical principles (Whitehead and Russell 1910-1913). Other outstanding mathematicians who were involved in the investigation of cognitive operations were Norbert Wiener [1894-1964] and Claude E. Shannon [1916-].

Most of the other significant contributions to the development of the new science of mind belong to the field of psychology. However, the Neobehaviorists among them had to be converted from their allegiance to some form of the S-R theory before they could feel comfortable with the language of the investigators of cognition, meaning, attention, and thought. Coming from mathematics or other fields, the students interested in the way in which the mind processes information were not shackled by the Behaviorist tradition in the manner in which many able psychologists were. But for those brought up in the neobehaviorist approach to learning, some preparation was necessary. This preparation was provided by none other than Karl Lashley, who had been, in his own words, a "twitch psychologist" in his younger days. Others had published pointed criticisms of Skinner's position, but they had largely gone unanswered. It was Karl Lashley's demand that psychology be released from its long indenture to the behaviorist tradition that opened the way for psychologists to speak of the mind or of mental states without enclosing these terms within quotation marks.

Lashley pointed out the limitations of Behaviorism at the Hixon Symposium. This symposium was held in 1948 and was the forerunner of a number of interdisciplinary symposia that proved so productive in advancing cognitive science. Lashley's paper (1951) was entitled "The Problem of Serial Order in Behavior". In this paper he began by asserting:

> My principal thesis today is that the input is never into a quiescent or static system, but always into a system that is already actively excited and organized. In the intact organism, behavior is the result of interaction of this background of excitation with input from any designated stimulus.

He goes on to point out how impossible it is to account for the meaningful sequence of words in a sentence on the basis of some kind of stimulus-response chain. Without a serial order imposed by a higher integrating center, syntax is lost. His devastating critiques of Behaviorism and Neobehaviorism were received with great enthusiasm and sparked animated discussions that helped clear the path of the cognitive revival.

Linguistic behavior provides one of the best opportunities to study cognitive functions, and it is in this area that psychologists became directly involved in the revival of cognitive studies, because language involves a high level of cognitive operations. Serious study of language had been inaugurated by Wilhelm von Humboldt [1767-1835]. He took a strongly rationalist position, maintaining that the human being is born with the basic structures of language. Wundt was impressed with Humboldt's linguistic analysis and followed him in his *Völkerpsychologie* (a term coined by Humboldt). Ferdinand de Saussure [1857-1913], emphasizing the sign-significance aspect of language, opposed the rationalist position of von Humboldt. The beginnings of the current interest in psycholinguistics dates from a meeting of six psychologists for a seminar at Cornell in 1951 (Hilgard 1987: 251). One of those who took part in the seminar was George A. Miller [1920-], of the Harvard Center for Cognitive Studies. His *Language and Communication* (1951) opened up the discussion of the psychological factors involved in language. B. F. Skinner's book, *Verbal Behavior*, appeared in 1957. It was vigorously attacked as soon as it appeared by Noam Chomsky (1959) in particular, who had been developing his own approach to the origins of language along the lines of Humboldt's rationalist position. Chomsky's concept of generative grammar depended heavily on innate structures, and introduced the rationalism-empiricism debate into the issues of the cognitive revival. Among other things, his generative grammar served to indicate why artificial intelligence could not effectively simulate language. Chomsky at MIT was working with the team at the Harvard Center for Cognitive Studies. His devastating refutation of Skinner's attempt to account for verbal behavior in terms of association and his ingenious demonstrations of transformational grammar did much to convert George A. Miller from Neobehaviorism and engage him as an effective member of the team working on cognitive psychology.

In defending the importance of generative grammar, Chomsky took support from Humboldt's position of a century before and even revived some of Descartes' notions of the innate structures of thought. His position on language parallels in some measure the position of Lev Vygotsky referred to in connection with Russian psychology in Chapter 6. However, Vygotsky's socio-historical theory holds that the structural aspects of grammar can be explained without recourse to inborn structures.

Another area in which psychologists made important contributions to the cognitive revolution was that of memory. It will recalled that the first study of memory by a psychologist was done by Ebbinghaus (1885). Ebbinghaus used nonsense syllables in order to study memory apart from meanings or other higher thought processes. His work became the model of memory studies, and interest readily shifted to verbal memory as numerous studies developed to test the memory of word lists. When memory was taken up by Claude E. Shannon [1916-] at the Bell Laboratories, he shifted the stage to information processing, in which meanings and their retention become important. Shannon introduced the term "bit" (short for binary digit) for the unit of information readily translatable into computer language. Memory involved in information processing became an area of great interest, both in this country and in Great Britain. Studies requiring the subject to listen to a passage of some length, and, after an interval, to repeat it, yielded interesting empirical results. Out of this new approach came a view of memory as a complex process involving registration, storage and retrieval. The process of memory was divided correspondingly into the three stages of "immediate memory", "short term memory", and "long term memory".

George Miller (1956) is credited with having established seven as the number of discrete items that are attended to and held in immediate memory.[21] On the whole, the new

---

[21] Hilgard (1987: 244) points out that Miller's basic idea had been expressed in the much earlier work of Hamilton (1859: 177), and that "Hamilton's results were quoted by William James (1890), and the truths that he reported were familiar to Woodworth (1938) and hence available to

look at information processing and memory is the best example of the importance of the breakthrough in computer theory and development to the revival of cognitive science. Of all the areas that received new impetus from the cognitive revolution, creativity or productive thinking ranks among the highest. It is also the topic that will retain the interest of psychologists well into the next century.

Psychologists of the Gestalt persuasion were the first to draw attention to this interesting field of psychology. John Dewey's [1859-1952] *How We Think: A Restatement of the Relation of Reflective Thinking to the Educative Process* (1910) was an attempt to set down the five steps presumably involved in scientific discovery. This was followed by Wolfgang Köhler's [1887-1967] demonstration of insightful behavior on the part of chimpanzees in their native environment (1917). *The Mentality of Apes* appeared in the English translation in 1925 and opened up the debate between the behaviorists and the followers of Gestalt psychology in this country. Karl Duncker [1903-1940] was another Gestalt psychologist who was interested in creative thinking. His work on productive thought appeared in German in 1935, but the first English edition appeared in *Psychological Monographs* in 1945. It stimulated his former teacher, Max Wertheimer [1880-1943], to continue the investigation into the field of problem solving and creative thinking in a work that received wide attention, *Productive Thinking* (Wertheimer a.1943). Meantime, J. P. Guilford [1897-] had made the distinction between convergent and divergent thinking on the

psychologists generally. It was not the reassertion of these facts that made Miller's paper so important, but the placing of them in the context of the new cognitive psychology of information processing and the limitations on the amount of information that could be handled at once."

basis of his factorial analysis of intelligence test scores, and offered some observations on creativity in an article in the *American Psychologist* in 1950, followed by his discussion of the nature of intelligence in 1967 (see also Guilford 1968).

All this contributed to the excitement over the investigation of intelligence, problem-solving and creativity by means of the new methods of studying higher thought processes opened up by the computer-aided information processing, creative memory and mathematical logic. Jerome Bruner [1915-] was lured from work on the analysis of public opinion by the interesting prospects of studying human intelligence at the Harvard Center for Cognitive Studies, where he found a congenial teammate in George A. Miller, who had sparked the establishment of the Center. Bruner brought a rich academic background to his study of creativity. He had more than a passing familiarity with Gestalt psychology, and had worked closely with William McDougall and Gordon Allport. He had also spent some time at Cambridge, working with Frederick C. Bartlett [1886-] and D. E. Broadbent [1945-], both of whom had done extensive work on memory and on verbal learning. The Cambridge connection enabled Bruner to engage some British talent in the cognitive project, and to move his own interest into the field of cognitive growth. In this enterprise, he was able to make use of Piaget's ingenious methods of studying the development of logical thinking in the child. Bruner's work with George Miller at the Harvard Center over a period of ten years, together with his own writings, represent one of the most significant contributions of all the elements that went into the so-called Cognitive Revolution.

Before leaving the creativity aspects of the cognitive revolution, we should mention the work of Ulric Neisser [1928-]. Considerably younger than the persons we have been considering, he was an undergraduate at Harvard and later a student for the Ph.D. in psychology while the Center for Cognitive Studies was still active. An appointment to Cornell University brought him into close contact with James J. Gibson [1904-1979], whose work on visual perception went back to the study of how pilots land an airplane, research done in conjunction with the war effort. Gibson had demonstrated the perceptual activity that he called "active sensing" (see Gibson 1950, 1966). Results of this work at Cornell were to move Neisser's interest towards the function of selective attention in responding to visual and auditory signals. This interest is reflected in Neisser's *Cognition and Reality* (1976), which is recognized as one of the best syntheses of the various strands that went into the cognitive revolution.

THE EXISTENTIAL WILL

The cognitive revolution, by opening up the study of creativity, selective attention, and productive thinking, has renewed interest in topics that are related to but lie somewhat outside the province of cognition strictly viewed. Attention is one of the mental activities that had been well recognized and accepted in the beginnings of experimental psychology under the name "determining tendencies", but had been forced out of the field by Watson's narrow definition of behavior. It is brought back now as a necessary element in the creative process. Directed attention is a necessary condition for the creative act to begin. This initial direction of attention must be sustained by a clear concept of the goal, if the effort is to succeed. Such goal direction requires that the end to be attained must be in the mind before the work begins. This involves teleology or purposiveness, words that have been taboo since Francis Bacon [1561-

1626] published his design for scientific investigation in *The New Atlantis* (Bacon 1624). The mechanical sciences may very well do without any teleological concepts, but the life sciences cannot, without gravely inhibiting their understanding of evolution. Ragnor Granit has pointed this out in a recent work with the unusual title *The Purposive Brain* (Granit 1977). It is also a point that becomes clear when the role of *signs* is discussed in general, as Peirce discovered (see Deely 1990: Chapter 6).

Selective attention, goal direction, and purposiveness are all operations that involve some power of self-direction. This has been referred to as "will" or "volition", but this concept, never at home in experimental psychology because of psychologists' concern about being accepted by the scientific community, needs to be reinstated in order to make the cognitive revolution complete. However, to understand the existential will it is necessary to have a much more complete understanding of the emotions and of the manner in which they interact with our cognitive life. That chapter of experimental psychology exists only in the barest outline, but emotions have at last achieved recognition and are being investigated in their own right. We are still a long way from the straightforward recognition of the contribution of the emotions to our intellectual life. This was strikingly expressed by a practicing psychiatrist, J. W. Appel, in one of his contributions to the later revisions of *Discovering Ourselves* (Strecker and Appel 1931; Strecker, Appel, and Appel 1958: 103): "The emotions and feelings supply the energy which makes the mind work."

With knowledge of the brain now being assimilated and extended and the cognitive revolution broadened to include purposiveness and the goal direction of productive thinking, the agenda of the twenty-first century is rich in possibility.

The hopes for the new psychology are more sober than a century ago, but they are well founded.

Chapter 12

FROM SENSATION TO SIGN

Having sketched the history of psychology through something more than a century, one is impressed by the fact that the discipline has steadily progressed. The shifts of emphasis and interest have not been based on relatively minor differences but have gone to the very bedrock of the science. Such was the shift from the analysis of consciousness under Wundt to the denial of consciousness by Watson and the affirmation of the unconscious by Freud. But in all of those radical changes one thing has remained constant at the core of scientific psychology. The one constant in all of this restlessness and change has been elementarism, with its related doctrine of Associationism: the idea that the basic activity of the mind is associating elements of experience that come through the senses. It was the unquestioned acceptance of associationism that caused the study of learning and learning theory to occupy the central position in American psychology from the 'twenties through the 'fifties. It was not until the cognitive revolution entered the field and problems of creative thinking and discovery began to be seriously examined that it became clear that not all cognitive functions could be explained in terms of S-R bonds.

It so happened that the beginning of the Cognitive Revolution coincided with the official self-examination conducted by the American Psychological Association and published under the title *Psychology: A Study of a Science* (Koch 1959 and after). The study, as we noted in Chapter 10, came up with a rather devastating criticism of the whole direction that psychological theory and research in learning had pursued. The negative conclusions concerning the worth of learning studies, based on various forms of Associationism, had little to do with the cognitive revival but have served to usher in a new age for American psychology.

If cognitive psychology, after an exciting breakthrough, showed signs of some kind of unified attack on the problem of creative thought, it would be worthwhile to pursue this as a conclusion to this review. At the moment, however, cognitive psychologists represent a wide range of thought lacking a unified thrust.[22]

---

[22] Shank (1990: 2-3) submits the following observations on this point: "On the surface, the cognitive revolution looks like a genuine interdisciplinary attempt to solve questions that have plagued psychology since its earliest days as a science. Workers in such diverse fields as linguistics (Fodor, Bever and Garrett 1975), neuroscience (Sperry 1982, Geschwind 1984, Gazzaniga 1970), and artificial intelligence (Aleksander 1984, Forsyth and Naylor 1986, Arnold and Bowie 1986), have joined together with psychologists to address crucial questions about the nature and operation of thought and thinking processes. Philosophers have debated such issues as the nature of cognitive control

Let us rather turn our attention to the elementarism that was able, especially as giving rise to Associationism, to play such a dominant role in the first one hundred years of psychology, both in Europe and in America.

THE FLAWED CORNERSTONE OF PSYCHOLOGY'S FIRST HUNDRED YEARS

There is general agreement that Associationism is correctly traced back to the chapter titled "The Association of Ideas" in the fourth edition (1700) of John Locke's *Essay Concerning*

---

processes (Dennett 1978, Fodor 1981), the fundamental properties of cognition (Churchland 1981), and even the likelihood of a computational model of thinking as the basis of cognitive psychology in the first place (Dreyfus 1979, Searle 1984). Finally, psychology itself has pursued exciting new research in such areas as knowledge representation (Rosch and Mervis 1975, Schank and Abelson 1977) and the modeling of cognition along such non-traditional lines as language (Pribram 1971) and the arts (Hofstadter 1979). When looking at an overview of the field of cognitive science, such as that provided by Stillings and his colleagues (1987), one is struck by the breadth and diversity of the field.

"As the cognitive revolution enters the final decade of the twentieth century, though, it finally betrays its roots in the Cartesianism that has hamstrung all of its predecessors in their attempts to provide an overarching model for a psychology that deals with theory, research, and practice in a coherent fashion. Out of the refreshing array of perspectives that characterized the early formulation of the revolution, we have a settling in of an approach that reinstates the mind-body problem as the fundamental principle of psychological research. This approach is called 'connectionism'. Connectionism is a view of cognitive science that says that thinking is necessarily a brain function, and that we cannot understand cognition without understanding the brain at the same time (Feldman 1985, Rumelhart and Zipser 1985, Bechtel 1988). The fact that the 1990s have been declared, by funding advocates of psychology, to be the 'decade of the brain', only accentuates this state of affairs.

"As psychology enters the twenty-first century, then, what are its options for growing and maturing as a branch of empirical inquiry?"

Human Understanding. However, Locke's reference to the association of ideas bears little resemblance to the doctrine of Associationism which was later elaborated by men like Hartley, the Mills, and others. As time went on Associationism came to mean, as we noted in note 1 to Chapter 1, the dogma that associating is the basic cognitive function, and that the whole process of thinking involves nothing more than the formation of associative bonds between elements of knowledge already formed. This constituted the sensism opposed by the Gestalt psychologists, including a number of the non-Pavlovian Russian psychologists. Locke, himself, was far from going to this extreme, but his radical empiricism—anticipatory of positivism, as we have seen—and his exaggerated notion that sensory data are meaningful in themselves, rather than signs to be interpreted, were the major philosophical influences leading to the doctrine of Associationism.

Centuries of freely referring to sensation as the simplest conscious phenomenon have prevented us from realizing that sensation is anything but simple. By the time sensory experience can be spoken of, it is already more than on the way to a meaning. Before any kind of recognition occurs, a number of things have happened in a continuous process that developments in neuroscience have helped us to understand: threshold, excitation, transmission of the nerve-impulse through the sensorium to the specific area of the brain that determines the conscious character of the stimulation.

In drawing attention to the source of the stimulation, the sensory impulse sets up a relationship between environment and the organism. This makes it imperative that in addition to cognitive analysis of the stimulus the organism make an immediate somatic response of advance, withdrawal, or indifference. This is provided for by the fact that the incoming nerve impulse alerts the reticular activating system, which is in close connection with the autonomic centers, and provides for the quick reaction of the organism as a whole. At the same time the sensory input to the cortex initiates the perceptual process in search of the meaning of the sensory stimulation. Thus it is clear that sensation is far from a simple flashing of a meaning on the screen of consciousness, and asks far more questions than it answers.

This evaluation of the sensory input puts sensation in its proper perspective, viz., a sign to be interpreted. Hence to regard the contribution of the sense-organ as a sign to be interpreted, rather than as the atomic building block of meaning, could do much to retrieve the importance of sensory psychology and provide a sound basis for further developments of the creative and discovery aspects of learning. This promising alternative to the Sensationalism of the British Empiricists also goes far toward putting the mind-body problem to rest. Since the somatic response to stimulation goes on simultaneously with the cognitive effort to recognize the object and assume an attitude toward it, recognizing the stimulation as semiosic (as an action of signs) frees us at once from the tired realisms which require us to assume in advance that we know "what the stimulus is" objectively—that is to say, in its own being as physical.

A NEW CORNERSTONE FOR THE SECOND CENTURY?

By a strange sequence of events, it happens that even as Associationism traces back to John Locke's famous *Essay Concerning Human Understanding,* today this most promising alternative for sensationism received its name from that same author. This is in his reference to *semiotic* as "the doctrine of signs" in the important division of knowledge he introduced to conclude his *Essay*. In the closing chapter of his famous *Essay*, John Locke introduced into Aristotle's twofold division of knowledge into *speculative* and *practical* a third term, for which he coined the name *semiotics*.

The terms "speculative" and "practical", in the Aristotelian sense Locke employs, may be unfamiliar to the contemporary reader, so we may note that, of the things we come to know and study, the resulting knowledge is called by Aristotle *speculative* when it results from the investigation of objects deemed primarily to exist independently of human initiative (as in the case of geology, astronomy, physics, chemistry, biology, and the like), and *practical* when it concerns objects that primarily depend in their being on human initiative (as in the case of art, technology, politics, ethics, economics, and the like). It is precisely between this dichotomy of objects which exist independently of our minds and objects which depend upon our minds that Locke places his third term, his new study of what these opposed types of object have in common precisely insofar as they are objects known. The new study would focus on the means whereby all knowledge—speculative and practical alike—is acquired, developed, and communicated. Semiotics, in short, unites the divisions of knowledge in terms of their common foundation as sign-dependent cognitive structures erected within experience. This would tie modern psychology closely to logic in line with the cognitive revival.

In suggesting the development of semiotics as a doctrine of signs, however, Locke also speaks of signs as being predominantly words, thus leading the way to a neglect of non-verbal signs, an area that has such rich connotations for psychological research. We have already had occasion to mention above in passing that Locke's earlier contemporary, John Poinsot [1589-1644], had penetrated far more deeply into this matter of the semiotic foundations (or sign-dependent character) of knowledge and experience generally when he supplanted the limited commentaries on Aristotle's logical treatise *On Interpretation* with an extensive treatment of the doctrine of signs (Poinsot 1632). The very extent of the work, along with the rationale of its treatment, is sufficient evidence of the importance Poinsot gave to the doctrine of signs as fundamental to all questions bearing on the nature of experience and theory of knowledge. But, more importantly, viewed from the vantage point of contemporary psychology, Poinsot's extended discussion shows that the study of signs takes one back to the very basic psychological concepts of stimulus, sensory impulse, and the subtle transformation of the impulse to the basic change in consciousness that alerts the organism to a change in the environment—sometimes only an increase or decrease in the level of excitation. Whatever is acting on the receptor engages the attention of the subject, and by that very engagement becomes a sign demanding to be interpreted. All this takes place before what the Empiricists called "sensation" has registered, because for them the sensation is already meaningful and, at the human level, is ready to be named.

At the subhuman level, the clear evidence that any change in the environment operates and has value as a sign is that the organism reacts, either draws nearer or draws away from the situation. This is the sign operating at the most basic psychological level, i.e., establishing a relationship of experience between a living organism and its environment. Regarding the matter in this light opens up a whole new way of looking at psychology, tying human and comparative psychology together at the level of a most basic function they have in common: the irritability of the organism.

SEMIOTICS AND THE FUTURE OF PSYCHOLOGY

To exploit the field of psychology from this perspective it would seem necessary for the psychologist to recognize the fundamental meaning of the sign, namely, that it is *a relation* (Deely 1990: 32-49), and specifically a relation between the organism and some environmental change that needs to be evaluated in terms of the organism's immediate interests and ultimate survival.

Already some psychologists are moving into this understanding of their field. Unfortunately, the rich possibilities of the verbal sign bedazzle many of the investigators and divert their attention from the more basic sign function of the irritability that is a property of all living things and a part of the infrastructure even of the sensory processes involved in the production and reception of verbal signs. By contrast, the whole area of non-verbal communication among subhuman animals and the parallels between this and true language, an area demarcated and unified especially through the work of Sebeok under the provocative label of *zoösemiosis* (the study of the action of signs among animals as such—from Sebeok 1963), is a rich mine for comparative psychology. This whole range of non-verbal communication has recently aroused lively interest. It is an area awaiting exploitation with the new sign approach provided by semiotics.

In terms of the revival of interest in information processing, the study of the sensory process would seem to offer the best basis upon which to build a sound and well-rounded theory of cognition. A revised theory of learning which emphasizes discovery and creativity as highly important aspects of learning would follow naturally from this.

The failure of Associationism to provide an adequate theoretical framework for the integration of sensation with the higher thought processes, thus, would be a tragedy to American psychology only if there were no alternative view to integrate human cognition. Fortunately there is an alternative of great potential, the perspective given its name by John Locke (1st edition, 1690)—even earlier than his introduction of the association of ideas into the modern mainstream (4th edition, 1700). This new perspective contrasts with any perspective based on elementarism in a very striking way that is of the greatest importance for psychology. For those who adopt an elementarist view, the problem of connecting the elementary sensations either leads to a passive view of mind, as in the doctrine of Associationism, or to an active view of mind which is essentially external to the data to be related, as in Wundt's voluntarism (or, in the terms of modern philosophy, idealism generally). On the semiotic view, by contrast, the action of signs is at work from the first moment of sensory stimulation and before, allowing the activity of the mind to elaborate further connections, indeed, but connections already based on and extending what the sign action of the sense organ itself suggests here and now in an ongoing process.

This is a gain of the first importance, suggesting that the sign, traced in its workings through the various orders from the amoeba to Homo Sapiens, offers the most direct and one of the simplest means of dealing with the mind-body problem in all its aspects. A semiotic approach simply by-passes Wundt's problem of dealing with the relations of inner consciousness and the region of incoming experience, and his difficulty in handling the dilemma of Associationism vs. High German Idealism, since sensory experience is not flashed upon a blank screen but is borne in upon a consciousness already engaged in the survival of the organism. "Inner" and "outer", thus, form a continuum in the experience of the person mediated by sign-relations. Getting rid of the artificial separation of mind and body can do much to simplify the terms of psychological discussion. The exaggerated emphasis on the distance between mind and body, the mental and the physical, has too long dominated the psychological field without more effective challenge than behaviorism.

Semiotics provides, for example, an answer to the question as to whether psychology should be viewed as predominantly a biological or a social discipline. It is neither. The point at which the social signs of subhuman animals become cognitively clear and fully capable of logical treatment in terms of analogy, metaphor, and symbol will always remain blurred, but somewhere in the evolutionary sequence the sign activity emerges as unmistakably human. When signs no longer trigger instinctive reaction, but human choice emerges, it is clear that subhuman communication has now become true language. No longer is there any need to discuss whether psychology is a social or a biological discipline. Biology naturally prepares the way for full-blown social interaction, something that has been demonstrated with particular effectiveness in semiotics with reference to the biological studies of Jakob von Uexküll (1899-1940, 1934, 1940; see Sebeok 1979).

Rich and rewarding as the insights into semiotic activity are at the lower levels of the evolutionary scale, it is at the level of social interaction in which the dimension of communicative exchange reaches the plane of true language—capable of dealing flexibly with object-sign-symbol, as the situation dictates—that the full potential of semiosis is reached. There exists at this level an extensive literature that has been largely dominated by non-psychological linguists. The full psychological significance of this work has yet to be exploited. The data it provides, analyzed from the psychologist's point of view, has many valuable results to yield.

Within the perspective semiotic provides, it would seem, we are as far from psychophysical parallelism à la Wundt as we are from reductivistic materialism à la Sechenov. With the possibility of such an understanding opened up, one wonders how long psychology can afford to ignore the rich and flexible area of signs, how much longer psychology can afford to neglect *semiosis* as a distinctive process.

Perhaps one of the clearest and most striking contemporary testimonies concerning the importance of signs and the far-reaching extent of their action in human affairs has been provided in terms that no one can mistake by Jacques Maritain (1938: 299, 1957: 51-52): "The sign is in the human world a universal instrument, just as is motion in the physical world". In other words, to try to understand human thought and action while ignoring consideration of the sign and the way it operates in human cognition is like trying to develop a science of physics with motion left out of the picture.

Under the yoke of Associationism and the S-R bond theory, academic psychology in America has missed valuable opportunities to advance, but the intense activity of a century has not been wasted. The inviting areas of investigation that have ended in blind alleys have served to prove that this is not the direction to go. Within the last quarter century the cognitive revolution has demonstrated that there are alternatives out there full of interest and promise. Undoubtedly the most radical and daring of these is the semiotic trail, already beckoning for exploration in this, psychology's second century.

ALPHABETIZED CHRONOLOGY

Here we list the names of all those mentioned as contributing to the shaping of psychology, along with their dates of birth and death. An asterisk in place of a death date indicates that the individual in question was thought to be alive at the time of the compilation (June 1990).

Abelard, Peter	1079-1142
Ach, Narziss Kaspar	1871-1946
Adler, Alfred	1870-1937
Adorno, Theodor	1903-1969
Adrian, Edgar Douglas	1889-1977
Albert the Great	1193/1206-1280
Alexander the Great (King of Macedonia)	356-323BC
Allport, Floyd H.	1890-1978

Allport, Gordon Willard	1897-1967
Anastasi, Anne	1908- *
Angell, Frank	1857-1939
Angell, James Rowland	1869-1949
Anselm of Canterbury	1033-1109
Appel, John W.	
Appel, Kenneth Ellmaker	1896- ?
Aquinas, Thomas	1224/5-1274
Archimedes	c.287-212BC
Ardigò, Roberto	1828-1920
Aristotle	c.384-323BC
Asch, Solomon E.	1907- *
Augustine	354-430
Bacon, Francis	1561-1626
Bain, Alexander	1818-1903
Bartlett, Frederick C.	1886-1969
Beers, Clifford Wittingham	1876-1943
Békésy, George von	1890-1972
Bekhterev (=Bechterew), Vladimir Mikhailovich	1857-1927
Bell, Charles	1774-1842
Bergson, Henri	1859-1941
Berkeley, Bishop George	1685-1753
Bernheim, Hippolyte	1840-1919
Binet, Alfred	1857-1911
Bingham, Walter Van Dyke	1880-1952
Boethius	480-524
Boring, Edwin Garrigues	1886-1968
Brentano, Franz	1838-1917
Broadbent, D. E.	1945- *
Broca, Paul	1824-1880
Bruner, Jerome	1915- *
Bühler, Karl	1879-1963
Burnham, William Henry	1855-1941

Carr, Harvey A.	1873-1954
Cattell, James McKeen	1860-1944
Charcot, Jean-Martin	1825-1893
Chelpanov, G. I.	1862-1936
Chiarugi, V.	1759-1820
Claparède, Edouard	1873-1940
Clark, Kenneth	1914-
Comte, Isadore Auguste Marie François	1798-1857
Descartes, René	1596-1650
Dessoir, Max	1867-1947
Dewey, John	1859-1952
Dollard, John	1900-1980
Doob, Leonard W.	1909- *
Doyle, Charles I.	1889-1973
Drever, James	1873-1950
DuBois-Reymond, Emil	1818-1896
Duncker, Karl	1903-1940
Durkheim, Emile	1858-1917
Ebbinghaus, Hermann	1850-1909
Eccles, John Carew	1903- *
Ehrenfels, Christian von	1859-1932
Erikson, Erik	1902-
Fechner, Gustav Theodor	1801-1887
Flourens, Pierre Jean Marie	1794-1867
Flournoy, Théodore	1854-1920
Ford, Clellan S.	1909-
Franz, Shepherd Ivory	1874-1933
Freud, Sigmund	1856-1939
Frisch, Karl von	1886-1982
Fritsch, Gustav Theodor	1838-1927
Fromm, Erich	1900-1980
Gale, Harlow	1862-1945
Gall, Franz Joseph	1758-1828

Galton, Francis	1822-1911
Gannon, Timothy Joseph	1904-1991
Gazzaniga, Michael S.	1939- *
Gemelli, Agostino	1878-1959
Gibson, James J.	1904-1979
Golgi, Camillo	1843-1926
Granit, Ragnor	
Gruender, Hubert	-1940
Guilford, Joy Paul	1897-1987
Hall, Granville Stanley	1844-1924
Harlow, Harry Frederick	1905-1981
Hartley, David	1705-1757
Healy, William	1869-1963
Hebb, Donald O.	1904-1985
Helmholtz, Hermann von	1821-1894
Herbart, Johann Friedrich	1776-1841
Hilgard, Ernest R.	1904- *
Hitzig, Eduard	1838-1907
Hobbes, Thomas	1588-1679
Horney, Karen	1885-1952
Hovland, Carl I.	1912-1961
Hull, Clark Leonard	1884-1952
Humboldt, Wilhelm von	1767-1835
Hume, David	1711-1776
Husserl, Edmund	1859-1938
Itard, Jean Marie-Gaspard	1775-1838
James, William	1842-1910
Janet, Pierre	1859-1947
Jastrow, Joseph	1863-1944
Judd, Charles Hubbard	1873-1946
Jung, Carl Gustav	1875-1961
Kant, Immanuel	1724-1804
Kierkegaard, Søren Aabye	1813-1855

Kiesow, Federico	1858-1940
Koch, Sigmund	1917- *
Koffka, Kurt	1886-1941
Köhler, Wolfgang	1887-1967
Kornilov, Konstantin Nikolaevich	1879-1957
Kraepelin, Emil	1856-1926
Krech, David	1909-1977
Kretschmer, Ernst	1888-1964
Külpe, Oswald	1862-1915
Lange, Karl Georg	1834-1900
Lashley, Karl Spencer	1890-1958
Le Bon, Gustave	1841-1931
Leibniz, Gottfried Wilhelm von	1646-1716
Lenin, Vladimir Ilyich	1870-1924
Leontiev, Alexi N.	1903-1979
Lewin, Kurt	1890-1947
Liébeault, Ambroise-Auguste	1823-1904
Locke, John	1632-1704
Lombroso, Cesare	1835-1909
Lorenz, Konrad	1903-1989
Luria, Alesandro Romanovich	1902-1977
MacLean, Paul D.	1913-
Mahowald, George H.	? -1966
Marbe, Karl	1869-1953
Maritain, Jacques	1882-1973
Maslow, Abraham Harold	1908-1970
May, Rollo	1909- *
McCarthy, Raphael	1889-1979
McDougall, William	1871-1938
Meinong, Alexis	1853-1920
Mercier, Desiré	1851-1926
Meyer, Adolf	1866-1950
Michotte, Albert Edward	1881-1965

Mill, James	1773-1836
Mill, John Stuart	1806-1873
Miller, George A.	1920- *
Miller, Neal E.	1909- *
Misiak, Henryk	1911- *
Moerbeke, William	c.1215-1286
Montessori, Maria	1870-1952
Moore, Thomas Verner	1877-1969
Morgan, Conwy Lloyd	1852-1936
Mosso, Angelo	1846-1910
Mowrer, Hobart Orval	1907-1982
Müller, Johannes	1801-1858
Münsterberg, Hugo	1863-1916
Murchison, Carl	1887-1961
Murphy, Gardner	1895-1979
Murphy, Lois	1902-
Murray, Henry A.	1893-1988
Neisser, Ulric	1928- *
Newcomb, Theodore M.	1903-1984
Newell, Alan	1927- *
Newton, Isaac	1642-1727
Ockham, William of	c.1289-1349
Pace, Edward Aloysius	1861-1938
Patrick, George Thomas White	1857-1949
Pavlov, Ivan Petrovich	1849-1936
Peirce, Charles Sanders	1839-1914
Pestalozzi, Johann Heinrich	1746-1827
Piaget, Jean	1896-1980
Pinel, Philippe	1745-1826
Pinter, Rudolf	1884-1942
Plato	c.428/7-348/7BC
Plotinus	205-270
Poinsot, John	1589-1644

Porphyry	c.232-300/306
Pribram, Karl H.	1912- *
Prince, Morton	1854-1929
Reid, Thomas	1710-1796
Ribot, Theodule Armand	1839-1916
Rogers, Carl	1902-1987
Rorschach, Hermann	1844-1922
Ross, Edward Alsworth	1866-1951
Russell, Bertrand	1872-1970
Sarlo, Francesco de	1864-1937
Saussure, Ferdinand de	1857-1913
Scott, Walter Dill	1869-1955
Scotus, John Duns	c.1265-1308
Scripture, Edward Wheeler	1864-1945
Sears, Robert R.	1908-1989
Sechenov, Ivan V.	1829-1905
Séguin, Edouard	1812-1880
Shakow, David	1901-1981
Shank, Gary D.	1949- *
Shannon, Claude E.	1916- *
Sheldon, William Herbert	1898-1977
Sherrington, Sir Charles Scott	1857-1952
Simon, Herbert A.	1916- *
Skinner, Burrhus Frederick	1904-1990
Socrates	c.470-399BC
Spearman, Charles Edward	1863-1945
Sperry, R. W.	1913- *
Spranger, Eduard	1882-1963
Spurzheim, Johann Kaspar	1776-1832
Staudt (Sexton), Virginia	
Stern, William Louis	1871-1938
Stewart, Dugald	1753-1828
Stratton, George Malcolm	1865-1957

Strecker, Edward Adam	1886-
Stumpf, Carl	1848-1936
Sullivan, Harry Stack	1892-1949
Summers, Walter G.	1889-1938
Tarde, Gabriel	1843-1904
Tawney, G. A.	1870-1947
Terman, Lewis Madison	1877-1956
Thorndike, Edward Lee	1874-1949
Thurstone, Louis Leon	1887-1955
Titchener, Edward Bradford	1867-1927
Tolman, Edward Chase	1886-1959
Trendelenburg, F. A.	1802-1872
Turing, Alan Mathison	1912-1954
Vygotsky, Leon Semenovich	1896-1934
Warren, Howard Crosby	1867-1934
Wasmann, Erich von	1859-1931
Watson, John Broadus	1878-1958
Watt, Henry Jackson	1879-1925
Weber, Ernst Heinrich	1795-1878
Wertheimer, Max	1880-1943
Whitehead, Alfred North	1861-1947
Wiener, Norbert	1894-1964
Witmer, Lightner	1867-1956
Wolfe, H. K.	1858-1918
Woodworth, Robert Sessions	1869-1962
Wundt, Wilhelm	1832-1920
Yerkes, Robert Mearns	1876-1956
Zusne, Leonard	1924- *

The collaboration on this book began in earnest in December of 1988, when Gannon brought the draft of the first five chapters to Belo Horizonte, Minas Gerais, Brasil, where Deely was a Visiting Fulbright Professor. The editing and completion of that first draft was accomplished by the following December, and used for a team-taught Spring 1990 honors course at Loras College in Dubuque, Iowa. In early March the diagnosis of terminal cancer was made, making the completion of the work in publishable form a race against time which the collaborators, thankfully, won. This photograph of them was taken at the home of Professor Eugene Smith, a colleague of Gannon in psychology, on the occasion of Gannon's 86th birthday, April 2, 1990. The photograph was taken by Gannon's close friend, Monsignor Robert R. Vogl, a Professor of Religious Studies at Loras College.

The Shaping of "Shaping Psychology"

BIOGRAPHICAL APPENDIX

Besides the shaping influences upon the development of psychology as a science, which are set forth in the substance of this book, some readers may further be interested in the specific set of influences that led to the writing of the book, confluences of local circumstance that placed the two of us in the position of bringing the book into being.

These confluences form the subject matter of this appendix. The aim is to acquaint the interested reader with the personal background of the author relative to the coming into being of this book, which itself recounts the shaping influences upon the development of psychology as a science as these were perceived and personified by the principal author of the manuscript over a career in psychology that spanned his sixty years as a professor at Loras College in Dubuque, Iowa.

The reader interested simply in the perspective on the science at large—after all, the main subject of the book—can well afford to skip this appendix, as it gives only some local color and biographical background to the larger subject.

Timothy Gannon brought a unique perspective to the understanding of the basic issues which had motivated the founders of his discipline. On completing in Rome a doctorate in theology in 1929, Gannon was assigned, in the Fall of 1930, as a priest of the Archdiocese of Dubuque, Iowa, to the faculty of the College founded in 1839 by the first Bishop of Dubuque, Matthias Loras [1792-1858] (Gannon himself had gone to Creighton). The following Fall Gannon began teaching in the Department of Philosophy, covering the areas of logic, ethics, and history. The then-Chair of the Philosophy Department, William B. Collins, a Louvain Ph.D., had been the first to introduce the "new psychology"—i.e., an experimentally informed emphasis on the study of the human being in contrast to an emphasis on philosophically derived conceptions and doctrines—as a course in the Loras curriculum under the auspices of the Philosophy Department. In 1930, Psychology was separated from the Department of Philosophy and listed with Education in a newly established Department of Psychology and Education, with the psychology course continuing to be taught by members of the Philosophy Department. To his credit, Collins recognized the need for a full development of this then-novel aspect of the Loras curriculum, and he found in his new colleague Gannon ready material to support the new development.

The 1933-1934 academic year Gannon spent in Washington, DC, acquiring an M.S. in psychology at the Catholic University of America, as the first step toward acquiring a psychology Ph.D. On returning to Loras in 1934 to resume teaching duties, he promptly set to work on filling the lacuna of an introductory psychology text that was hierarchical in structure, i.e., that gave a coherent over-all view of the new psychology. The then-available texts he found to be "like a string of beads, one chapter after another, with no rhyme or reason for the sequence", and certainly without historical sequence. Over the next five years, while teaching a 6-hour introductory psychology course along with the history of philosophy and ethics at the undergraduate college, Gannon worked concurrently on revisions of this introductory text and on the research for and drafting of his doctoral dissertation, *A Statistical Analysis of Some Psychiatric Diagnostic Traits among Young Men* (Gannon 1939).

His introductory textbook in mimeograph form was used, updated, and revised for years at Loras College, and in 1953, in an offset form, was also adopted at the neighboring Clarke College for women. Finally the textbook appeared in published form as *Psychology. The Unity of Human Behavior* (Gannon 1954), and it still makes good reading today. Not surprisingly, the book anticipates some of the themes traced now historically in the present study, in particular the importance of personality as a psychological concept and of Aristotelian naturalism as a scheme for understanding the proper relations of psychology to biology and, more pointedly, of mind to body. "Instead of making the approach to psychology at the level of the mind-body dilemma, Aristotle began with a consideration of a much more fundamental contrast—the difference between living and non-living matter", Gannon noted (1954: 19). He thus took as his starting point a view that Wundt himself had suggested in passing with the closing pages of the 4th edition (1893) of his celebrated *Principles*—long after its seminal impetus (1873-1874) had sent the first psychological generation of researchers in completely other directions. Gannon expanded his foundational point in a lengthy contrast of "Aristotelian Unity vs. Psychophysical Parallelism" (Gannon 1954: 22), a passage which I have incorporated into the present work (footnote 17, p. 136), and which may be capitulated in the point that "consciousness depends upon life, not life upon consciousness".

Gannon was well aware (1954: 25) that "the reason most frequently alleged for rejecting the soul", namely, "that consideration of the soul involves one in supernaturalism", was as entrenched as it was ill-conceived. His rebuttal was pungent and to the point (ibid.): "in Aristotle's sense the soul is by definition no more supernatural than the foot". Gannon is to be admired for his willingness to stage an uphill battle from a marginal position on the academic mainstream! His work achieved nonetheless considerable regional success, and there is room to wonder whether his insistence on the relevance of biological considerations to the foundations and superstructure of psychology as a science in its own right may not eventually become more common wisdom in the national mainstream, if only by way of the unexpected avenue he opens up in concluding the present book. But this is to get ahead of the story, which has only reached Gannon's doctorate in psychology earned in 1939.

The eight years from 1939 to 1947 Gannon was charged with many duties at Loras, but the constant he insisted upon keeping in place and developing was the introductory psychology course. Blessed with the support of his department chair and academic dean, he was further intent on making something more of this than a private success. His aim was to overcome the general satisfaction with the curricular status-quo by establishing at Loras College a full-fledged department of scientific psychology, for which purpose he deemed a second staff member essential.

In 1947 he approached one of his former students, Francis Friedl, now Assistant Pastor at Nativity Parish in Dubuque, with the proposal that he go get a Ph.D. in psychology and join the Loras faculty for the purpose of soon establishing a full-fledged independent Department of Psychology. This plan met with the support of the President of the College and the Archbishop, and in 1954, Friedl returned from the Catholic University of America with his Ph.D. in hand.

Unfortunately for the fledgling department plans, the then-President of Loras was so appreciative of the new faculty member's administrative skills that he co-opted his time almost from the first with administrative tasks and functions,[23] leaving the problem of higher level courses requisite for a Psychology Major problematic.

Gannon, now freed at least from the introductory course load, developed a history of psychology course, one of the early such in the new psychology curriculum (for example, there was no such course at the University of Iowa at that time), and an upper division course in Personality and Adjustment (later "the Healthy Personality"). The remaining requisite upper level courses for a Psychology Major he began to piece together from elsewhere in the curriculum. Statistics he got from the Department of Business; educational psychology was taken from the Department of Education; abnormal (later "Behavior Pathology") was covered by hiring a local psychiatrist part-time; a course in "Directed Readings" and a thesis requirement rounded out the early picture. In

---

[23] Eventually, Friedl's administrative skills led him from the Psychology Department in 1965 to the office of Academic Dean, and thence to the office of President of the College in 1971--a path to be followed in 1977 and 1988 by another of Gannon's hand-picked Psychology Department members, Fr. James Barta, who had joined the psychology faculty in 1961.

1954 a Major in Psychology was announced as part of the Loras curriculum.

The independent Department of Psychology was formally established in its own right in the 1956-1957 academic year, with two full-time faculty members and Gannon as Head. From there it has continued to grow under a series of Chairmen (James Barta, 1972; Tom Sannito, 1975; Bruce Moore, 1978; Steve Milliser, 1988), to a full-time faculty of eight in the 1990-1991 academic year, with one half-time and three adjunct faculty. Over this period, even after promotion to Emeritus in 1974, Gannon continued active involvement with the curricular structure and teaching load of the department.

Thus, when the 1983-1984 *Bulletin* of courses was published, the announcement of a pioneering interdisciplinary major in Gerontology came as no surprise to those who had watched Gannon patiently develop the project through a series of preparatory and experimental course offerings over several years. In 1987, using the same patient method of preparatory experimental offerings, he put together a team of core professors (Drs. Mary Johnson and Brooke Williams) to work along with him in initiating an interdisciplinary women's studies course under the title "The Gender Trap: Shaping Women's Reality". In 1990, this project too became a permanent part of the Loras curriculum.

My own association with Monsignor Gannon began in a casual way in 1976, when I joined the Loras faculty as Chair of the Department of Philosophy. By those days, Gannon was in the category of a mythological figure in the Loras community, alongside his even more senior colleague George Schulte, also now a Monsignor, who was to the Chemistry Department at Loras College a mentor somewhat comparable to what Gannon had been to psychology. (As I write this Appendix in January of 1991, bronze plaques commemorating the work of both these gentlemen have been placed at Loras College in the last months of 1990, located, respectively, in the Saint Joseph Hall of Science and Hennessey Hall which houses the laboratory and department of psychology—with Schulte's plaque fittingly having been dedicated a few weeks earlier.) The close ties between the Philosophy Department's program of courses and the Psychology Major remained in the form of our required, if ill-named, "Philosophy of Man" course, and this historical connection led to some early, extremely pleasant, but basically social visits between the distinguished Dean of Loras psychology and the neonate Chair of Loras philosophy.

I had been hired by Gannon's first protegé, the now-Monsignor Francis Friedl, then-President of Loras College. In the hiring interview, we had spoken together of semiotics as the perspective I thought had the best chance of revivifying the role of philosophy in the curriculum of a liberal arts college, views which Friedl received with interest and support. That was in 1976. At that time, semiotics had made no appreciable penetration into the philosophy curriculum outside the narrow circles of Peircean exegesis, so it was not surprising that my own departmental colleagues responded with justifiable skepticism to this new word, which, for all they knew, might be nothing more than that as far as philosophical doctrine is concerned. After all, rewriting the history of Latin renaissance and early modern philosophy around the work of an author as little heard of as John Poinsot, to say nothing of the evaluation of contemporary developments in light of such rewriting, is not likely to strike the superficial observer as a plausible enterprise worthy of participation and support.

Yet is was in just this regard that an improbable bridge sprung up between the emeritus professor of psychology and the associate professor of philosophy. I went to Gannon's room early in 1986, shortly after the publication of my critical edition of Poinsot's *Tractatus de Signis*, to ask him for a letter of recommendation supporting my promotion to the rank of full Professor. Among the materials to give evidence of professional achievement, I included a copy of the Poinsot book. Gannon had already read my earlier essay, *Introducing Semiotic* (1982), and now expressed open delight at the chance to examine directly the basis of the claims.

It was with considerable surprise and not a little pleasure that I listened, over a series of meetings, to the Monsignor's comments, observations, and questions concerning Poinsot's position in particular and semiotics in general, all based on an evidently attentive reading of the text.

Eventually I was led to ask him point-blank why it was that he, a senior academician by any standard, was able so easily to grasp the perspective required for understanding semiotics, when the majority of my colleagues, much younger than he, professed to see "only a word" signifying "nothing of value". Because it is evident, he replied, that we aren't going to get anywhere by continuing to go in circles on the realist-idealist argument. He would occasionally remark, in the course of many conversations, that the situation of semiotics on our campus today reminded him of the situation there of psychology half a century ago.

It was at a dinner with Gannon in Spring Green, Wisconsin, prior to my leaving in the summer of 1987 on a Fulbright award to teach semiotics at the Universidade Federal de Minas Gerais in Belo Horizonte, Brasil, that the subject casually came up of a series of lectures he had given some years before on the history of psychology, lectures which were just now become available on cassette at the Loras Instructional Resource Center.

Thinking in terms of two or three cassettes, I expressed an interest in listening to the tapes, and Gannon arranged for complimentary copies to be made for me. Imagine my surprise on picking up the tapes to discover there were eighteen of them! I lost no time in suggesting to Gannon that, given his age and perspective on the discipline of psychology, there had to be historical value in the record these tapes contained, but that the vocal medium was not likely to be effective for the transmission of that value. I proposed that he have the tapes transcribed, and that we work together to edit them with an eye to eventual publication. He showed outwardly only the mildest interest in this proposal. That was where things stood when, shortly thereafter, I left for Brasil.

When, in early December, Gannon showed up in Belo Horizonte to spend two weeks as our house guest, bringing with him the first half of the tapes transcribed, I knew that he had after all taken my proposal more seriously than had appeared. I began at once the editor's task, particularly the historical layering of the references which I knew to be essential to bring out the full force and value of the project.

The remaining tapes were transcribed during my second semester in Brasil, and I edited them on my return in the Fall semester of 1989. The resulting manuscript, a completely revised version of the transcription, under the working title of "Psychology and Philosophy in Historical Review", we submitted to the Loras College Honors Committee as a proposed basis for the invitation-only Spring 1990 All-College Honors course. This proposal was adopted by the Committee.

The selected handful of students in this course learned something about psychology, and perhaps even more about libraries and the demands of bibliographical research, for we made them into a team charged with running down details of Gannon's casual references to the considerable literature of psychology's youth in the late 1800s and early 1900s. It took our undergraduates half the semester to realize that this was a matter of work indeed, for we schooled and disciplined them according to the canon of the historical layering of sources, which is the heart of the interdisciplinary Style Sheet developed by the Semiotic Society of America for its publications program. Our students learned what even the academic world has only begun to realize, namely, the importance of establishing a data base which approximates invariance across the lines of different linguistic communities, historical epochs, and derivative editions.

The best of our students, Paul Barton, became the central bibliographer for the group, and his yeoman work in collating and polishing the results of our neophyte bibliophiles was of the greatest assistance—especially to me, who had expected and dreaded to wind up with the full brunt of the bibliographical task of determining the historical layers within Gannon's scientific memoir.

When Gannon proposed that I should be the one to introduce and comment upon the semiotic connection at appropriate points, I simply refused, as the purpose of the project was to establish the record of his own perceptions of his field. If anything were to be said about semiotics and psychology, the Monsignor would have to draft the statement himself.

When the news of cancer in the spine arrived about halfway through the course, we both had to wonder if the task would see completion. Gannon proposed that we bring in someone with a Ph.D. in psychology as a guest-speaker in the course to introduce to the class the connection of semiotics with psychology, and we invited Dr. Gary Shank of St. Meinrad College for the purpose. Professor Shank gave a masterly presentation, attended by some invited faculty auditors, and, enthusiastic over the manuscript which he felt filled a kind of vacuum in the contemporary consciousness of the psychology profession, Shank offered to draft some pages for the final chapter tying in semiotics with psychology via the so-called "cognitive revolution".

This he nicely did (see Shank 1990), in a sparkling display of familiarity with the latest literature (see, for example, note 22, p. 232); but Gannon, on reading Shank's pages, professed discomfort with using sources he had not himself truly studied first-hand, and, while finding the remarks "both useful and stimulating", decided to set his own hand to the task. The result is the now-Chapter 12. "Here", he said with a mischievous twinkle. "Let's see what this might stir up."

As for the work as a whole, I consider it a little masterpiece. I hope it will benefit the discipline of psychology at large by contributing to a *prise de conscience* within the discipline, not merely of the advantage to the learned world adopting in its work a semiotic point of view (with the inevitable consciousness raising that results), but, more specifically, of an awareness of the historicity of the human condition and of the centrality of history to our understanding of any discipline in what is foundational to it, namely, human experience as a public affair of the ages, not reducible merely to our time (still less to our individual understanding) as the measure of all things—least of all in psychology, which pretends at its best to be a science integrative of the person in the experience of hopes as well as needs, a future as well as a present, and a past which harbingers both.

The sketch of psychology's history which Gannon provides is a synoptic one, yet one clearly drawn from the perspective of an American psychologist whose interests encompass the whole discipline, both in its European provenance and in its philosophical overtones and past. As regards the whole discipline, he is clearly more sympathetic to the clinical and counseling extensions or amplifications of psychology than narrow academicians will find comfortable. As regards the philosophical past, he outlines it in the main as it has actually influenced scientific psychology heretofore, not as it might have or should have influenced it from a more informed point of view. Thus the contributions of the later Latin age, the so-called Renaissance period, are not to be found here. Even so, in Gannon's grasp of semiotic doctrine stemming from Poinsot, he well suggests a point in the late Latin development from which later researchers in the history and background of psychology will no doubt uncover much to report, just as has begun to happen in philosophy itself, where too, for good or ill, the present changes the past.

The weakness of the memoir in this regard is also its strength—"il a les defauts des ses qualités"! We see here a rich picture of what has been, but, at the same time, a sketch of something more, of what may well become: a future which will be illuminative of a fuller past as that future present will be. To that richer time, the present work provides a footpath.

Born on April 2, near midnight of the 1st, 1904, in Grand Junction, Iowa, Timothy Gannon died on the morning of January 26, 1991, near noon. Of this book only some proofreading remained to be done. Now there is only to share its results with all of our colleagues near and far who have an interest in the human being as subject matter for understanding and research. And as for the friends of Timothy Gannon, both those who have met him and those who will meet him only through his published work (a bronze plaque, as it were, writ large), I pass on to them the paraphrase he suggested to me of Christopher Wrenn's plaque in St. Paul's Cathedral in London: *Si monumentum queris, circumspice hoc librum.*

MONSIGNOR
TIMOTHY J. GANNON
PSYCHOLOGY LABS

In honor of Msgr.
Timothy Gannon, Professor Emeritus,
who has distinguished himself
for 60 years at Loras College
as professor, psychologist,
author and priest.
Given this sesquicentennial year
of 1989–1990.

Twenty by twenty-four inch bronze plaque erected in Gannon's honor at Loras College in a ceremony Wednesday, September 5, 1991. The plaque is placed in Hennessey Hall, which houses the psychology department, outside the laboratories. Photograph by Michelle Mihalakis.

REFERENCES

ADORNO, Theodor W., Else FRENKEL-BRUNSWIK, Daniel J. LEVINSON, and R. Nevitt SANFORD.
    1950.   *The Authoritarian Personality* (New York: Harper & Bros.).
ALEKSANDER, I.
    1984.   *Designing Intelligent Systems* (New York: UNIPUB).
ALLEN, R. E.
    1984.   *The Dialogues of Plato* (New Haven, CT: Yale), Vol. 1.
ALLPORT, Floyd Henry.
    1924.   *Social Psychology* (Boston: Houghton Mifflin).
ALLPORT, Gordon W.
    1937.   *Personality: a psychological interpretation* (New York: Henry Holt and Company).
    1940.   "The Psychologist's Frame of Reference", *Psychological Bulletin* 37.1 (January), 1-28.
    1942.   *The Use of Personal Documents in Psychological Science* (New York: Social Science Research Council).
    1954.   *The Nature of Prejudice* (Garden City, NY: Doubleday).

265

1960. *Personality and Social Encounter*, selected essays (Boston: Bacon Press).

1967. "Gordon W. Allport", in Boring and Lindzey 1967: 1-25.

1967a. "The Historical Background of Social Psychology", delivered by Allport before his death for publication in the 2nd edition of Lindzey and Aronson 1985, and "lightly abridged by Gardner Lindzey" for inclusion in the 3rd ed. of Lindzey and Aronson 1985: 1-46 cited in this work.

ALLPORT, Gordon W., and P. E. VERNON.

1931. *A Study of Values: A Scale for Measuring the Dominant Interests in Personality* (Boston: Houghton Mifflin; a 3rd ed. with G. LINDZEY appeared from the same publisher in 1959).

ANASTASI, Anne.

1937. *Differential Psychology. Individual and Group Differences in Behavior* (New York: MacMillan). 3rd rev. ed. 1958.

ANSELM OF CANTERBURY.

i.1070-1078. *Proslogion*, translated by M.J. Charlesworth, in *Philosophy yin the Middle Ages. The Christian, Islamic, and Jewish Translations*, edited by Arthur Hyman and James Walsh (Indianapolis: Hackett, 1973), 149-151.

ANSHEN, Ruth Nanda.

1957. *Language: An Enquiry into Its Meaning and Function* (New York: Harper & Row).

AQUINAS, St. Thomas.

c.1266-1273. *Summa theologiae*, ed. P. Carmello cum textu ex recensione leonina (Turin: Marietti, 1952).

c.1266. *Commentarium in librum Aristotelis de Sensu et Sensato*, in the Parma ed. of the *Opera Omnia*, Vol. XX: 245ff.

c.1266a. *Commentarium in librum Aristotelis de Memoria et Reminiscentia*, in the Parma ed. of the *Opera Omnia*, Vol. XX: 197ff.

    Note: two other commentaries, on Aristotle c.330 and c.330a (*In librum de Somno et Vigilia* and *In librum de Somniis*), formerly regarded as authentic but now considered spurious, can be found in the Parma ed. vol. XX, 215 and 229.

c.1268. *In Octo Libros Physicorum Aristotelis Expositio*, ed. P. M. Maggiolo (Rome: Marietti, 1954).

c.1369. *In Decem Libros Ethicorum Aristotelis ad Nicomachum Expositio*, ed. Raymundus Spiazzi (3rd ed.; Turin: Marietti, 1949).

c.1269-1273. *Aristotle's De Anima in Version of William of Moerbeke and the Com-*

mentary of St. Thomas Aquinas, trans. Foster and Silvester Humphries (New Haven: Yale, 1941).

ARDIGÒ, Roberto.

1870. *La psychologia come scienza positiva*, reprinted in Ardigò's *Opere filosofiche*, 11 vols. (1882-1912: vol. I, Mantua; vols. II-XI, Padua; vol. 11, 2nd ed., Padua 1918).

ARISTOTLE.

Note: our citations here are from the 12-volume Oxford edition prepared under W. D. Ross Ed. 1928-1952 (q.v.); for the convenience of the reader, after the abbreviation RM, we also give the pages where applicable to the more readily available one-volume edition of *The Basic Works of Aristotle* prepared by Richard McKeon using the Oxford translations (New York: Basic Books, 1941). Chronology for the works is based on Gauthier 1970, as follows:

c.360-330BC. *Organon*, Oxford Vol. I (RM 1-212).

c.360.   *Categories* (trans. E. M. Edghill; RM 1-37 complete).

c.353a.   *Topics* (trans. W. A. Pickard-Cambridge; RM 187-206 incomplete).

c.353b.   *Refuting Sophisms* (trans. Pickard-Cambridge; RM 207-212 incomplete).

c.348-7a. *Prior Analytics* (trans. Jenkinson; RM 62-107 incomplete).

c.348-7b. *Posterior Analytics* (trans. G. R. C. Mure; RM 108-186 complete).

c.330   *On Interpretation* (trans. Edghill; RM 38-61 complete).
         It should be noted that, in some ways more consistent than the Latin development of Aristotle's notion of Logic as the instrument common to all thought, it was the custom in the Arabic tradition of Aristotelian commentary to include the *Rhetoric* (composed c.335-4) and the *Poetics* (c.335-4) as part of the *Organon* itself, corresponding, as it were, to the logic involved in practical knowledge.

c.335-4BC. *Nicomachean Ethics*, Oxford Vol. IX 1094a1-1181b25 (trans. W. D. Ross; RM 927-1112 complete).

c.330BC. *On the Soul*, Oxford Vol. III 402a1-435b26 (trans. J. A. Smith; RM 533-603 complete).

c.330aBC. *On Sense and the Sensible*, Oxford Vol. III 436a1-449a33 (trans. J. I. Beare).

c.330bBC. *On Memory and Reminiscence*, Oxford Vol. III 436a1-453b11 (trans. J. I. Beare; RM 607-617 complete).

c.330, c.343-2BC. *On Sleep and Sleeplessness*, Oxford Vol. III 453b12-458a33 (trans. J. I. Beare).

c.330a, 343-2BC. *On Dreams*, Oxford Vol. III 458b1-462b12 (trans. J. I. Beare; RM 618-625 complete).

c.330, 343-2bBC. *On the Interpretation of Dreams*, Oxford Vol. III 462b12-467b8 (trans. J. I. Beare; RM 626-630 complete).

ARNOLD, Magda B.
    1960. *Emotion and Personality* (New York: Columbia University Press), 2 vols.

ARNOLD, Magda B., Editor.
    1970. *Feelings and Emotions: The Loyola Symposium* (New York: Academic Press).

ARNOLD, W. R., and BOWIE, J. S.
    1986. *Artificial Intelligence: A Personal Commonsense Journey* (Englewood Cliffs, NJ: Prentice-Hall).

ASCH, Solomon E.
    1956. *Studies of Independence and Conformity* (Washington, DC: American Psychological Association, psychological monographs v. 70, no. 9).

AUGUSTINE of Hippo.
    399. *Confessions*, with an English translation by William Watts, 1631 (New York: Macmillan, 1919).

BACON, Francis.
    1623. *De Dignitate et Augmentis Scientiarum*, edited by William Rawley (Paris: Typis Petri Mettayer, c.1624).
    1624. *New Atlantis*, ed. A. B. Gough (Oxford, 1915).

BALDWIN, Mark and James CATTELL.
    1894. *The Psychological Review* vol. 1 (Washington: American Psychological Association).

BANDURA, A. L., and R. H. WALTERS.
    1963. *Social Learning and Personality Development* (New York: Holt, Rinehart & Winston).

BEACH, Frank A., Donald O. HEBB, Clifford T. MORGAN, and Henry W. NISSEN.
    1960. *The Neuropsychology of Lashley. Selected Papers of K. S. Lashley* (New York: McGraw-Hill).

BECHTEL, W.
    1988. "Connectionism and Rules Representation Systems: Are They Compatible?", *Philosophical Psychology* 1, 5-16.

BECHTEREW, W. von (=Bekhterev, Vladimir Mikhailovich).
    1907-1910. *Obiektivnaia psikhologiia*, authorized trans. into German as *Objektive Psychologie oder Psychoreflexologie die Lehren von den Assoziati-*

onsreflexeny (Leipzig und Berlin: B. G. Teubner, 1913); *La Psychologie objective*, trans. from the Russian by Nicolas Klstyleff (Paris: Alcan, 1913).

BEERS, Clifford W.

1908.   *A Mind That Found Itself; an autobiography* (New York: Longmans, Green and Company).

BÉKÉSY, George von.

1947.   "The Variation of Phase along the Basilar Membrane with Sinusoidal Vibration", *Journal of the Acoustical Society of America* 19, 452-460.

BEKKER, Immanual, Editor.

1831-1870. *Aristotelis Opera* (Berlin: G. Reimer), 5 vols.

BELL, Charles.

1811.   *Idea of a New Anatomy of the Brain* (London), circulated in a private printing of 100 copies, of which but three are known to be extant: see Olmsted 1945: 104.

BINET, Alfred, and Théodor SIMON.

1905.   "Sur la nécessité d'établir un diagnostic scientific des états inférieurs de l'intelligence", *L'Année Psychologique* XI (1905), 163-190.

1911.   *La Mesure du développement de l'intelligence chez le jeunes enfants* (Paris: F. Alcan), authorized trans., with preface and an appendix containing an arrangement of the tests in age and diagnostic groups for convenience in conducting examinations, Clara Harrison Town, *A Method of Measuring the Development of the Intelligence of Young Children* (Lincoln, IL: The Courier Co.). See also the limited facsimile ed. with marginal notes by Lewis M. Terman and a new Preface by Lloyd M. Dunn titled *The Development of Intelligence in Children* (Nashville, TN: Williams Printing Co., 1980).

BLUMENTHAL, Arthur L.

1975.   "A Reappraisal of Wilhelm Wundt", *American Psychologist* 30, 1081-1088.

BORING, Edwin G.

1929.   *A History of Experimental Psychology* (1st ed.; New York: D. Appleton-Century Co., Inc.).

1950.   *A History of Experimental Psychology* (2nd ed., revised; New York: Appleton-Century-Crofts, Inc.).

BORING, Edwin G., and Gardner LINDZEY, Editors.
1967.   Volume V of *A History of Psychology in Autobiography* (New York: Appleton-Century-Crofts).
BORING, Edwin G., Heinz WERNER, Herbert S. LANGFELD, and Robert M. YERKES, Editors.
1952.   *A History of Psychology in Autobiography* (Worcester, MA: Clark University Press).
BRENTANO, Franz.
1874.   *Psychologie vom Empirischen Standpunkt*, translated by Linda McAlister, A. Rancurello, and D. B. Terrell as *Psychology from an Empirical Standpoint* (New York: Humanities Press, 1973).
BROCA, Paul.
1861.   "Perti de Parole, Remollissement Chronique et Destruction Partielle du Lobe Anterieur Gauche du Cerveau", *Bulletin de la Societé Anthropologique*, Paris, 2, 235-238.
CATTELL, James.
1906.   *American Men of Science* (New York: Science Press).
1915.   *The Scientific Monthly* (Washington: American Association for the Advancement of Science).
CHAPLIN, J. P.
1985.   *Dictionary of Psychology* (2nd rev. ed.; New York: Laurel/Dell Publishing Co.).
CHOMSKY, Noam.
1959.   Review of *Verbal Behavior* (Skinner 1957) in *Language* 35, 26-58.
CHURCHLAND, P. M.
1981.   "Eliminative Materialism and the Propositional Attitudes", *The Journal of Philosophy* LXXVIII.2, 67-90.
CLARK, Kenneth E.
1957.   *America's Psychologists. A Survey of a Growing Profession* (Washington, DC: American Psychological Association, Inc.).
COLE, Michael, Vera JOHN-STEINER, Sylvia SCRIBNER, and Ellen SOUBERMAN, Editors.
1978.   *L. S. Vygotsky. Mind in Society. The Development of Higher Psychological Processes* (Cambridge, MA: Harvard). A collection of separate essays put together with "significant liberties", i.e., "not a literal translation of Vygotsky but rather our edited translation of Vygotsky"—Editors' Preface, p. x.
CURRAN, Charles A.
1969.   *Religious Values in Counseling and Psychotherapy* (New York: Sheed & Ward).

DARWIN, Charles.
    1859.   *On the origin of the species by means of natural selection, or, The preservation of favored races in the struggle for life* (London: J. Murray).

DEELY, John.
    1971.   "Animal Intelligence and Concept-Formation", *The Thomist* XXXV.1 (January), 43-93.
    1986.   "The Coalescence of Semiotic Consciousness", in Deely, Williams and Kruse 1986: 5-34.
    1987.   "A Maxim for Semiotics", Editor's Preface to the Proceedings of the Twelfth Annual Meeting of the Semiotic Society of America, *Semiotics 1987* (Lanham, MD: University Press of America, 1988), iii-vi.
    1990.   *Basics of Semiotics* (Bloomington, IN: Indiana University Press).

DEELY, John, Terry PREWITT, and Karen HAWORTH.
    1990.   "On the SSA Style Sheet", *Semiotic Scene* n.s. 2.2 (Fall), 9.

DEELY, John, Brooke WILLIAMS, and Felicia KRUSE, Editors.
    1986.   *Frontiers in Semiotics* (Bloomington, IN: Indiana University Press).

DENNETT, D.
    1978.   *Brainstorms* (Cambridge, MA: MIT Press).

DESCARTES, René.
    1637.   *Discours de la Methode Pour Bien Conduire sa Raison & Chercher la Verité dans les Sciences*, trans. Laurence J. Lafleur in *Discourse in Method* (Indianapolis: The Bobbs-Merrill Company Inc., 1964).
    1641.   *Meditationes de Prima Philosophia*, trans. Laurence J. Lafleur as *Meditations on First Philosophy* (Indianapolis: The Bobbs-Merrill Company Inc., 1964).

DESMET, Firmin, Editor.
    1927.   *Le Cardinal Mercier (1851-1926)* (Bruxelles: Éditions Louis Desmet-Verteneuil).

DEWEY, John.
    1910.   *How We Think: A Restatement of the Relation of Reflective Thinking to the Educative Process* (Boston: D.C. Heath and Company).

DREVER, James.
    1952.   *Dictionary of Psychology* (London: Penguin).
    1968.   "Some Early Associationists", Chapter 2 of *Historical Roots of Contemporary Psychology*, ed. Benjamin B. Wolman (New York: Harper & Row, 1968), 11-28.

DREYFUS, H.
    1979.   *What Computers Can't Do: A Critique of Artificial Reason* (2nd ed.; New York: Harper and Row).

DUBOIS-REYMOND, Emil H.
   1884.   *Untersuchungen über Thierische Electricität*, 2 vols. in 3 (Berlin: G. Reimer).
DUNCKER, Karl.
   1935.   *Zur Psychologie des produktiven Denkens*, trans. L. S. Lees as "On Problem-Solving" in *Psychological Monographs* 58 (Whole no. 270, 1945).
DURKHEIM, Emile David.
   1897.   *Suicide, étude de sociologie* (Paris: Felix Alcan) trans. from French by John A. Spaulding and George Simpson as *Suicide, a Study in Sociology*, with introduction by George Simpson (Glencoe, IL: Free Press, 1951).
EBBINGHAUS, Hermann.
   1885.   *Über das Gedächtniss*, translated by Henry A. Ruger and Clara E. Bussenius as *Memory: A Contribution to Experimental Psychology* (New York: Dover Publications, 1964).
ERIKSON, Erik.
   1963.   *Childhood and Society* (2nd ed.; New York: Norton).
FECHNER, Gustav.
   1860.   *Elemente der Psychophysik*, translated by Helmut E. Adler as *Elements of Psychophysics* (New York: Holt, Rinehart, and Winston, Inc., 1966).
FELDMAN, J. A.
   1985.   "Connectionist Models and Their Applications: An Introduction", *Cognitive Science* 9, 1-2.
FELDMAN, S.
   1932.   "Wundt's Psychology", *American Journal of Psychology* XLIV.4, 615-629, as reprinted in Rieber 1980: 207-227, to which reprint page reference is made in this work.
FODOR, J. A.
   1981.   *Representations: Philosophical Essays on the Foundations of Cognitive Science* (Cambridge, MA: MIT Press).
FODOR, J. A., T. G. BEVER, and M. F. GARRETT.
   1975.   *The Psychology of Language* (New York: McGraw-Hill).
FORSYTH, R. and NAYLOR, C.
   1986.   *The Hitch-Hiker's Guide to Artificial Intelligence* (New York: Chapman and Hall).
FREUD, Sigmund and Joseph BREUER.
   1895.   *Studien über Hysterie*, authorized trans. A. A. Brill as *Studies in Hysteria*, with an introduction by A.A. Brill (New York and

Washington: Nervous and Mental Disease Publishing Company, 1936).

FRISCH, von Karl.
1950. *Bees, their Vision, Chemical Senses, and Language* (Ithaca, NY: Cornell).

FRITSCH, G. and E. HITZIG.
1870. "Über die Elektrische Erregbarkeit des Grosshirns", *Archiv fur Anatomie, Physiologie, und Wissenschaftliche Medizin*, 37, 200-332.

GALL, Franz Joseph, and J. K. SPURZHEIM.
1810-1819. *Anatomie et physiologie du système nerveux en général, et du cerveau en particulier* (Paris: Schoell), 4 vols.

GALTON, Francis.
1869. *Hereditary genius: an inquiry into its laws and consequences* (London: Macmillan).

GANNON, Timothy J.
1939. "A Statistical Study of Certain Diagnostic Personality Traits of College Men", *Studies in Psychology and Psychiatry*, IV.4 (January), 1-44.
1954. *Psychology. The Unity of Human Behavior* (New York: Ginn and Company).

GARDNER, Howard.
1985. *The Mind's New Science. A History of the Cognitive Revolution* (New York: Basic Books).

GAUTHIER, René Antoine.
1970. "Introduction" to *L'Ethique a Nicomaque, traduction et commentaire*, R. A. Gauthier et Jean Yves Jolif (12th ed., avec une introduction nouvelle; Paris: Beatrice-Nauwelaerts), Tome I, première partie.

GAZZANIGA, M. S.
1970. *The Bisected Brain* (Englewood Cliffs, NJ: Prentice-Hall).

GAZZANIGA, M. S., J. E. BOGEN, and R. W. SPERRY.
1962. "Some Functional Effects of Sectioning the Cerebral Commissures in Man", *Proceedings of the National Academy of Sciences* 48, 1765-1769.

GEMELLI, Agostino.
1952. "Agostino Gemelli" in Boring et al. 1952: 97-121.

GESCHWIND, N.
1984. "The Biology of Cerebral Dominance: Implications for Cognition", *Cognition* 17, 193-208.

GIBSON, James J.
1950. *The Perception of the Visual World* (Boston: Houghton-Mifflin).

1966. *The Senses considered as Perceptual Systems* (Boston: Houghton-Mifflin).

GRANIT, Ragnor.

1977. *The Purposive Brain* (Cambridge, MA: The M.I.T. Press).

GRUENDER, Hubert.

1911. *Free Will; The Greatest of the Seven World-Riddles* (St. Louis, MO: B. Herder).

1920. *An Introductory Course in Experimental Psychology* (Chicago, IL: Loyola University Press).

GUILFORD, J. P.

1950. "Creativity", *American Psychologist* 5, 444-454.

1967. *The Nature of Human Intelligence* (New York: McGraw-Hill).

1968. "Intelligence Has Three Facets", *Science* 160.3828 (10 May), 615-620.

HALL, Calvin Springer and Gardner LINDZEY.

1957. *Theories of Personality* (New York: John Wiley and Sons, Inc.).

HALL, G. Stanley.

1887. *American Journal of Psychology* vol. 1 (Urbana: University of Illinois Press).

1891. *Pedagogical Seminary* vol. 1 (Provincetown: Journal Press).

HAMILTON, Edith, and Huntington CAIRNS.

1961. *The Collected Dialogues of Plato Including the Letters* (Princeton, NJ: Princeton University Press, Bollingen Series LXXI).

HAMILTON, Sir William.

1859-1860. *Lectures on Metaphysics and Logic*, ed. H. L. Mansel and John Veitch (Edinburgh), 4 vols.

HARTLEY, David.

c.1757. *Hartley's Theories on the Human Mind, On the Principle of the Association of Ideas*, ed. Joseph Priestley (London: J. Johnson, 1775).

HATHAWAY, Starke, and Jovian MCKINLEY.

1943. *Minnesota Multiphasic Personality Inventory* (Minneapolis: University of Minnesota).

HEBB, Donald Olding.

1949. *The Organization of Behavior: A Neuropsychological Theory* (New York: John Wiley and Sons, Inc.).

HELMHOLTZ, Hermann von.

1866. *Handbuch der Physiologischen Optik, Band II*, translated by J. P. Southall as *Treatise on Physiological Optics, vol. II* (Rochester: Optical Society of America, 1924).

HERBART, Johann Friedrich.
    1824-1825. *Psychologie als Wissenschaft neu gegründet auf Erfahrung, Metaphysik und Mathematik* (Königsberg: A. W. Unzer).
HERKEN, Rolf, Editor.
    1988. *The Universal Turing Machine: A Half-Century Survey* (Oxford, England: Oxford University Press).
HILGARD, Ernest R.
    1987. *Psychology in America. An Historical Survey* (New York: Harcourt Brace Jovanovich).
HILGARD, Ernest R., Editor.
    1978. *American Psychology in Historical Perspective. Addresses of the Presidents of the American Psychological Association, 1892-1977* (Washington: American Psychological Association, Inc.).
HOFSTADTER, D.
    1979. *Gödel, Escher, and Bach: An Eternal Golden Braid* (New York: Basic Books).
HORNEY, Karen.
    1937. *The Neurotic Personality of Our Time* (New York: W. W. Norton and Company, Inc.).
HUBEL, D. H., and T. N. WIESEL.
    1968. "Receptive Fields and Functional Architecture of Monkey Striate Cortex", *Journal of Physiology* 195, 215-243.
HULL, Clark Leonard.
    1943. *Principles of Behavior* (New York: Appleton-Century-Crofts).
    1951. *Essentials of Behavior* (New Haven, CT: published for the Institute of Human Relations by Yale University Press).
    1952. *A Behavior System* (New Haven: Yale).
HUME, David.
    1748. *Philosophical Essays Concerning Human Understanding* (London: Printed for A. Millar, 1748).
    1750. *Philosophical Essays Concerning Human Understanding*, 2nd edition, (London: Printed for A. Millar, 1750).
JAMES, William.
    1890. *Principles of Psychology* (New York: Henry Holt and Company).
    1892. *Psychology: Briefer Course* (New York: Henry Holt and Company).
KENNEDY, Eugene C., Editor.
    1975. *Human Rights and Psychological Research: A Debate on Psychology and Ethics* (New York: Crowell).
KIERKRGAARD, Soren.
    1844. *Bergrebet Angest* (Copenhagen: Bianco Luno Press), trans. from

Danish by Reidar Thomte in collaboration with Alberta B. Anderson as *The Concept of Anxiety* (Princeton: Princeton University Press, 1980).

KIMBLE, Gregory A.
1989.   "Psychology from the Standpoint of a Generalist", *American Psychologist* 44.3 (March), 491-499.

KOCH, Sigmund.
1959.   "Epilogue" to Koch ed. 1959b: 729-802.
1985.   "The Nature and Limits of Psychological Knowledge: Lessons of a Century qua 'Science'", in Koch and Leary 1985: 75-97.

KOCH, Sigmund, Editor.
           Psychology: A Study of a Science, a multi-volume series in two studies.
           STUDY I. CONCEPTUAL AND SYSTEMATIC:
1959.   Volume 1, *Sensory, Perceptual, and Physiological Foundations* (New York: McGraw-Hill).
1959a.   Volume 2, *General Systematic Formulations, Learning, and Special Processes* (New York: McGraw-Hill).
1959b.   Volume 3, *Formulations of the Person and the Social Context* (New York: McGraw-Hill).
           STUDY II. EMPIRICAL SUBSTRUCTURE AND RELATIONS WITH OTHER SCIENCES:
1962.   Volume 4, *Biologically Oriented Fields: Their Place in Psychology and in Biological Science* (New York: McGraw-Hill).
1963.   Volume 5, *The Process Areas, the Person, and Some Applied Fields: Their Place in Psychology and in Science* (New York: McGraw-Hill).
1963a.   Volume 6, *Investigations of Man as Socius: Their Place in Psychology and the Social Sciences* (New York: McGraw-Hill).
           POSTSCRIPT TO THE STUDY
nd.   *Psychology and the Human Agent: A View of Problems in the Enaction of a Science*: projected volume completed in autumn of 1964 but never submitted, revised in manuscript several times since. See discussion in Chapter 10 above.
1985.   "The Nature and Limits of Psychological Knowledge: Lessons of a Century qua 'Science'", in Koch and Leary 1985: 75-97.

KOCH, Sigmund, and David E. LEARY, Editors.
1985.   *A Century of Psychology as Science* (New York: McGraw-Hill).

KOFFKA, Kurt.
1959.   *The Growth of the Mind: An Introduction to Child Psychology*, translated by Robert Morris Ogden (Patterson: Littlefield Adams).

KÖHLER, Wolfgang.
1921. *Intelligenzprüfungen an Menschenaffen* (Springer), trans. from German by Ella Winter as *The Mentality of Apes* (3rd ed., rev.; New York: Vintage Books, 1959).

KRETSCHMER, Ernst.
1921. *Körperbau und Charakter*, trans. W. J. H. Sprott from the 2nd rev. ed. as *Physique and Character: An investigation of the Nature of Constitution and of the Theory of Temperament* (New York: Harcourt, Brace, 1925).

KULPE, Oswald.
1893. *Grundriss der Psychologie*, translated by Edward B. Titchner as *Outlines of Psychology, Based on Results of Experimental Investigation* (New York: Macmillan and Co., 1895).

LANGE, Karl Georg.
1885. *Om sindsbevaegelser; et psyko-fysiologisk studie* (Copenhagen: Lund); authorized trans. from the Danish by Hans Kurella as *Über Gemütsbewegungen: eine psycho-psychologische Studie* (Leipzig: T. Thomas, 1887); in turn, Kurella's German text became the basis for a French trans. by Georges Dumas as *Les Émotions; études psychophysiologique* (Paris: Alcan, 1895), and the English trans. by I. A. Haupt (Baltimore: Williams & Wilkins, 1922).

LASHLEY, Karl S.
1929. *Brain Mechanisms and Intelligence: A Quantitative Study of Injuries to the Brain* (Chicago: The University of Chicago Press).
1951. "The Problem of Serial Order in Behavior", reprinted in Beach et al. 1960: 506-528.

LE BON, Gustave.
1895. *La Psychologie des Foules* (Paris), trans. as *The Crowd: A Study of Popular Mind* (London: T. F. Unwin, 1896; Boston: Houghton Mifflin, 1896).

LENIN, Vladimir I.
1929-1930. *Philosophical Notebooks*, being the title given after 1933 to the writings first published in *Lenin Miscellanier IX and XI*, including the *Notebooks on Philosophy* titled and compiled by Lenin in 1914-1915; from *V.I. Lenin Collected Works*, vol. 38, trans. by Clemens Dutt and ed. by Stewart Smith (Moscow: Foreign Language Publishing House).

LEO XIII, Pope.
1879, August 4. Encyclical letter, *Aeterni Patris* (on the restoration of Christian philosophy), initiating the modern revival of Thomism,

in Pennacchi and Piazzesi eds. 1894: 97-115, q.v.; English trans. in *The Papal Encyclicals 1878-1903*, ed. Claudia Carlen Ihm (Salem, NH: McGrath Publishing Co., 1981), 17-26.

LEWIN, Kurt.

1936. *Principles of Topological Psychology*, trans. Fritz Heider and Grace M. Heider (New York: McGraw-Hill).

LINDZEY, Gardner, and E. Aronson, Editors.

1985. *Handbook of Social Psychology*, 3rd Ed., Vol. 1, *Theory and Method* (New York: Random House).

LOCKE, John.

1690. *An Essay Concerning Humane Understanding* (London: Thomas Bassett).

1700. 4th edition of the *Essay*.

LOMBROSO, Cesare.

1876. *L'Uomo Delinquente in rapporto all'antropologia, alla giurisprudenza ed alle discipline carcerarie* (Rome: Napoleone Editore s.r.l., 1971).

LURIA, Alexander Romanovich.

a.1977. *The Making of a Mind. A Personal Account of Soviet Psychology*, Michael and Sheila Cole, eds. (Cambridge, MA: Harvard University Press, 1979).

MacLEAN, Paul D.

1973. *A Triune Concept of the Brain* (Toronto: University of Toronto Press).

MAGENDIE, François.

1818. *Physiological and Medical Researches into the Causes, Symptoms, and Treatment of Gravel*, trans. by a member of the Royal College of Surgeons (London).

1822. "Experiénces sur les fonctions des racines des nerfs qui naissent de la moelle épinière", *Journal de Physiologie Expérimentale* 2 (June).

MARITAIN, Jacques.

1938. "Signe et Symbole", *Revue Thomiste* XLIV (avril), 299-300; trans. H. L. Binsse as "Sign and Symbol" in *Redeeming the Time* (London: Geoffrey Bless, 1943), text pp. 191-224, Latin notes from Poinsot 1632 and a.1644 on pp. 268-276.

1957. "Language and the Theory of Sign", reprinted from Anshen 1957: 86-101, with full critical apparatus relating text to Maritain 1938 and Poinsot 1632, in Deely, Williams, and Kruse 1986: 51-62, to which reprint reference is made in the present work.

1958.   "Foreword" to the 1959 English edition of *The Degrees of Knowledge*, trans. Gerald B. Phelan (New York: Charles Scribner's Sons, 1959), xvii-xix.

MASLOW, Abraham H.

1954.   *Motivation and Personality* (New York: Harper).

MAY, Rollo.

1950, 1977.   *The Meaning of Anxiety* (New York: Ronald Press; rev. ed.; New York: Norton, 1977).

MAY, Rollo, Editor.

1961.   *Existential Psychology* (New York: Random House).

McCARTHY, Raphael C.

1934.   *Training the Adolescent* (New York: Bruce Publishing Co.).

1937.   *Safeguarding Mental Health* (New York: Bruce Publishing Co.).

McDOUGALL, William.

1908.   *An Introduction to Social Psychology* (London: Methuen & Co.).

1924.   "Fundamentals of Psychology", *Psyche* 5, 13-32, the substance of remarks made before the Psychological Club of Washington, D.C., on 5 February 1924 in reply to Dr. J. B. Watson's exposition of behaviorism; subsequently published in Watson and McDougall 1929: 40-85, with an added "Postscript" dated September 1927 pp. 86-96.

McKEON, Richard M., Editor.

1941.   *The Basic Works of Aristotle* (New York: Basic Books, 1941).

MERCIER, Désiré (Cardinal).

1894.   *Psychologie* (2nd ed.; Louvain: Uystpruyst-Dieudonne), 2 vols.

1897.   *Les Origines de la psychologie contemporaine* (Louvain: Institut Supérieur de Philosophie), trans. W. B. Mitchell as *Origins of Contemporary Psychology* (New York: P. J. Kennedy and Sons, 1918).

1900, May 9.   "La Psychologie expérimentale et la Philosophie spiritualiste", *Bulletin de la Classe des Lettres et des Sciences Morales et Politiques et de la Classe des Beaux-Arts*, 421-450, crudely translated by Edmund J. Wirth as *The Relation of Experimental Psychology to Philosophy*, (New York: Benziger Brothers).

MILES, L.

1835.   *Casket of Knowledge: Phrenology*, (Philadelphia: Carey, Lea and Blanchard, 1935).

MILLER, George A.

1951.   *Language and Communication* (New York: McGraw-Hill Book Company, Inc.).

1956.   "The Magical Number Seven Plus or Minus Two: Some Limits on our Capacity for Processing Information", *Psychological Review* 63, 81-97.

MILLER, Neal E., and John DOLLARD.
1941.   *Social Learning and Imitation* (New Haven, CT: Yale University Press).

MISCHEL, Theodor.
1970.   "Wundt and the Conceptual Foundations of Psychology", *Philosophy and Phenomenological Research* 31, 1-26.

MISIAK, Henryk, and Virginia M. STAUDT.
1954.   *Catholics in Psychology. A Historical Survey* (New York: McGraw-Hill Book Company).

MISIAK, Henryk, and Virginia Staudt SEXTON.
1966.   *History of Psychology. An Overview* (New York: Grune & Stratton).

MOORE, Thomas Verner.
1924.   *Dynamic Psychology. An Introduction to Modern Psychological Theory and Practice* (Philadelphia, PA: J. P. Lippincott Co.).
1939.   *Cognitive Psychology* (New York: J. B. Lippincott Co.).
1943.   *The Nature and Treatment of Mental Disorders* (New York: Grune & Stratton).
1956.   *The Life of Man with God* (New York: Harcourt, Brace).

MORGAN, Conwy Lloyd.
1894.   *Introduction to Comparative Psychology* (London: W. Scott; New York: Scribner).

MORGAN, C. D., and H. A. MURRAY.
1935.   "A Method for Investigating Fantasies: The Thematic Apperception Test", *Archives of Neurology and Psychiatry* 34, 289-306.

MÜLLER, Johannes. [1801-1858]
1833.   *Handbuch der Physiologie des Menschen* (Coblenz, Germany: Holscher).

MÜNSTERBERG, Hugo.
1913.   *Psychology and Industrial Efficiency* (Boston: Houghton Mifflin Company).

MURCHISON, Carl, Editor.
1924.   *Journal of Genetic Psychology*, vol. 1 (Provincetown: Journal Press).
1926.   *Psychologies of 1925* (Worcester, MA: Clark University Press).
1930.   *A History of Psychology in Autobiography*, Volume I (Worcester, MA: Clark University Press; reprinted New York: Russell & Russell, 1961).
1930a.   *Psychologies of 1930* (Worcester: Clark University Press).

MURPHY, Gardner, and Lois B. MURPHY.
1931.   *Experimental Social Psychology* (New York: Harper). A rev. ed. was issued in 1937 with T. M. NEWCOMB as a third author.
MURRAY, Henry A., Editor.
1938.   *Explorations in Personality: A Clinical and Experimental Study of Fifty Men of College Age by Workers at the Harvard Psychological Clinic* (New York: Oxford University Press).
NEISSER, Ulric.
1976.   *Cognition and Reality* (San Francisco: Freeman Press).
NEWCOMB, Theodore Mead.
1943.   *Personality and Social Change; attitude and social formation in a student community* (New York: Dryden Press).
NEWELL, Allen.
1985.   "Duncker on Thinking: An Inquiry into Progress in Cognition", in Koch and Leary 1985: 392-419.
NEWELL, Allen and Herbert A. SIMON.
1972.   *Human Problem-Solving* (Englewood Cliffs, NJ: Prentice-Hall, Inc.).
OCKHAM, William of.
i.1317-1328. *Summa Totius Guielmi Occham Anglici Logicorum Argutissima Nuper Correcta*, partial edition by Philotheus Boehner entitled *Summa Logicae* (St. Bonaventure, NY: Franciscan Institute Publications, 1954).
OLMSTED, J. M. D.
1945.   *François Magendie* (New York: Schuman's; reprinted by Arno Press, 1981).
PAVLOV, Ivan Petrovich.
1904.   "Sur la sécrétion psychique des glandes salivaires (phénomènes nerveux complexes dans le travail de glandes salivaires)", *Archives Internationales de Physiologie* 1, 119-135.
1927.   *Lektsii o rabote bolishikh pulusharifi golovnogo*, trans. G. V. Anrep as *Conditioned Reflexes; An Investigation of the Physiological Activity of the Cerebral Cortex* (London: Oxford University Press).
1932.   "The Reply of a Physiologist to Psychologists", *Psychological Review* 39, 92-127.
PENNACCHI, Josephus, and PIAZZESI, Victorius, Editors.
1894.   *Acta Sanctae Sedis* (Rome: S. Congr. de Prop. Fide), Vol. XII.
PLATO. (Chronology is based on Allen 1984: 15, q.v.)
c.399BC.   *Laches*, trans. B. Jowett in Hamilton and Cairns 1961: 123-144.
c.388-387BC. *Meno*, trans. W. K. C. Guthrie in Hamilton and Cairns 1961: 353-384.

POINSOT, John.
  1632.   *Tractatus de Signis. The Semiotic of John Poinsot*, trans. and ed. John Deely in consultation with Ralph Austin Powell (1st ed.; Berkeley: University of California Press, 1985).
  a.1644. *Cursus Theologicus Tomus Octavus* (*De Sacramentis*), ed. P. Combesis (Paris: 1667, posthumous); volume IX of the Ludovicus Vivès ed. (Paris 1885).
POLICY AND PLANNING BOARD OF THE AMERICAN PSYCHOLOGICAL ASSOCIATION.
  1952.   "Annual Report", *The American Psychologist 7*, 563-568.
PORPHYRY.
  c.271.   *Porphyrii Isagoge et in Aristotelis Categorias Commentarium* (Greek text), ed. A. Busse (Berlin, 1887). English trans. by Edward W. Warren, *Porphyry the Phoenician: Isagoge* (Toronto: Pontifical Institute of Mediaeval Studies, 1975).
PRIBRAM, K. H.
  1971.   *Languages of the Brain* (Englewood Cliffs, NJ: Prentice-Hall).
REID, Thomas.
  c.1803. *Essays on the Power of the Human Mind*, edited by Dugald Stewart in *The Account of the Life and Writings of Thomas Reid* (Edinburgh: Printed Bell and Bradfute, 1803).
RIEBER, R. W., Editor.
  1980.   *Wilhelm Wundt and the Making of a Scientific Psychology* (New York: Plenum Press).
ROBINSON, Anthony Lewin.
  1943.   *William McDougall, M.B., D.Sc., F.R.S.: A Bibliography together with a Brief Outline of His Life* (Durham, NC: Duke University Press).
ROBINSON, Daniel N.
  1989.   *Aristotle's Psychology* (New York: Columbia University Press).
ROE, Anne, and George Gaylord SIMPSON, Editors.
  1958.   *Behavior and Evolution* (New Haven, CT: Yale University Press).
ROGERS, Carl R.
  1942.   *Counseling and Psychotherapy: Newer Concepts in Practice of Freud* (Boston: Houghton Mifflin Company).
  1969.   *Freedom to Learn: a view of education* (Columbus, OH: C. E. Merrill).
RORSCHACH, Hermann.
  1921/1942. *Psychodiagnostik: Methodik und Ergebnisse eines wahrnehmungsdiag*

nostischen Experiments (Bern and Leipzig: Ernst Bircher). English trans. P. Lemkan and B. Kronebert Huber as *Psychodiagnostic Test Based on Perception* (2nd ed.; New York: Grune & Stratton, 1942).

ROSCH, E., and MERVIS, C. B.
1975.   "Family Resemblances: Studies in the Internal Structure of Categories", *Cognitive Psychology* 7, 573-605.

ROSS, E. A.
1908.   *Social Psychology: An Outline and Source Book* (New York: Macmillan).

ROSS, W. D.
1928-1952. *The Works of Aristotle Translated into English*, in XII vols. (Oxford: The Clarendon Press).

RUMELHART, D. E., and ZIPSER, D.
1985.   "Feature Discovery by Competitive Learning", *Cognitive Science* 9, 75-112.

SCHANK, R. C., and ABELSON, R. P.
1977.   *Scripts, Plans, Goals and Understandings: An Inquiry into Human Knowledge Structures* (Hillsdale, NJ: Lawrence Erlbaum Associates).

SCOTT, Walter Dill.
1903.   *The Theory of Advertising: A Simple Exposition of the Principles of Psychology in their Relation to Successful Advertising* (Boston: Small, Maynard & Company).

SEARLE, J.
1984.   *Minds, Brains, and Science* (Cambridge, MA: Harvard University Press).

SEBEOK, Thomas A.
1963.   "The Notion of Zoosemiotics", excerpted under an editorially assigned title from the review article, "Communication among social bees; porpoises and sonar; man and dolphin", *Language* 39, 448-466, and reprinted in Deely, Williams, and Kruse 1986: 74-75.

1979.   "Neglected Figures in the History of Semiotic Inquiry: Jakob von Uexküll", in Sebeok 1989: 263-267.

1989.   *The Sign & Its Masters* (2nd ed.; = Sources in Semiotics VIII; Lanham, MD: University Press of America).

SECHENOV, Ivan Mikhailovich.
1863.   "Reflexes of the Brain", English trans. of original text reprinted in *Psikhologicheskie etiudy* (St. Petersburg: F. S. Sushchinski, 1873), 1-102.

The only copy of *Psikhologicheskie etiudy* extant in the United States is in the Goddard Library of Clark University; two translations of the "Reflexes of the Brain" section are extant, an older one in Subkov Ed. 1935: 263-336, and a more recent one made from a Russian text ed. by K. Koshtoyants in book form, *Reflexes of the Brain*, trans. S. Belsky with editing by G. Gibbons and notes by S. Gellerstein (Cambridge, MA: The M.I.T. Press, 1965).

1873.   "Who Must Investigate the Problems of Psychology and How?", English trans. of original text in *Psikhologicheskie etiudy* (see immediately preceding entry), trans. into English in Subkov Ed. 1935: 337-391.

This was the only English version of this text we were able to locate.

SEMIOTIC SOCIETY OF AMERICA STYLE SHEET.

1986.   In *The American Journal of Semiotics* 4.3-4, 193-215; and in *Semiotics 1984*, 715-739.

SHAKOW, David.

1964.   *The Influence of Freud on American Psychology* (New York: International Universities Press).

1969.   *Clinical Psychology as a Science and Profession. A Forty-Year Odyssey* (Chicago: Aldine).

SHANK, Gary.

1990.   Memorandum on "Cognitive Psychology" submitted to the author in May of 1990 as a summary and expansion of class discussion in the Spring 1990 Loras College All-College Honors course after the guest-lecture by Dr. Shank (April 5) entitled "Psychology: Cognitive Skirmish or Semiotic Revolution?" This memorandum was subsequently incorporated into the paper, "Psychology and the Semiotic Horizon", forthcoming in *Semiotics 1990*, ed. Karen Haworth, John Deely, and Terry Prewitt (Lanham, MD: University Press of America, 1991), but page numbers are not available in time for use here.

SHELDON, W. H., S. S. STEVENS, and W. B. TUCKER.

1940.   *The Varieties of Human Physique; An Introduction to Constitutional Psychology* (New York: Harper & Bros.).

1942.   *The Varieties of Temperament: A Psychology of Constitutional Differences* (New York: Harper & Bros.).

SHERRINGTON, Sir Charles E.

1906.   *The Integrative Action of the Nervous System* (New York: Charles Scribner's Sons). This work was reprinted with a new Foreword by the author and a Bibliography of his writings, New Haven, CT: Yale University Press, 1947.

SHNEIDMAN, Edwin S., Editor.
1981.   *Endeavors in Psychology: Selections of the personology of Henry A. Murray* (New York: Harper Row).

SHOBEN, E. L., Jr.
1956.   "Counseling", *Annual Review of Psychology* 7, 147-172.

SIMON, H. A., and A. NEWELL.
1958.   "Simulation of Cognitive Processes: A Report on the Summer Research Training Institute, 1958", Social Science Research Council *Items* 12, 37-40.

SKINNER, B.F.
1938.   *The Behavior of Organisms* (New York: Appleton-Century-Crofts).
1957.   *Verbal Behavior* (Englewood Cliffs, NJ: Prentice-Hall, Inc.).

SLIFE, Brent D., Editor.
1990.   "Introduction and Overview of the Special Issue on Aristotle", *Theoretical and Philosophical Psychology* 10.1 (Spring 1990), 3-6.

SOTO, Dominic.
1529, 1554. *Summulae* (1st ed. Burgos; 3rd rev. ed. Salamanca).

SPEARMAN, Charles.
1904.   "General Intelligence" objectively determined and measured by C. Spearman, reprinted from the *American Journal of Psychology* XV (2), 201-292.

SPERRY, R. W.
1982.   "Some Effects of Disconnecting the Cerebral Hemispheres", *Science* 217, 1223-1226.

SPRANGER, Eduard.
1913.   *Lebensformen*, trans. from the 5th ed. by P. J. W. Pigors as *Types of Men: The Psychology and Ethics of Personality* (Halle: Niemeyer, 1928).

STERN, William.
1906.   *Person und Sache: System der philosophischen Weltanschauung*, vols.
1917.   "Die Psychologie und der Personalismus", *Zeitschrift für Psychologie*, 78.
1927.   "William Stern", translated for the Clark University Press by Mrs. Susanne Langer from *Philosophie der Gegenwart in Selbstdarstellungen*, Volume 6 (1927), ed. Raymund Schmidt, and published in Murchison 1930: 335-388.
1935.   *Allgemeine Psychologie auf personalistischen Grundlage* (Den Haag: Martinus Nijhoff), trans. Howard Davis Spoerl as *General*

Psychology From the Personalistic Standpoint (New York, Macmillan, 1938).

STILLINGS, N. A., M. H. FEINSTEIN, J. L. GARFIELD, E. L. RISSELAND, D. A. ROSENBAUM, S. E. WEISLER, L. BAKER-WARD.

1987. *Cognitive Science: An Introduction* (Cambridge, MA: MIT Press).

STRECKER, Edward A., Kenneth E. APPEL, and John W. APPEL.

1958. *Discovering Ourselves* (3rd ed.; New York: Macmillan Company). The original ed. of 1931 was prepared by the first two of these three authors.

SUBKOV, A., Editor.

1935. *I. Sechenov Selected Works Abridged* (Moscow-Leningrad: State Publishing House for Biological and Medical Literature, 1935; Harvard University Library Photographic Department Film No. 61-2004; hardcopy available at the University of Missouri Library, Columbia).

SUTICH, Anthony J. and Miles A. VICH.

1969. "Introduction" to Sutich and Vich Eds. 1969: 1-18.

SUTICH, Anthony J. and Miles A. VICH, Editors.

1969. *Readings in Humanistic Psychology* (New York: The Free Press).

SYMONDS, J.P., Editor.

1937. *Journal of Consulting Psychology*, Vol. 1 (Lancaster: American Psychological Association).

TARDE, Gabriel de.

1890. *Les Lois de l'imitation* (Paris: Felix Alcan), trans. Elsie Worthington Clews Parsons from the 2nd French ed. as *The Laws of Imitation* (New York: H. Holt and Company, 1903).

TERMAN, Lewis Madison.

1916. *The Measurement of Intelligence. An Explanation of and a Complete Guide for the Use of the Stanford Revision and Extension of the Binet-Simon Intelligence Scale* (Boston: Houghton Mifflin Company).

THORNDIKE, Edward L.

1903. *Educational Psychology* (New York: The Science Press).

1906. *The Principles of Teaching Based on Psychology* (New York: A. G. Seiler).

THURSTONE, Louis L.

1928. "Attitudes Can Be Measured", *American Journal of Sociology* 19, 441-453.

TOLMAN, Edward Chase.

1932. *Purposive Behavior in Animals and Men* (New York: Appleton-Century).

1937.   "The Determiners of Behavior at a Choice Point", Presidential Address delivered to the American Psychological Association (September 3) and published in the *Psychological Review* 45, 1-41; reprinted in Hilgard Ed. 1978: 337-370, to which page reference citation is keyed.

von UEXKÜLL, Jakob.

1899-1940. *Kompositionslehre der Natur. Biologie als undogmatische Naturwissenschaft,* selected writings edited and with an introduction by T. von Uexküll (Frankfurt a. M.: Ullstein).

1934.   *Streifzuge durch die Umwelten von Tieren und Menschen* (Berlin), trans. by Claire H. Schiller as "A Stroll through the Worlds of Animals and Men" in *Instinctive Behavior: The Development of a Modern Concept,* ed. by Claire H. Schiller (New York: International Universities Press, Inc., 1957), 5-80.

1940.   "Bedeutungslehre", Bios 10 (Leipzig), trans. by Barry Stone and Herbert Weiner as "The Theory of Meaning" in *Semiotica* 42.1 (1982), 25-82.

VYGOTSKY, Lev Semyonovich.

1930.   "Tool and Symbol in Child Development", edited trans. constructed from a previously unpublished ms., included as Ch. 1 in Cole, John-Steiner, Scribner, and Souberman, Eds. 1978: 19-30, q.v.

WASMANN, Erich von.

1897.   *Vergleichende studien über das seelenleben der Ameisen und der hohern Thiere* (Freiburg im B.: Herder); authorized Engl. trans. (from the 2nd German ed.) *Comparative Studies in the Psychology of Ants and of Higher Animals* (2nd ed., rev. and enlarged; St. Louis, MO: B. Herder, 1905).

1899.   *Instinct und Intelligenz im Thierreich: ein Kritischer Bezur modernen Thierpsychologie* (2nd ed. enlarged; Freiburg im Br.: Herder); authorized Engl. trans. *Instinct and Intelligence in the Animal Kingdom. A Critical Contribution to Modern Animal Psychology* (2nd ed., rev. and enlarged; St. Louis, MO: B. Herder, 1903).

WATSON, John B.

1913.   "Psychology as the Behaviorist Views It", *The Psychological Review* vol. 20, 158-177. This essay has come often to be referred to as "The Behaviorist Manifesto", although in fact no tract actually bearing this title exists from John B. Watson.

        The *point of view* Watson introduces here as "Behaviorism" he contrasts, in the 1915 entry below, with a *method appropriate to implementing the behaviorist point of view.* Cf. Deely 1990: Chapter 2, "Semiotics: Method or Point of View?", pp. 9-21.

1914.	*Behavior: an Introduction to Comparative Psychology* (New York: Henry Holt and Company).

1915.	"The Place of the Conditioned Reflex in Psychology", Presidential Address delivered in December to the American Psychological Association and published in the *Psychological Review* (1916) 23, 89-116; reprinted in Hilgard Ed. 1978: 139-161, to which page reference citation is keyed.

1919.	*Psychology from the Standpoint of a Behaviorist* (Philadelphia: J.B. Lippincott Company).

WATSON, John B., and William McDOUGALL.

1929.	*The Battle of Behaviorism. An Exposition and an Exposure* (New York: W. W. Norton & Co., Inc.). A 1928 edition was published in London by Kegan Paul, Trench, Trubner & Co., according to A. Robinson 1943: 14, entry #31.

WATSON, Robert I.

1953.	"A Brief History of Clinical Psychology", *Psychological Bulletin* 50.5 (September), 321-345.

1971.	*The Great Psychologists* (3rd ed.; Philadelphia, PA: J. B. Lippincott).

WAUCK, Leroy A.

1979.	"The Story of Psychology at Loyola [of Chicago], 1929-1979", pp. 20 (archives of the department).

WEBER, Ernst Heinrich.

1846.	"Der Tatsinn und das Gemeingefühl" ("The Sense of Touch and Common Sensibility"), in R. Wagner, ed., *Handworterbuch der Physiologie*, vol. 3.

WERTHEIMER, Max.

1912.	"Experimentelle Studien über das Sehen von Bewegung" ("Experimental Studies on the Viewing of Motion"), *Zeitschrift für Psychologie* 60, 321-378.

a.1943.	*Productive Thinking* (published posthumously; New York: Harper, 1945).

WHITEHEAD, Alfred North, and Bertrand RUSSELL.

1910-1913. *Principia Mathematica* (Cambridge), 3 vols.

WOODWORTH, Robert S.

1918.	*Dynamic Psychology* (New York: Columbia University Press).

1938.	*Experimental Psychology* (New York: Holt).

1931.	*Contemporary Schools of Psychology* (New York: The Ronald Press Company).

1948. *Contemporary Schools of Psychology* (rev. ed.; New York: The Ronald Press Company).

WOODWORTH, Robert S., and H. SCHLOSSBERG.

1950. *Experimental Psychology* (rev. ed. of Woodworth 1938; New York: Holt).

WUNDT, Wilhelm.

1873. *Grundzüge der physiologische Psychologie*, Introduction, Parts 1 and 2 (Leipzig: Wilhelm Engelmann).

1874. *Grundzüge der physiologische Psychologie*, Parts 3, 4 and 5 (Leipzig: Englemann).

1880. *Grundzüge*, Second edition.

1887. *Grundzüge*, Third edition.

1893. *Grundzüge*, Fourth edition.

1896. *Grundriss der Psychologie* (Leipzig: W. Engelmann), trans. by Charles Hubbard Judd as *Outlines of Psychology* (Leipzig: Wilhelm Engelmann; London: Williams & Norgate; New York: Gustav E. Stechert, 1897).

i.1900-1920. *Völkerpsychologie* (Leipzig: W. Engelmann), a work whose course Boring describes (1950: 326) as follows: "The new century . . . brought [Wundt] the leisure to return to the unfilled task, outlined in the *Beitrage* of 1862—the writing of the *Völkerpsychologie*, the natural history of man, which alone, Wundt thought, could give the scientific answer to the problems of the higher mental processes. The first volume of this work appeared in 1900, was later revised and finally became two volumes in a second revision. The second volume was published in 1905-1906 and became two volumes on revision. Then, from 1914-1920, six more volumes appeared, making ten in all. . . . Even his death seems to have accorded with his systematic habits. All the revisions had been completed. The *Völkerpsychologie* was at last finished. He wrote his life's psychological reminiscences in 1920, and died shortly thereafter, on August 31 at the age of eighty-eight."

1902-1903. *Grundzüge*, Fifth edition. This edition was partially translated into English by Edward B. Titchener as *Principles of Physiological Psychology* (London: Sonnenscheim; New York: The Macmillan Co. 1904).

1908-1911. *Grundzüge*, Sixth edition.

ZUSNE, Leonard.

1968. *Biographical Dictionary of Psychology* (Westport, CT: Greenwood Press).

INDEX

291

Colophon

Design:
John Deely and Czeslaw Jan Grycz
Composition:
Letterheads to Books
using 12/31/90 release of WordPerfect 5.1
Text:
Palatino 14/16 with Leading Adjustment 1.02, 1.02; Footnotes, References, and Index 11/13
Display:
Main Title Page—series identification 13, editors 11 italic; title 38, subtitle 23, author 18,
editor 15; Dummy title pages 23; Copyright 10; Headers—fixed 11 italic, variable 11; rules
advance down 9, 378 x 1.44 100%; Chapter identifiers 14 italic; Chapter titles 20; Subheads
and captions 11 ital; Margins 81, 126, 117.36, 108 (top, right, bottom, left); Sinks for chapters
180.3, 216.3, 395.7
Page Output:
Adobe Postscript cartridge-controlled Hewlett-Packard LaserJet III with resolution
enhnancement on; actual output reduced 20% in final production